AN ECONOMIC AND SOCIAL HISTORY OF EUROPE FROM 1939 TO THE PRESENT

An Economic and Social History of Europe from 1939 to the Present

FRANK B. TIPTON AND ROBERT ALDRICH

The Johns Hopkins University Press
Baltimore

Printed in Hong Kong

First published 1987

Published by The Johns Hopkins University Press
701 West 40th Street
Baltimore, Maryland 21211

Library of Congress Cataloging-in-Publication Data

Tipton, Frank B., 1943–
An economic and social history of Europe from 1939
to the present.
Bibliography: p.
Includes index.
1. Europe—Economic conditions—1918–1945. 2. Europe—
Economic conditions—1945– . 3. Europe—Social
conditions—20th century. I. Aldrich, Robert, 1954–
II. Title.
HC240.T563   1987   330.94′055   87–3870
ISBN 0–8018–3538–0

CONTENTS

ACKNOWLEDGEMENTS

We would like to thank our research assistants, Janell Mills and Ayling Rubin, for their invaluable assistance in finding information, giving suggestions and providing a critical reading of our work; they have been involved in this project from the outset. We would also like to thank Mark Hayne for reading the manuscript and John Roberts of the Department of Geography at the University of Sydney for preparing the maps.

Note: throughout, the number 'billion' is used in the sense of 'thousand million'.

Für Elise

FBT

To Livia Yanowicz

RA

INTRODUCTION

EUROPE FROM 1939 TO THE PRESENT

Europe in 1939 was a world on the brink of war, a war which all foresaw yet none felt able to prevent. Conflict had already erupted in China, in Spain, in Ethiopia and in Albania, but Europeans looked with fatalistic foreboding towards a new and larger conflict. When that new war came it was Adolf Hitler, the master of Germany, who chose its time and place and determined its form and extent. The Second World War was 'Hitler's War' – but it was also something more. Hitler's Nazi movement espoused the most virulent of the conservative, anti-modern ideologies of the interwar years, but the virulence of Nazism resulted from the fact that it was the most extreme and consistent version of ideas which many Europeans in all countries held in common. To many Europeans the problems confronting them seemed so serious that they could not be solved by discussion and compromise. They thought stronger medicine was needed and therefore supported authoritarian regimes and extreme 'emergency' measures by governments which retained their parliamentary form.

The fact that so many Europeans supported authoritarian regimes and programmes indicates that the situation which led to the Second World War had its origins in the period from 1890 to 1939. The social and political problems arising from more rapid economic development had led directly to the First World War. The spread of industrial development had led to increased competition, and the rise of a new working class had led to demands for political change. Political leaders attempted to use foreign expansion and war as a means of defusing domestic discontent. They were willing to risk war in part because none foresaw the extent of destruction which the war of 1914–18 would bring; shell-

1

shocked, the survivors attempted to restore the prewar world. They failed, and the old problems re-emerged in new and even more difficult forms. The problem of national competition was compounded by the emergence of new states and the problem of representation of the working class by the attempt to quarantine the new Soviet Union. The attempt to restore the prewar economic system not only failed but led directly to the depression of the 1930s. Political institutions remained inadequate to absorb the impact of economic and social change; they came under attack from the left for their refusal to recognise the legitimacy of working-class demands and from the right for their failure to protect conservative interests from the thrust of economic change. The depression added desperation to these cries, and in the absence of political consensus only authoritarian solutions seemed to promise a way out of the impasse. Once in power authoritarian governments proved not only conservative and nationalist, but also militaristic and expansionist. Rearmament lifted economies out of the depression but also made war more likely.

The Second World War therefore was the culmination of unresolved conflicts arising out of the previous two generations. However, the Second World War also was a historical divide, for out of the war emerged the structures of the contemporary world. The old competitive state system became a world dominated by two 'superpowers'. Europe's dominance over Latin America, Africa, Asia and the Pacific became a much more difficult relationship with the 'Third World'. Technology opened new vistas, but the atomic bomb and the Holocaust called into question the most fundamental nature of European society. All these movements contributed to a relative decline in the position of Europe in the world. Within Europe the expansion and then the contraction of the Axis powers shattered existing economic, social and political structures. The progress of the war determined the shape of the postwar world by imposing solutions to the problems which Europe had been unable to solve peacefully.

The victorious Allied powers intended that the period of 'reconstruction' would be precisely that. Rather than attempt to 'restore' Europe as had the interwar generation, they consciously set about creating a new and more stable structure. The war had pre-empted some of their decisions; the emergence of the United States and the Soviet Union as superpowers meant their wishes would be paramount, and the position of the armies largely dictated which superpower's wishes would be granted in each particular case. Germany naturally became the proving ground for their competing visions of the postwar world, and their competition led to the division of Germany and of Europe into 'east' and 'west'. However, despite the competition between the superpowers, a broad range of international institutions was established to restrain the expansionist nationalism which twice had led to world war. For Europe this meant the creation of supranational organisations for economic, social and political cooperation among national states, but it also contributed to the loss of empires by fostering the rise of nationalist movements in Europe's possessions overseas.

The institutions created during the reconstruction period proved their worth during the 1950s and 1960s. Despite their differences, the states of both eastern and western Europe embarked on an unprecedented period of rapid development and increasing affluence, the 'great boom'. In both east and west the boom was marked by the increasingly close interrelations of economic, social and political developments. International institutions – the European Economic Community, the European Free Trade Association and the Council for Mutual Economic Assistance, as well as the burgeoning array of United Nations agencies – became a prominent feature of the world scene. Europe found itself playing a new and complex role in a multicentred world system.

Just as the more enthusiastic were announcing that Europe's problems had been solved, the great boom ended. In the 1970s and 1980s Europe found itself locked into a crisis. Institutions which had appeared flexible and creative during the great boom now seemed rigid and unresponsive; the previous two decades rapidly became objects of nostalgia. The institutions remained, however; there was no fundamental challenge to the existing structure. Europe's problems had become problems of affluence, which might require hard choices and even a reduction in accustomed living standards but which could not compare to the conditions in the newly-emerging societies of the Third World or to the situation in Europe itself before 1939.

The period from 1939 to the present therefore possesses a unity equal to that of the period from 1890 to 1939 but qualitatively different. The preceding two generations had been marked by the failure to solve the social problems arising out of economic development and the resulting conflict. Out of the Second World War, in contrast, emerged institutions based on a new consensus. In important respects the new split between east and west dominated the structure of those institutions. Nevertheless, Europe remained a unit. Each nation had its own history, and the two groups of 'eastern' and 'western' European nations did not simply 'converge' around some standard pattern. But all of the European nations did address the same problems, all developed means to overcome those problems, and as they did so all moved along the same trajectory of development. In overcoming their economic, social and political problems, they also overcame the internal instability which had played such a major role in leading to the depression and the two world wars of the first half of the century.

CONTEMPORARY ECONOMIC AND SOCIAL HISTORY

Like all historians, economic and social historians aim to explain events as well as describe them. However, their subject-matter is more problem-oriented than that of some other sorts of historians – the desire to understand the process of economic development and to understand the ways in which societies function has immediate relevance to the historian's own time. In addition, the close connection of economic and social history to the analogous social sciences leads them to a relatively great interest in general theories. This can take several forms. The historian may want to explain developments by demonstrating that, given certain conditions, the result could have been predicted by some general theory. Alternatively, the historian may want to know which of two competing theories better explains actual developments: for example, the question of whether theories of elite domination or of social modernisation best explain changes in Europe's class structure after 1939. A third case, and perhaps the most common, recalls Sherlock Holmes asking why the dog did *not* bark in the night; historians become very interested indeed when general theories *fail* to predict what actually happened, or appear to do so in one period but not in another: for example, the way in which Keynesian economic theory seemed to explain the pattern of development in Europe during the 1950s and 1960s but then seemed to fail to explain the very different pattern of the 1970s and 1980s.

Economic history deals with things: their production, their exchange and their consumption and the relations among those who produce, exchange and consume them. These all underwent a substantial transformation during the Second World War and reconstruction period. The war accelerated the spread of the technologies of the 'second industrial revolution' – steel, machine tools, chemicals and electricity – and stimulated further technological advances, most spectacularly in the case of atomic energy. During the reconstruction period Europe could take advantage of these advances and of the entire backlog of innovations delayed by the depression of the 1930s. This was certainly one of the factors behind the great boom. Conversely, Europe lagged in the beginnings of the 'third industrial revolution' of automation and electronics, losing ground particularly to Japan, and this contributed to the crisis of the 1970s and 1980s. These developments were mediated through different institutional structures in east and west, and both eastern and western Europe found that changing international structures played a large role in their domestic economies. Exploration of these relationships has provided a fascinating field of study for economic historians.

Social history looks at the same domain as economic history, but from the other side, emphasising people rather than things. People are both individuals and members of collectivities. They may be producers, but they also belong to occupational classes and exercise greater or lesser degrees of authority. They may be consumers, but they also belong to families, ethnic groupings, churches and a broad range of other formal and informal associations. Social historians have had to consider both underlying continuities and some startling new developments since the Second World War. Trends in population movements and occupational distribution continued along lines extending back into the nineteenth century; on the other hand, political change, a revolution in higher education and the fundamental change in the position of women were among the features of postwar society which marked it off from previous epochs. Some old problems were 'solved'; forced migration reduced the number of national minorities, for instance. Others remained, such as the continuing difficult situation of small farmers in both east and west.

Neither economic nor social developments could be considered apart from the political realm after 1939. The Second World War and the reconstruction period saw the completion of the process of interpenetration of economy, society and politics which had begun before the First World War. All European governments assumed responsibility for managing the economy and controlling society during the war, but after the war they did not withdraw from economic and social life as most had attempted to do after the First World War. Western European governments adopted an indirect 'Keynesian' approach while their eastern European counterparts preferred the 'Soviet' model, but all agreed that economic development could and should be 'planned' and that social policy could and should both foster economic development and minimise its possible negative effects.

All governments claimed to represent the interests of all their citizens, but not all of them were convinced. Politics is not only the area where economics and society overlap but is also divided into a 'formal' realm governed by constitutional regulations and an 'extraparliamentary' realm of informal pressure, protest and violence. One of the great achievements of postwar Europe was the establishment of an impressively broad consensus. Nevertheless, consensus was not universal, and one of the characteristic features of the period was extraparliamentary agitation by groups which either sought inclusion in the ruling consensus or rejected it altogether.

Though not a revolutionary time, the decades following the Second World War were far from quiet, punctuated as they were by the protests of workers, farmers, youth, women, homosexuals and national minorities. The expansion of the political sphere also broadened the range of political conflict, and the continued emergence of self-conscious 'marginal' groups ensured that conflict would continue.

The history of Europe from 1939 to the present is 'contemporary' history. Obviously, at some point contemporary history becomes the story of the historian's own time. This can pose problems of materials and perspective. Traditionally, diplomatic historians were restricted by the British government's 'fifty-year rule' for the release of documents to considering events more than a half-century in the past, and political historians concentrated their attention on the careers of leaders who were safely deceased. For the social and economic historian, however, the contemporary world suffers from no shortage of materials. Government and private agencies at all levels in all countries produce information intended to help determine economic and social policy or to evaluate its effect – that is, precisely the materials the historian needs. The material tends to be of high quality as well; the debates over policy and the division between east and west ensure that biased or incomplete accounts do not go unchallenged.

Perspective poses more of a problem than materials. Since the historian does not know what will happen tomorrow, it is difficult to know what is most important today. However, 'contemporary' does not mean merely the present; even more importantly, contemporary history refers to the origin and development of the institutions of the present-day world. Existing institutions pose no problem of identification, and their origin and development are clearly questions for historical analysis and explanation. Indeed the very rapid changes in institutions which mark the contemporary world make historical analysis and explanation imperative. With the interpenetration of economy, society and politics the historical fabric became denser. Nineteenth-century laissez-faire attitudes kept politics and diplomacy relatively separate from economy and society, whereas socialist planning,

Keynesian economics and the welfare state of the twentieth century brought them together. The technologies of the first and second industrial revolutions were only slowly felt by the masses of Europeans, whereas the inventions of the twentieth century, from automobiles and radios to televisions and computers, became omnipresent in only a short period of time. The electronics revolution in technology and the white-collar revolution in labour created new and immediate links among science, education and marketing. These new inventions, particularly in the fields of transportation and communications, also made Europe's relationship with the non-European world closer than in the days of sailing ships or steamers. The establishment of international organisations added a new level of governmental structures to the already complicated interplay of regional and national politics, while the media provided an added forum for extraparliamentary campaigns. The structure of contemporary European society thus differs radically from that of past epochs. More stable in some respects and more fluid in others, in both its aspects it is one on which historical debate is pertinent.

1
THE SECOND WORLD WAR

EUROPE ON THE EVE OF WAR: POLITICS, TECHNOLOGY AND ECONOMICS

Compared to the First World War the outbreak and progress of the Second World War seem to require little in the way of analysis or explanation. The Second World War seems clearly 'Hitler's War', one orchestrated by him at a time of his choosing, which lasted of necessity until the Nazi system had been destroyed. However, the straightforward battle against Nazism overlapped with the struggle between competing nationalisms, between socialist and capitalist powers to expand their spheres, among imperialist powers to extend their possessions, and between the imperialist powers and movements of national liberation.

Tension increased steadily through the 1930s as Europe's leaders prepared for war. As they had before the First World War, virtually all nations increased their military expenditure – defence, they said, against other nations' aggressive intentions. Yet even as they prepared for war, most leaders hoped for peace. The depression absorbed their energies and undermined their confidence. Their constituencies were divided; a majority opposed war, but many also felt something to be wrong with existing political and economic systems; many looked with sympathy on authoritarian regimes, and a noisy right wing glorified the supposed regenerative effects of violence. In Britain Winston Churchill himself approved of Mussolini's fascist regime, and British animosity to Hitler resulted less from moral considerations than from the knowledge that Germany posed a much greater potential threat to British interests than did

9

Italy. On the Continent, both the extreme left and the extreme right gained wide support, and in combating this double threat most governments moved in a rightward and authoritarian direction.

In the context of the 1930s, Hitler's Germany appeared merely one case among several in which the extreme right had defeated more moderate conservative elements. Nazi anti-Semitism occasioned little negative comment, for it seemed only another variant of feelings widespread in Europe. Prominent and respected western European intellectuals were openly anti-Semitic, and in eastern Europe violence against Jewish persons and property perpetrated by the Union of Young Poland, or the anti-Semitic legislation enacted in Rumania and Hungary, appeared to equal Nazi excesses. *Mein Kampf*, Hitler's manifesto, could be, and was, dismissed as the embarrassing juvenilia of a man now risen to the leadership of a great nation. The Nazis' anti-Soviet stance seemed merely a more forthright statement of opinions shared by a wide range of respectable individuals and groups, for the fear of communist insurrection remained strong. In the view of many conservatives a stronger, more stable Germany would not only be less likely to fall victim to such an insurrection, but would also provide a useful bulwark against the Soviet Union.

Hitler was able to exploit these crosscurrents and divisions in opinion with relative ease. By the end of 1937 he had ended the restrictions placed on Germany by the Treaty of Versailles and achieved virtually unquestioned domination over east-central Europe. However, Hitler did not rest content with his considerable successes. In 1938 the annexation of Austria passed quite smoothly, but the Munich agreement forcing Czechoslovakia to cede the German-speaking Sudetenland to Germany was reached only after a serious crisis. In the meantime public opinion in western Europe had been hardening. The momentary euphoria following the preservation of 'peace in our time' – the phrase used by British prime minister Neville Chamberlain on his return from the Munich conference – gave way to scepticism, bitterness and a widening conviction that Hitler must be resisted at all costs. Rearmament programmes accelerated, and when Germany annexed the remainder of Czechoslovakia in March 1939 Britain and France immediately pledged themselves to aid Poland against Germany. When Germany attacked Poland in September, Britain and France both declared war on Germany. In the meantime Hitler had scored a spectacular diplomatic coup by signing a pact with the Soviet Union; nevertheless in 1941 Germany invaded the Soviet Union without having defeated Britain, and then casually declared war on the United States as well after the Japanese attack on American possessions in the Pacific.

Why did Hitler blunder into a war he could not win? Politically, two interpretations of Hitler's policy seem possible. On the one hand, Hitler and key decision-making groups within Germany may have been essentially rational, but mistaken in their calculations. Hitler's previous successes may have bred overconfidence and a conviction that his opponents would always surrender. If the Nazi regime was logical but mistaken, then earlier and more forceful opposition to Hitler, and reasonable revisions in the Treaty of Versailles, might have strengthened the 'moderates' in Germany and held Hitler's personal ambition in check. On the other hand, Hitler and a large fraction of the German people may have been acting on the basis of irrational motives. Childhood trauma may have led Hitler to his compulsive anti-Semitism, while hatred of the Jews reflected the status anxieties of important classes in German society threatened by social change. Additionally, for the generation of Germans emerging from the First World War, wartime deprivation may have provided the unconscious trigger leading them to support a policy of conquest in the east – repeatedly portrayed in Nazi propaganda as an inexhaustible source of food. Again, for Hitler and other Germans, the shock of defeat in the First World War may have led to a drive to relive the earlier traumatic experience, including the bungled foreign policy, the hopeless two-front war and defeat. Hitler himself had identified the two-front war as the fatal mistake of the German imperial government in 1914, and insisted he wanted to reach an understanding or even alliance with Britain. Nevertheless, by pushing Britain into war, invading Russia and declaring war on the United States, Hitler wilfully recreated the coalition which had defeated Germany before. In this much less optimistic interpretation, Germany could be expected to choose war deliberately, regardless of other nations' policies.

Militarily, two interpretations again present themselves, one rational and limited, the other irrational and unlimited. Hitler prided himself on his military expertise and played an important role in the development of the concept of the *Blitzkrieg*, a way of exploiting modern technology while avoiding the strains which modern war had placed on Germany society during the First World War. If Hitler's commitment to the *Blitzkrieg* concept can be taken at face value, then his pursuit of his goals remained rational, and the military means of achieving them remained subordinate to the goals themselves. Tactically, the *Blitzkrieg* concept called for a mobile campaign to smash enemy resistance quickly. Elite armoured units reinforced from the air by fighters and light bombers would bypass fortifications and avoid masses of enemy troops, surprise and destroy the enemy command structure and leave enemy forces leaderless and disorganised. The enemy army in effect would be destroyed without having been engaged. Strategically and even more importantly, the *Blitzkrieg* was a series of short campaigns with limited objectives. Periods of rest between campaigns would allow for stockpiling strategic materials, and the series of campaigns could therefore be fought without increasing the share of the military in the economy. In minimising the role of large-scale industry, the *Blitzkrieg* came as close as possible to fitting the social composition and goals of the Nazi movement. Though modern war required modern industrial products, small elite units and short campaigns would require less than had the armed masses and frontal assaults of the First World War. Small businessmen, shopkeepers, white-collar workers and farmers, and more amorphous groups of consumers and workers as well, could rest easier because neither mobilisation nor war would require unacceptable disruption of their enterprises, deprive them of their labour supply or undermine the purchasing power of their salaries.

Hitler presented the *Blitzkrieg* strategy as a rational, coherent concept. Substantial aggregate evidence supports this view. Germany in 1939 was emphatically not a totally militarised state. Though military spending had played an important role in recovery from the depression, it had been only one aspect of a wide range of public investment. But not all of the evidence fits. Recent estimates suggest that rather than remaining static, German military spending continued to increase at a constant rate between 1938–39 and 1943–44 – which should not have been the case if the *Blitzkrieg* strategy had actually been followed. Rather than concentrating on the elite armoured units prescribed by the *Blitzkrieg* strategy, Hitler agreed to the army's plans for massive increases in conventional units as well. Simultaneous planned increases in aircraft production exceeded existing capacity; the plans had to be reduced after the Munich agreements, just as Germany's opponents were beginning to increase their output of new aircraft. Finally, despite his commitment to some sort of understanding with Britain, and despite a naval agreement signed with Britain in 1935, in 1936 Hitler approved the 'Z-programme' advocated by the navy, a new large fleet of both submarine and surface vessels whose only function could be to challenge Britain on the seas. The army, air force and navy pursued their goals with single-minded and competitive determination, and Hitler did not impose a set of priorities on their demands. He combined a consuming interest in the technical details of armaments and military organisation with a complete aversion to study of the economic implications of military decisions. Therefore the failure to plan for a long war may have arisen not so much from the logic of Hitler's *Blitzkrieg* strategy, as from a pathological need to have his wishes fulfilled without consideration of cost.

Economic explanations of the outbreak of the war can also be divided into those which see the Nazi regime as in some sense logical, or at least part of a logical system, and those which see it driven by irrational, contradictory and sometimes unconscious motives. The Marxist interpretation which identifies fascism as the political form of state monopoly capitalism seems to predict war. Under the capitalist mode of production, Marxists have argued, technical innovation and the resulting decline in the rate of profit lead to a restless search for new markets. The end to European overseas expansion left capitalist powers such as Germany with only one option – a war of conquest in Europe itself.

The Nazis' own theory of the 'economics of large areas' (*Grossraumwirtschaft*) also seemed to predict war. Taking the British Empire, the United States and the Soviet Union as models of states drawing on resources of continental dimensions, Nazi writers argued that the liberal period of economic development had ended, and that the world economy would henceforth be organised into autarkic empires. Within the *Grossraum* they envisaged for Germany, these writers postulated a regional specialisation of economic functions with corresponding racial types. The central industrial core, inhabited by Aryans, would be surrounded by extensive regions producing agricultural products and industrial raw materials, inhabited by Slavs. The creation of the German *Grossraum* therefore would require war with the Soviet Union, and many authors were more or less explicit in drawing this conclusion.

Though based on unacceptable irrational premises, the theory of *Grossraumwirtschaft* still possesses logical consistency. However, the theory fails to explain why Hitler stumbled into a two-front war – especially a two-front war involving Britain, since according to the theory each *Grossraum* would be a self-sufficient entity. Similarly, although there is much evidence to support the Marxist interpretation, much of Nazi policy remained explicitly anti-capitalist and anti-industrial. The support of big business interests played a crucial role in Nazi election campaigns before 1933, and big business profited from rearmament and German economic penetration of eastern Europe in the later 1930s. Some firms such as I.G. Farben, the Deutsche Bank and the major aluminium producers were deeply involved in the exploitation of conquered areas after the war began. However, the Nazi government taxed business profits heavily, placed restrictions on large retail shops and legislated in favour of small-scale artisan enterprises. New laws limited employment and educational opportunities for women. New forms of hereditary tenure were devised for peasants, and extensive plans were proposed for the settlement of German yeoman farmers in the east. The war when it came undermined the most important classes of Nazi supporters, and increased the contradiction between the Nazis' anti-modern, anti-industrial ideology and the modern, industrial means of increasing state power needed to prosecute the war successfully. Yet the goal of the war was the creation of a preindustrial utopia in which an Aryan elite would be served by masses of non-Aryan slaves. The contradictions and inconsistencies were open and obvious, but at the profoundest level, the Nazis meant exactly what they said. In Alan Milward's telling phrase: 'The National Socialist movement kept its inner momentum, which was driving it towards a different horizon from that of the business world, a horizon both more distant and more frightening'.

The ideological – and perhaps irrational – element in Nazi policy reveals itself in a comparison of Germany with other belligerents. Germany's opponents and allies alike found their military options limited by internal social and political considerations – in contrast to the Nazis, who openly proclaimed their unwillingness to be bound by any limits at all. Further, this seems true of both the 'democratic' systems of France and Britain on the one hand, and the allegedly 'totalitarian' systems of Italy and the Soviet Union on the other.

France was the worst-prepared of the major belligerents, and paid the price in defeat. Official French army doctrine called for the mobilisation of the 'people as a whole' and for the creation of an administrative framework for centralised direction of the entire economy in wartime. The army's thinking resulted directly from the experiences of the First World War; however, so did the opposition of property owners to increased taxes, government controls and inflationary finance, and so too did the opposition of French socialists to any large increase in the army's influence in public life. Only in 1938 did France finally create legislation providing for wartime economic organisation. In the meantime military service had been limited to twelve months, and the army had come to rely on the defence of fixed positions, embodied in the famous Maginot Line, a set of fortresses built along the Franco-German border.

After the defeat of 1940, many identified the 'Maginot

mentality' as the crucial weakness in French planning. However, the Germans never did take the line by frontal assault; by forcing the Germans on to predictable invasion routes and providing a shield behind which reservists could be mobilised, the line should have given the French the ability to withstand a German advance. German military planners agreed, and did not expect to win a clear victory. The problems lay behind the line. The army's bid for expansion and control over the economy – for a true nation in arms – remained in limbo. Charles De Gaulle argued for a much smaller force of elite, highly trained, mobile armoured units, but in 1940 the planned armoured divisions still did not exist. France possessed a superb shield, but neither broadsword nor rapier.

Britain began from a position similar to that of France, but developed a new successful consensus based on the deployment of overseas resources to meet the Nazi threat. In the late 1930s British leaders began to realise their need to defend British interests against Germany, Italy and Japan simultaneously. This realisation led Britain step by step to a level of mobilisation second only to the Soviet Union. The British in fact had taken Nazi assertions about the degree to which the German economy had been militarised too seriously. However, their overly-pessimistic evaluation of their own position led the British to emphasise those areas where they had the advantage, especially the construction of ships and long-range bombers to ensure continuity of overseas supplies and to neutralise Germany's presumed insurmountable lead in ground forces. Ships and highly sophisticated airplanes required long-range planning, coordination of scientific and technological developments and expansion of large-scale industrial production facilities. At the same time it became clearer that a large army would also have to be raised and equipped, which would add to the burdens which workers and consumers would have to bear. In taking these decisions, Britain wagered on a long war – one likely to be won by the nation with the highest level of domestic mobilisation and easiest access to overseas resources.

The Russians, and notably Stalin himself, were too optimistic about Hitler's intentions and timetable, but the

Third Five-Year Plan begun in 1937–38 had emphasised military preparedness. The share of defence industries in the budget doubled, and machine-building and engineering industries received special attention. By 1941 aircraft and tanks were being produced by production-line methods. The government began to stockpile some strategic raw materials, and industry was shifted eastward to less strategically vulnerable locations. This too was preparation for a long war, though of a different kind from that practised in Britain. Russia still lagged far behind western Europe in industrial development but possessed a huge economic potential and the experience of more than a decade of centralised planning which permitted exploitation of that potential when the crisis broke.

In 1931 the Soviet armed forces had undertaken a series of coordinated reforms, but in 1937 the purges struck the armed forces. Eight senior commanders were accused of treason and executed, and through 1937 and 1938 perhaps 35,000 officers perished. At the lower levels, newly promoted officers lacked experience, and at higher levels Stalin's 'political' generals owed their positions and their continued safety to their unquestioning loyalty rather than to their ability. Lack of imagination and fear undoubtedly contributed to the huge initial losses to the Germans in 1941–42. However, like Britain, the Soviet Union survived initial setbacks, and the system proved flexible enough to regroup and build new forces capable of eventual victory.

Mussolini had written that 'war alone brings up to its highest tension all human energy and puts the stamp of nobility upon the peoples who have the courage to meet it'. Despite their bombastic rhetoric and aggressive policy, however, Italian leaders had no desire to participate in a major war and had made no preparations for one. Italy possessed almost no supplies of coal or petroleum and all other strategic raw materials were in short supply as well, but virtually no stockpiles had been assembled. Italy produced only two million tons of steel a year in 1938, and the capacity of the armaments industry was similarly limited, but again no stockpiles existed and no new investment had been undertaken. Shortages of parts kept two-thirds of the aircraft on the ground. Mussolini himself supposedly exercised authority over the three independent and competitive service ministries, but he possessed no expertise and had not assembled a professional staff to advise him. He was aware of his country's weakness relative to Germany; he also realised that the invasion of Ethiopia and Albania had strained Italy's resources and that there was no popular support for a major war. He proclaimed Italy's neutrality the day following the German attack on Poland and only entered the war in June 1940, three days before the German occupation of Paris, and then only out of fear that German expansion would put an end to Italian ambitions.

AXIS EXPANSION

The war in Europe, 1939–42: Sitzkreig *and* Blitzkreig

Polish leaders confidently expected to hold the Germans at bay for six months, by which time France and Britain should have mobilised and attacked Germany in the west. Instead, the small Polish air force was destroyed on the ground, and German armoured divisions supported by fighters and divebombers advanced to the outskirts of Warsaw in a mere ten days. The government moved its command centre from Warsaw to the southeast corner of Poland, but Russian armies suddenly invaded from the east, and by the end of September, after less than a month of fighting, Germany and Russia had divided Poland between them.

Hitler intended to attack France as soon as possible, but weather prevented the planned invasion in November 1939 and again in January 1940. Journalists, without stories for their readers, referred to the 'phoney war' and the Germans' *Sitzkrieg* tactics. In the meantime, Soviet armies invaded Finland. The French and British hoping to break the shackles of the phoney war, aid Finland and strike a blow at Germany at the same time, planned to occupy the Norwegian port of Narvik, seize the iron mines of northern Sweden and then move to reinforce the Finns. Instead, the exhausted Finns capitulated to the Russians, and the Germans occupied

Norway and Denmark with startling speed. Caught by surprise by this brilliant operation, the British responded tardily and clumsily. Disappointment now led to a cabinet crisis in Britain. Churchill emerged as Britain's new leader – despite having been the minister responsible for the Norwegian fiasco.

The long-feared German attack on the Low Countries and France finally began on 10 May 1940. As the French and British forces moved towards their planned defensive positions in Belgium, German armoured divisions cut through the French lines much further to the east at Sedan, drove nearly 100 kilometres into France, then turned west – behind the French and British armies, and between them and their central headquarters. The thrust was a textbook illustration of the *Blitzkrieg* concept, and it would have given the French and British little comfort to know that the German commander had actually violated orders to stop and regroup after his initial breakthrough. The Germans reached the Atlantic on 20 May. Allied communications broke down. An attempted counterattack failed. The Belgian and Dutch armies surrendered, and though the British were able to evacuate some 200,000 of their own and 130,000 French troops from Dunkirk, all equipment was lost and Britain itself was open to invasion. The French government moved south twice, then capitulated. A new government, under the aged First World War commander Henri Pétain, signed the armistice dictated by the Germans on 22 June – in the same railway car in which the Germans had been forced to sign the earlier armistice of 1918.

Hitler firmly expected Britain to abandon the war after the fall of France. But British resistance continued, and Hitler, apparently with considerable reluctance, began to plan for an attack on Britain. Hermann Goering insisted that his *Luftwaffe* not only could defeat the British air force, but indeed could defeat Britain without the assistance of either the navy or the army. Hitler agreed, and the Battle of Britain was joined. The Germans had the advantage of numbers – some 1,200 bombers and 1,000 fighters, compared to a total of 900 British planes. However, most of the British fighters were both faster and more heavily armed than their German opponents, and they were flying directly over their own bases, while the best German fighters were confined to the region south of London. The German bombers were slow, requiring constant fighter protection, and therefore the Germans were restricted to using only 300–400 at any one time. Further, the British knew when they were coming. Since 1935 scientists and the military had been working together on a crash programme to develop an early warning system, and by 1939 a chain of twenty 'radar' (for radio detecting and ranging) stations guarded Britain's southern coast. In addition British fighters could be guided to the enemy bombers by a sophisticated radio ground-control system, developed on the assumption that radar would work even before the first stations had been built. By 1940–41 British fighters contained small radar sets, a further refinement which neutralised the Germans' use of radar beams to guide bombers to their targets.

The Germans finally began to show themselves error-prone as well. Goering broke off his assault on Britain's coastal defences before they had been destroyed, and moved instead to attacks on fighter bases. These very nearly succeeded, but then Goering broke them off in favour of attacks on aircraft factories and finally began large-scale attacks on the city of London. Hitler had demanded vengeance for a British bombing raid on Berlin, and in September 1940 the Germans launched a campaign of twenty-four-hour attacks on the British capital. German commanders shared the common belief that civilian populations would not be able to cope with air attacks. They were wrong, and German losses were high, so high that Hitler felt compelled to postpone the final invasion of Britain.

Hitler now decided to invade 'that degenerate Jewish sponge-fungus, Marxist Russia'. In June 1941 Operation Barbarossa launched 4,000,000 men, 3,300 tanks and 5,000 aircraft across the Soviet borders. Stalin ignored plain evidence of German intentions, and the Soviet armies were caught by surprise. Fearing to retreat, they fell victim to the Germans' planned pincers movements. Some 2,000 planes were lost, the Soviet tank force was reduced from 15,000 to

700 and more than 2,000,000 Russian soldiers were taken prisoner during three terrible months.

That the Soviet Union survived these blows seems astonishing – and there was a period of panic in Moscow as the advance German units approached – but Soviet survival owed something to German overconfidence and errors. Hitler did not coordinate his policies or cooperate with Japan, and since Japan did not attack Russia, Stalin was able to move a large new army from east to west. The Germans neglected to gather current intelligence and operated largely without accurate information on Soviet strength or morale. None of Hitler's senior planners dared question his conviction that the Soviet regime would collapse and Russia would revert to the chaos of the civil war period. Hitler indeed had begun to remove any of his commanders who did dare question his genius, and the survivors vied with one another to tell Hitler what he wished to hear.

The Russian invasion was delayed six weeks while Yugoslavia and Greece were conquered. This perhaps secured the southern flank of the invading armies, but the delay also placed the Germans in a much less favourable position with regard to the weather, and German planners took no account of the weather on the operation. Planning for 'Operation Barbarossa' in fact was a shambles, to the extent that psychohistorians have argued that Hitler unconsciously wanted to lose and bungled the planning to ensure failure. Hitler launched Barbarossa on the same day of the year that Napoleon had begun his invasion of Russia. Mismatched equipment and vehicles were gathered from all over Europe, and no provisions made for repair or replacement. Fuel, ammunition and winter clothing all were in desperately short supply, but Hitler argued his original timetable was correct and refused to consider alternatives. Partly because of these weaknesses in their supply system, German commanders launched into a headlong rush for immediate victories and conquests without an overall strategy. Soviet losses of men, matériel and resources were indeed immense, but the Soviet army was not destroyed, Soviet morale did not crumble and the Soviet potential to raise and equip new units was not exhausted. Furthermore, Hitler's declaration of war on the United States following the Japanese attack on American possessions converted the world's greatest manufacturing power into a full ally of both Russia and Britain.

The war in Asia

The recurrent economic crises of the 1920s and the depression of the 1930s had led to the rise of a militant right-wing authoritarianism in Japan, similar in many respects to the authoritarian movements of southern and eastern Europe. Right-wing agitation increased the weight of military opinion in determining policy. The army and navy had bitterly opposed the budget cuts and arms limitation treaties forced on them during the 1920s. They were convinced that the European powers and the United States, all with extensive colonial possessions, were systematically denying Japan the opportunity to acquire similar sources of raw materials and secure markets. Military planners saw in the Chinese province of Manchuria a crucial source of industrial raw materials, and feared that if the Chinese national government extended its effective control over the region, it would then exclude Japanese interests. In 1931 the army used a contrived 'incident' as a pretext for the conquest of all of Manchuria; the government ratified the action after the fact, and step by step, Japan was drawn into a full-scale war in China.

By late 1938 the Japanese controlled half of China, but they had not won the war. Two centres of resistance remained, communist in the northwest, nationalist in the southwest, and in Japanese-controlled areas both communists and nationalists continued guerrilla attacks on the occupying forces. The pessimists among Japanese military planners had been proved correct – Japan faced a military stalemate or worse in China and a looming war with the Soviet Union. Army and navy leaders agreed that Japan did not possess the necessary raw materials to prosecute such a war successfully, but the rising wave of popular enthusiasm in Japan swept them along. The war had increased demand in Japan, restoring employment and increasing wages, while the unbroken series of victories had led to an unrealistic optimism similar to the experience of European countries during the First World War.

The outbreak of war in Europe offered Japan a possible avenue of escape from this impasse, through the conquest of European colonial possessions in resource-rich southeast Asia. Japan signed the Tripartite Pact for mutual defence with Germany and Italy, and occupied French territory in northern Indochina with the consent of the Vichy government. China had been fighting virtually alone. Small amounts of aid from the United States had been more than offset by the benefits to Japan of continued trade with America, slightly larger amounts of Soviet aid declined after the Nazi-Soviet pact, and Britain and France had actually closed the southern routes from their colonies into China to avoid offending Japan. Now, however, the Japanese advance into southeast Asia brought the United States to more open support for China. The Americans imposed an embargo on oil shipments which would have deprived Japan of 90 per cent of oil imports and brought both the army and the navy to a complete halt within months. In reply, the Japanese decided on a pre-emptive strike at American military bases in the Pacific.

The German war economy

The decision to invade Russia finally imposed the need for greater organisation and more complete mobilisation of Germany's economic resources. At the outbreak of the war the economic and armaments office of the army generally opposed the *Blitzkrieg* strategy and argued for long-term industrial development under its control. The office of the Four-Year Plan under Goering concentrated on the development of strategic materials for use in the *Blitzkrieg* strategy. The economics ministry's authority over foreign trade led it into more or less continual disputes with the other two. In late 1941, when the German armies stalled in the ice and snow of the Russian front, Hitler appointed Fritz Todt (previously head of the successful highway construction agency) Minister for Armaments Production. Hitler never abandoned his belief that Russia would collapse. Accordingly

Todt's office initially represented only a fourth agency competing for power over the economy. Todt argued for increased investment in industrial plants for armaments production, and Hitler may gradually have become convinced of the need to increase the share of the military in the economy significantly. In January 1942 he issued an order directing increased numbers of armoured vehicles for use in Russia and of submarines for use in the Atlantic – so that by implication he accepted Todt's plans.

When Todt died in a plane crash Hitler replaced him with Albert Speer, previously known only as Hitler's architect. Speer's new role provided scope to realise his remarkable capacities. Using Hitler's obsession with the details of military planning to his advantage, Speer synthesised the masses of minuscule decisions made by Hitler – each invested with the full authority of the *Führer* himself – into production decisions. Speer controlled the corresponding decisions for the allocation of raw materials through a three-member committee established in April 1942. With control of raw materials Speer first forced competing ministries to conform to his wishes, then gradually absorbed them into his munitions ministry.

Under Speer's direction, German armaments production increased rapidly, more than trebling between early 1941 and early 1944. However, the importance and the direction of Nazi ideology remained unchanged even under Speer's economic regime and resulted in inefficiency which limited arms production. Jurisdictional disputes continued to hamper the war effort. The entire sprawling, inefficient economic empire ruled by the SS remained outside Speer's control. The extermination of the Jews continued, as did the relocation and employment of foreign labour under conditions ensuring low productivity and high mortality. These appalling human disasters interfered with the prosecution of the war, diverted and destroyed incalculable resources, and actually created resistance movements in important sections of western Russia. Speer's attempts to redirect resources into industry and armaments were resisted by Nazi party leaders at every level, sometimes effectively. Consumer expenditures declined by less than ten per cent in real terms during the first two years of his administration; the increase in arms production came at the expense of construction and new machinery. There was relatively little investment in research and development, and therefore the development of new and improved weapons was slow. Despite the desperate need for labour – the 7.5 million coerced foreign workers made up one-fifth of the total labour force – Germany mobilised a far smaller proportion of women than any other belligerent power. Female employment increased by only 600,000, compared to an increase of some 2,000,000 in Britain. In late 1944, 1.3 million persons were still employed as domestic servants in Germany. The determination of the Nazi regime to pursue its racial and social policies, even at the expense of efficient prosecution of the war to which those policies had led, was evident to the last.

Germany's ally Italy, in theory an equal partner, in fact proved unable to make a sustained contribution to the war effort. Italy was for instance completely dependent on German supplies of coal, a situation which German planners had failed to foresee and which led to shortages in Germany as well as severely restricting any increase in Italian industrial production. Italian national product actually reached its peak in 1939, declined slightly even during the period of Axis expansion and then began to drop precipitously during 1942. The next year Italy was invaded, leading to a substantial decline in agricultural production, and by 1945 Italian national income had reached the level of 1900–10. Before the Allied invasion the Italian money supply had already quadrupled, massive tax frauds had undermined government finances and food prices on the black market had risen to ten times the official levels.

The occupied territories

The more economically advanced countries provided the Nazis with their richest spoils. France was divided after the collapse of 1940 into an occupied zone and the theoretically independent rump state with its capital at Vichy, but the two regions came to receive much the same treatment. 'Occupation costs' were set at twenty million marks per day.

Bilateral trade agreements were imposed on the French similar to those in force in central and eastern Europe. French prisoners of war held in Germany, large numbers of French workers transferred to Germany, booty (including land seized by the German army), confiscated Jewish property and commandeered industrial plants made further contributions. Because the French economy was already highly developed, new industrial investment did not make as great an impact as in central and eastern Europe. Some Frenchmen benefited from the new regime, particularly in the creation of new industrial combines; as the German negotiator in the establishment of the dyestuffs trust told his French counterparts, 'you will have your place'. French agriculture, however, languished under Nazi domination. The agricultural labour force dropped by 400,000, and total output declined substantially. Nevertheless, though French food supplies never declined to starvation levels, France delivered greater supplies of foodstuffs to Germany than any eastern European country.

Belgium and the Netherlands were also intended by the Nazis to take their place as part of the Aryan industrial heartland, though both paid inflated occupation costs and suffered under discriminatory trade agreements. Industrially more developed, Belgium was proportionately more important in the German plans, and after 1943 the entire output of certain strategically important sectors of Belgian industry went to fulfil those plans. Certain manufacturing branches such as synthetic fibres expanded, but others such as non-ferrous metals (dependent on imported raw materials) declined, and total Belgian industrial production dropped to two-thirds of the already depressed prewar total. Dutch agricultural output rose, but Belgian agriculture declined parallel to France, and a well-developed black market arose, sometimes with the connivance of German authorities.

Denmark and Norway received relatively favourable treatment under the German occupation, although again their interests were subordinate to the Nazi vision of empire. Farmers were ordered to reduce production of animals fed on imported fodder and raise vast numbers of sheep, which would be pastured on land reclaimed from the heath.

Reorganisation by fiat failed in Denmark, and the dairy herds remained. In Norway, German military authorities seized extensive tracts of scarce agricultural land, the planned reclamation of the heath failed to materialise, production of bread grains could only be maintained by reducing fodder crops, the animal population declined rapidly and by 1944 Norwegians were suffering a severe food shortage. German authorities envisaged gigantic industrial investments in Denmark and in Norway. Installed horsepower, much of it in new power plants, increased in Denmark from 550,000 to 710,000 and in Norway from 2.2 to 2.4 million, but as the military situation worsened long-term development plans were increasingly relegated to the background.

After the initial shock of defeat, small resistance movements began to spring up throughout the occupied nations of western and central Europe, encouraged by the Nazis' failure to defeat Britain and more directly by Churchill's 'ministry of ungentlemanly warfare', the Special Operations Executive. By 1941 a network of resistance organisations was already in place, disseminating anti-German propaganda, aiding those wanting to escape, passing on military intelligence to the British and undertaking acts of sabotage. Many participants in the resistance hoped for social reform as well as liberation from the Nazis. This impulse was greatly strengthened by the addition of the well-organised communists to the resistance after the German invasion of Russia. Communists and non-communists remained suspicious of each other and openly hostile in some areas such as Poland, Yugoslavia and Greece. Nonetheless, resistance movements grew and developed into genuine mass movements, especially when the tide of war seemed to be turning against Germany after 1942. Savage German reprisals and increasing drafts of forced labour brought new recruits, and hope of German defeat gave increasing numbers the courage to aid active resisters when they could. Sabotage became a real problem for the Germans, and fairly substantial armed units awaited the signal of an Allied invasion to rise against the Nazis.

The countries of central and eastern Europe, already partially integrated into the German war economy, found the pressure of the 1930s intensified, though the relation of each to Germany varied with military and political conditions. German policy envisaged the integration of the industrial areas of Austria and Czechoslovakia into the Aryan industrial heartland. For the 'German' population of Austria this was to mean a general economic upswing, while of course no benefits were intended for the 'Slav' population of Czechoslovakia outside the Sudeten region. In both countries Jewish firms and other local concerns – especially the banks – were absorbed by German firms. In Austria some 200 firms which together possessed nearly two-thirds of the country's total incorporated capital passed into German control, as did virtually the entire Czech heavy industrial sector. Under 'trustee' agreements local owners were forced to 'lease' their property to Germans at bargain rates. Nazi leaders and German firms with government connections scrambled for the spoils. Under German administration central control over industry increased, and new plants were constructed. However, though output of armaments and capital goods rose, consumer industries and agriculture stagnated.

Nazi ideology dictated that the racially 'inferior' nations of Hungary, Rumania, Bulgaria and the puppet state of Slovakia should produce only agricultural products and raw materials for consumption in the Aryan industrial heartland, but the exigencies of war forced their development into a pattern similar to that of Austria and Czechoslovakia. The Germans discriminated against Hungarian industry until 1941, when the need for all possible industrial output and for plants outside the range of Allied bombers began to influence policy. Large aircraft plants and new aluminium works arose, and heavy industrial output increased rapidly. Similarly, in Slovakia new German investment raised industrial production nearly two-thirds over prewar levels by 1943. Rumanian oil output increased, and in both Rumania and Bulgaria heavy industrial investment expanded. Development of course was consciously one-sided, focused exclusively on Germany's need for armaments, heavy industrial goods and industrial raw materials. Bilateral arrangements obliged local governments to deliver goods to Germany, which Germany paid for in blocked and therefore useless credits. The German debt to Hungary for instance rose from 140 million marks in 1941 to

500 million in 1942, 1 billion in 1943 and 2.5 billion in 1944. Local governments in effect paid for deliveries to Germany by expanding domestic credit, which created severe inflationary pressures and required further extension of central economic control. Systematic rationing, quotas, control of distribution and direct price regulation increased not only the overall role of government, but also the size and importance of the central bureaucracy. The Hungarian government budget absorbed 33 per cent of gross national product in 1938–39 and 71 per cent in 1944.

Nazi myth and propaganda portrayed the east as a source of food above all else, but Nazi hopes were disappointed, and the failure shows once again the contradictions inherent in Nazi policies. The agricultural 'surpluses' recorded by eastern European countries in 1929–33 were illusory, a temporary result of depressed domestic consumption and the sudden decline in export markets. Eastern agriculture actually remained extremely backward. Large increases in output would have required correspondingly large increases in capital investment, especially in machinery and fertilisers. Instead agricultural investment was neglected and farm workers were mobilised for the army, shifted into local heavy industry or taken to Germany as forced labour. Throughout eastern Europe crop areas, livestock populations and total agricultural output declined drastically; though domestic rations were reduced ruthlessly, food shipments to Germany were never as large as those from the occupied countries of western Europe.

Poland and occupied Russia experienced an even more extreme form of Nazi tyranny. Western Poland was annexed to Germany, and after the invasion of Russia eastern Poland became the 'General Government of the Occupied Polish Territories' under the brutal administration of Hans Frank. In Russia, four huge 'Reich Commissariats' were established, but where they were put into operation, the new Nazi civilian administrations became merely one more overlapping authority competing for power. The army in theory remained in control of the actual 'war zones', Himmler's SS exercised authority in 'racial questions' and had formal responsibility for strengthening 'Germandom' in the east, and Goering's

Four-Year Plan office possessed formal responsibility for economic policy in occupied territories. These three or four agencies flatly refused to cooperate with one another, leading to egregious inefficiency even in the Nazi's own terms.

In Poland the first of the infamous *Einzatzgruppen* ('action teams') of SS personnel moved in behind the army and began to eliminate the entire Polish elite – government officials, professionals, industrial and commercial leaders and agricultural landowners. In addition, some one million Poles and Polish Jews were expelled from the annexed territories and 'resettled' in the territory of the General Government. By 1943 they had been replaced by a nearly equal number of ethnic Germans from enclaves in eastern Europe and Russia as well as from Germany itself. In the General Government the Germans originally planned simply to demolish all industrial plants. This approach changed to the systematic exploitation of all existing plants for German benefit, but the Nazis continued to view Poland essentially as a source of agricultural products, industrial raw materials and labour. All schools above the fourth grade level were closed, and some two million forced labourers were taken to Germany.

In Russia the German army was expected both to supply itself from the conquered areas and also to begin the development of those areas of sources of food, raw materials and labour. However, Hitler had told his army commanders this was to be 'a war of extermination'. Communist Party commissars serving with Soviet army units were summarily executed. The masses of Russian prisoners who fell into the Germans' hands were simply penned in huge fields fenced with barbed wire, where they began to die of hunger and exposure. Beginning in 1942 the survivors were shipped to Germany to work as forced labourers. Of the approximately five million Russian prisoners taken by the German army, some two million seem to have died in captivity, and another million are unaccounted for. The civilian population fared no better. Anyone connected with the Communist Party or the Soviet government was apt to be shot out of hand, and the German army enforced its rule through a system of hostages and mass reprisals against civilians for any show of opposition to German administration. Behind the army came the SS.

The *Einsatzgruppen* were expanded, and their field of operations extended. Himmler ordered a study of the skulls of Communist Party members, to determine if they differed in any systematic way from the average Russian. Some 1.5 million Russian civilians were rounded up as forced labourers and suffered approximately the same death rate as military prisoners. A query came from a German administrator in the Ukraine: 'If we shoot the Jews, liquidate the war prisoners, starve the major part of the big cities' population, and in the coming year reduce also a part of the peasants through famine there will arise a question: who is going to produce the economic goods?'.

In eastern Europe, the German invasion was initially seen by some as an opportunity rather than a disaster. Hungary was at least nominally an ally of Germany, for instance. The Germans were welcomed by the national minorities in the Soviet Union, especially in Byelorussia and the Ukraine, but the experiences of collectivisation and the purges also led many in 'Great Russia' to greet the Germans as saviours. The Germans' brutal behaviour quickly reversed these sentiments. Though in some districts, particularly in the Ukraine, the resistance for a time remained anti-Soviet as well as anti-Nazi, the movement soon crystallised around Soviet soldiers who had evaded capture during the initial German advances. Since Russia had not been defeated, these groups had more tangible basis for their hope of eventual victory than others, and of course the Soviet government made every effort to encourage them and integrate their contribution into the total war effort. Partisans were organised in bands ranging from 300 to 2,000 in size and may have totalled some 200,000 by 1943. As the Soviet armies moved west they were absorbed into regular military units. In the meantime they harassed the Germans and performed the invaluable political function of maintaining the reality of the Soviet Union for the populations of the occupied regions.

The Holocaust

Anti-Semitism lay at the core of Nazi ideology and therefore the extermination of the Jews became the culmination of

Nazi policy. The Nazis planned the elimination of other social groups; tens of thousands of homosexuals, for example, perished in the concentration camps. The Nazis also contemplated the elimination of other ethnic groups; to make room for German settlers in the region of the General Government, Nazi leaders debated whether to deport sixteen to twenty million Poles, or to kill them. But the Jews remained the focus of the Nazi vision, and their fate remains the true measure of the Nazi regime. Late in the war Hitler could calmly contemplate the destruction of Germany, but boasted to his private circle that though the war might be lost, he had at least accomplished his goal of eliminating Europe's Jews.

The question of what to do with the Jews had always exercised Nazi leaders, but with the conquests of the early war years more Jews came under Nazi authority and discussion of the 'Jewish question' became more urgent. Large numbers of Jews were forcibly resettled in officially established ghettos in the General Government in 1939–40. The defeat of France opened the possibility of deporting all European Jews to the French colony of Madagascar, a plan enthusiastically supported by a section of the Foreign Office and by Reinhardt Heydrich, an officer in the SS and Gestapo. However, the plan required a definitive peace treaty with France (and was impossible in any case until the end of the war with Britain) and was dropped without alternative destinations being discussed.

The invasion of Russia opened new vistas. In March 1941 Himmler's *Einsatzgruppen* were given permission to operate in the newly conquered areas, and Frank revealed that Hitler had assured him that the General Government 'in recognition of its accomplishments would become the first territory to be free of Jews'. A plan to declare German Jews stateless persons was rejected by Hitler because it was 'not necessary . . . after the war there would not be any Jews left in Germany anyhow'. In May 1941 further emigration of Jews from France was forbidden because the 'final solution of the Jewish question' was now in sight, and on 31 July 1941 Goering ordered Heydrich to prepare a plan for all 'organisational and financial matters for bringing about a complete solution of the Jewish question in the German sphere of influence in Europe'. Deportations and concentration in eastern ghettos had already begun; indeed mobile killing units were already in operation and extermination centres were already under construction. More cooperation was required among various government agencies, however, and accordingly in January 1942 a conference attended by representatives of all relevant government departments met in Heydrich's office in the Berlin suburb of Wannsee to discuss his plans. The Jews, announced Heydrich, would be deported to immense labour camps in 'the east'. There, 'undoubtedly a majority would fall away through natural decline'. The remainder – the truly dangerous Jews, because they would be the people capable of rebuilding Jewish life – 'would have to be treated accordingly'.

The Nazis intended the entire operation to be self-financing. Money and property confiscated from deported Jews would be used to pay the railway authorities for the use of their trains, police agencies for guards and local governments along the chosen routes for food supplies. The Jews concentrated in the ghettos would work – in the Lodz ghetto for instance every person over the age of nine eventually worked twelve hours a day, six and a half days a week, under threat of immediate 'resettlement' if they refused. At the killing centres, those physically fit would continue to work, and the personal property, clothing and gold fillings from the teeth of the victims would be systematically extracted. The administrative costs would be further reduced by forcing the leaders of the Jewish communities themselves to select and hand over stipulated numbers of candidates for 'resettlement'.

The Nazis cloaked the entire operation in an obsessive legality. Legislation restricting the rights of Jews multiplied, eventually leaving them isolated as objects of compulsory 'emigration'. This occasionally posed problems. Since only Jewish individuals had 'emigrated', the Finance Ministry at first experienced difficulty sequestering the property of Jewish community organisations, which had not 'emigrated'. Case-by-case dispositions eventually were authorised by Adolf Eichmann, acting as the official in charge of such organisations. Similarly, since non-Jews at the killing centres could only die of 'natural causes', the problem of overcrowding had to be periodically relieved by forced marches, denial of medical attention and occasionally by fatal injections. Several camp commanders were tried and convicted of 'corruption' – the murder of Jews was the purpose of the camps, and brutality and even torture beyond that authorised as part of ongoing 'medical' experiments could be overlooked, but individual profiteering, sexual relations with Jewish women, or habitual drunkenness could not be tolerated.

The operation also was conducted in great haste. The *Einsatzgruppen* may have killed as many as a million Jews before the first of the killing centres opened, and mobile gas vans were operating at Chelmno, in the portion of Poland annexed in 1939, in late 1941. The organisational and institutional arrangements still had not been completed before the deportations began. Deportees began to arrive in thousands in makeshift ghettos near the killing centres before they had been completed. In addition to Chelmno, four more killing centres were constructed in the General Government – Treblinka, Sobibor, Belzec and Lublin – and one in Upper Silesia – Auschwitz. The trains ran day after day. The daily trains from Warsaw to Treblinka which began running in July 1942 each contained 5,000 Jews, but this was an exceptional diversion necessitated by a breakdown in the railway line to Sobibor. The normal trainload was approximately 1,000 persons, and they came from all over Europe – three million Jews in three years, and a total of between seven and eight million persons altogether, of whom only a third survived.

The killing centres had to be efficient, and they were. The Nazis, and the SS in particular, were already experienced in the construction and administration of concentration camps, such as Belsen, Buchenwald and Sachsenhausen, in which political opponents and other undesirables could be systematically worked to death. A considerable amount of experience had also already been gained in the construction and use of mobile gas vans and gas chambers using carbon monoxide. These techniques were extended and improved in the Polish centres, though the pressure for speed meant that construction and operations were always behind schedule.

Finally, at Auschwitz, the Nazis found the space and isolation, combined with good transportation connections, for which they had been searching. The Auschwitz complex employed a new, more effective gas as well – hydrogen cyanide – marketed commercially as an insecticide under the name Zyklon B. Auschwitz also boasted improved combined killing units – each with its anteroom, gas chamber and oven to dispose of bodies. The technical, construction and supply problems, especially the problem of a reliable gas supply, all were overcome by Rudolf Höss, the camp commandant, a man overbearingly proud of his 'improvements' and cordially hated by his professional rivals at the other killing centres. The five crematoria at Auschwitz when completed could dispose of a maximum of 12,000 bodies a day. Occasionally the killings exceeded even this total. The Jews from Lodz for instance were killed in large batches of 20,000 a day. The excess bodies were burned in pits measuring approximately four by sixty metres. The fat was drained out of the bottom of the pits and poured over the tops of the fires to speed combustion. To save time and expense, children were sometimes thrown onto the fires without being gassed or shot first.

Even aside from the gross act of exterminating millions of persons, the Holocaust was economically and militarily irrational to its core. The first 50 trainloads of Jews from Germany were shipped eastward in November 1941 – just as the German army was making its last offensive in the Moscow region and desperately needed transportation for additional supplies. Large industrial plants were established around the camps, notably the I.G. Farben works at Auschwitz, to make use of the huge pool of forced labour. However, the locations of the plants were inconvenient, their construction slow and their operations inefficient. The life expectancy of workers in the I.G. Farben synthetic rubber and acetic acid plants was three to four months and in the coal mines supplying I.G. Farben's needs only about one month. Abuse of labour on this scale was itself inefficient, and in addition the camp's poor industrial results resulted from shortages elsewhere in the economy, shortages which resulted in part from the operation of the camps themselves.

Europe's Jews made virtually no resistance to the slaughter. The uprising in the Warsaw ghetto in April 1943 occurred only after 310,000 of the 380,000 Jews in the ghetto had already been deported and was easily suppressed by the Germans. Confronted by an event without precedent in human history, most Jews reacted with incomprehension, disbelief, denial and finally despair. They were isolated. They received no help in Germany or in the occupied countries of eastern Europe and very little in western Europe – though all but a few of Denmark's small Jewish community were spirited away to Sweden, and a few individual Swedish and other neutral diplomatic representatives did what they could. Early reports of the Holocaust from Polish sources were dismissed in Allied countries as propaganda. By the time the Russian armies arrived it was too late for most of the Nazis' intended victims. In the meantime, leaders of local Jewish communities were compelled to cooperate with German authorities in 'resettlement'. They considered resistance hopeless and believed that if 'resettlement' were left to the Germans it would be worse and certainly more brutal. In Lodz Jewish leaders selected first criminals, then the aged and then small children. They hoped that the Nazis, who seemed to want workers and continued industrial output, would spare those able to work, and in the meantime they tried desperately to delude themselves concerning the fate of those who had been 'resettled'. They were wrong – in August 1944 the remaining Jews of Lodz including the leaders of the community were sent to Auschwitz.

The perpetrators of the Holocaust pose even more of a problem. There are sadists in every social group; something of the sadist lurks in every individual personality, and that latent sadism can emerge easily when one individual is given absolute power over another. But the systematic, rational manner of operation of the killing centres is still worse. Many people were involved – those who rounded up and transported the Jews, the large number of guards who rotated through the camps and back to their SS units fighting at the front, the financial and industrial leaders who authorised the industrial plants and often visited the sites, the engineers and administrators in charge of construction and operation of the camps themselves and of the industrial plants and ultimately everyone who knew that the Jews were disappearing and being eliminated somehow. German police reports indicate that most Germans knew of the deportation of Jews, that many knew of the mass murders committed in Poland and Russia by the *Einsatzgruppen* through reports of witnesses and participants and that rumours about the actual killing centres were also widespread.

The perpetrators employed a series of psychological defence mechanisms. Most directly, others could be ordered to perform the actual acts. Teams of camp inmates searched the bodies for jewellery and extracted the dental fillings, and they were themselves regularly eliminated. Code words concealed the reality both from outsiders and from the perpetrators themselves. Gassing a group of prisoners was a 'special action'. Technical legality could be a pretext, and an emphasis on administrative detail could help conceal reality as well. This seems the origin of the compulsive use of forms and official authorisations for every action. The failure to question official euphemisms served as both a psychological and a personal defence; it was simply not safe to ask where or exactly how the Jews were to be 'resettled' or what would happen to them when they arrived, and it was more comfortable not to know. As Speer later said: 'I did not investigate – for I did not want to know what was happening there'. The rapid institutionalisation of the killing process also bred a certain mentality. Höss already had extensive experience in the camp system before his Auschwitz appointment. Finally, and most importantly, the perpetrators relied on superior authority. As Himmler himself said: 'The *Führer* has charged me with carrying out this very difficult task'. And so it seemed to many who were involved – a difficult, unpleasant task undertaken by very ordinary human beings in the course of very ordinary careers. And this, perhaps, is the ultimate horror.

THE DEFEAT OF THE AXIS

The Allied war economies

From its peak in 1942 the Nazi empire collapsed in three short years. In retrospect, this seems almost a matter of simple arithmetic. Despite the ruthless exploitation of their conquests, Germany and Japan could not possibly match the combined resources of the British empire, the Soviet Union and the United States. By 1944 the Allies' total production of weapons and military supplies had reached a level three times that of the Axis states, and as German and Japanese output peaked and began to decline Allied output continued to increase.

Britain's war economy rested on consent – the shared beliefs that the war must be won and that the burdens would be distributed fairly. The government immediately imposed strict controls on imports and exports. Restrictions were placed on profits and even more severe restrictions on consumption. Taxes, forced savings and rationing reduced consumers' purchases by over one-fifth from 1938 to 1944. Paradoxically, many British citizens enjoyed a higher standard of living under the wartime rationing regime than they had during the depressed 1930s. This may have made them more willing to accept the strict limits on personal liberty imposed by the 1941 National Service Act. Men aged 18–50 and women aged 20–30 were made liable for either military or essential civilian service, and the upper limits were later extended. British employment increased by three million during the war, and the increase included two million women. By 1942 British military production already exceeded German output in several important areas. The agricultural area under cultivation actually rose by over one-half; the shortage of labour in agriculture was alleviated by some 224,000 prisoners. Also, Britain never lost access to overseas sources of supply and largely succeeded in denying such access to Germany.

Britain initially could take up slack from the depression; the Soviet Union in contrast lost about half its total industrial capacity to the German invaders, and in any case had no cushion of civilian production available for redirection into the war effort. Between July and November 1941, under conditions of extraordinary hardship, the essential machines in 1,360 factories were dismantled, loaded on railway cars, shifted eastward and reassembled. One factory required 8,000 railway cars; some factories were dismantled and loaded as German artillery shells dropped around them. Some ten million persons accompanied the plants eastward. There, without adequate food, clothing or housing, they scraped together buildings to shelter the machines and put the plants back into operation. These plants, the nucleus of manufacturing establishments already operating in the east and a remarkable programme of new plant construction increased output so that by 1944 Russian military production actually exceeded 1940 levels and had surpassed that of Germany. In February 1942 the Soviet government mobilised all men aged 16–55 and all women aged 16–45. From 1940 to 1942 the proportion of women in the Soviet labour force rose from two-fifths to over half. Labour productivity increased in every year of the war, in contrast to Britain, where it remained approximately constant, and to Germany, where it declined. The Russians also made an extraordinary effort to maintain agricultural output but could not make good the loss of nearly half their agricultural land. In 1942 agricultural production equalled only one-third the prewar level and there was widespread starvation. The food supply improved during the next year, but by the end of the war average real wages had declined by over half. The Great Patriotic War deserves its title. The deadly threat of Nazism welded Soviet society together. The challenge was met and surmounted by young, inexperienced graduates of the new technical schools – who replaced the victims of the purges and became the new elite in the Soviet system.

The United States added the final crushing weight to the scales. Much of America's immense productive capacity still lay idle in 1941. During the next three years employment increased by nineteen million, while average plant utilisation rose from 40 to 90 hours per week between 1939 and 1944. Output per hour of labour – already double German levels and five times that of Japan – rose further. Entering the war late and remaining secure from attack, the United States could afford the luxury of relatively extensive planning of increases in military output, and as in Britain the government could rely on a large measure of voluntary sacrifice. In fact, not much sacrifice was required; consumer spending actually increased twelve per cent from 1939 to 1944, while by 1942 the United States already produced more armaments than all enemy nations combined.

American output was channelled to Britain and the Soviet Union by the Lend Lease programme. From 1941 to 1945 shipments to Britain totalled 13.8 billion dollars and shipments to Russia 9.5 billion. The United States and Britain achieved quite good coordination of production and supply, based on a general agreement to treat all resources as part of a common pool. This was true of technological developments as well; the Americans copied British aircraft engine designs, and the British copied American motor vehicles. America supplied 7 per cent of British munitions in 1942, 27 per cent in 1943 and 29 per cent in 1944. However, Lend Lease shipments were not gifts; payment was only deferred until the end of the war, and consequently in 1945 Britain suddenly had to deal with an immense debt despite a drastic reduction in resources.

The United States and the Soviet Union did not establish any joint planning mechanism. The Soviet government presented lists of requests to the United States authorities, but without statements of priorities. It is still unknown exactly what was delivered, what fraction of total Russian supplies the shipments constituted or how the Russians used the shipments. Large amounts of flour, sugar, canned meat (an important part of Soviet army rations), raw materials, semi-manufactured goods such as copper and steel, railway equipment, locomotives and industrial machinery flowed through Lend Lease channels. The United States supplied a large fraction of Russia's motor vehicles (138,000 in 1943 alone), and perhaps slightly over 10 per cent each of the tanks and aircraft employed by the Soviet armed forces.

American goods not only had to be produced but also delivered. As in the First World War, shipments across the Atlantic were threatened by the German submarine fleet.

Hitler neglected U-boat construction until 1940, but then ordered increased numbers when Britain refused to yield. Between June 1940 and December 1941 Britain lost one-third of total tonnage, and was only able to replace some 30 per cent of the losses. The German invasion of Russia and the Japanese attack on the United States added new allies, but also imposed the necessity of supplying Russia via the very dangerous route to Murmansk and also required the United States to shift naval forces from the Atlantic to the Pacific. Allied losses peaked in early 1943, but nonetheless the addition of American shipbuilding capacity resulted in a continuous increase in the size of Allied fleets after mid-1942. In addition the increased availability of long-range bombers, small escort aircraft carriers and improved microwave radar tipped the balance against Germany. Allied losses declined by half from March to April 1943, and in May the Germans lost 41 U-boats and never again posed a serious threat to Atlantic supply routes. Russian ships could carry supplies to Vladivostock because Russia was not yet at war with Japan. In addition the Allies opened a new route to Russia through the Middle East. In August 1941 Britain and Russia invaded Iran and forced the establishment of the more friendly regime of Mohammed Riza Pahlevi. Existing roads and railways were improved and extended, and by mid-1943 over 100,000 tons of American goods per month were flowing through Iran into the southern Soviet Union.

Allied victories

The military tide turned in 1942. In the Pacific, the battles of the Coral Sea and Midway ended Japanese expansion. In Russia, Hitler split the German forces to drive both towards the oil fields in the Caucasus and towards Stalingrad, the key to Russia's north-south communications. The Germans attacked Stalingrad in September, but were held off by the garrison's desperate defence, while Soviet armies massed to the north and south on their exposed flanks. Hitler refused to permit a retreat, and the pincers closed in late November, trapping 330,000 German troops; when the remnants defied Hitler and surrendered in February 1943, fewer than 100,000 remained alive. In north Africa the Germans and Italians lost nearly 950,000 men, mostly captured, and the final mass surrenders pushed Italy close to the point of collapse. Italy's obvious weakness led the British to prevail on the Americans to postpone the invasion of France to knock Italy out of the war. Popular enthusiasm for the war had never been high, and now plummeted; Mussolini lost control of the government and was dismissed, and the new government declared the Fascist Party dissolved, began to seek an armistice and finally surrendered in September. The Germans replied by seizing the major cities and disarming remaining Italian units, and the ensuing long, difficult campaign was not completed until the German collapse of spring 1945.

In the east, the Russians began a sustained offensive after Stalingrad despite their losses. Russia's immense population still provided reserves of manpower. Germany's population pool was nearing the bottom, and even the supposedly 'racially pure' elite SS units needed topping up with conscripts from occupied territories. Russian troops were also increasingly better armed. Russia was now producing some 2,000 tanks a month compared to Germany's 350. The terrible seige of Leningrad was lifted in January 1943, and by January 1944 Soviet forces were on the Polish border. By mid-1944 the Russians had penetrated into East Prussia and southern Poland and had advanced across southern Russia into Rumania, Bulgaria and Yugoslavia. In Yugoslavia the Russians cooperated with Tito's partisans in the final expulsion of the Germans. However, when the anti-Soviet Polish Home Army rose against the Germans in Warsaw in August 1944 they received no aid from the Russians and were massacred by the Germans. The Russians then resumed their advance in the north, occupying the Baltic states, capturing Warsaw in January 1945, and pressing across the Vistula towards Berlin.

In the west, the delayed landings in Normandy began in June 1944, and the American and British forces broke out after a sharp but brief resistance by the Germans. France and Belgium were quickly liberated, with some of the burden being borne by the Free French forces. There was one final German offensive, the Battle of the Bulge, but by early 1945

Allied forces were pressing into Germany from the west as the Russians penetrated from the east.

The air war

As the Allied armies massed on Germany's borders, day and night bombs rained down from the sky. The strategic air offensive highlighted the links between military and civilian, between technology and the economy and between science and technology. However, the results remain debatable, and the debate has called into question many of the assumptions regarding the psychology, economics and military means of waging modern war. The development and production of long-range bombers was fantastically expensive and difficult. Of the advanced economies only Britain, the United States and Germany possessed the necessary expertise, and only Britain and the United States in combination possessed the resources necessary to build both bombers and fighters. Even among this elite, no fundamental technical breakthroughs achieved operational significance. There were 19 models of the Spitfire and 1,100 design modifications from 1938 to 1945, increasing top speed from 356 to 460 miles per hour, but these were incremental improvements in an already existing design.

Because of Britain's presumed superiority in aircraft and inferiority in ground troops the bomber had become fundamental to British strategic thinking. The emphasis on the bomber assumed the validity of three assumptions: that 'the bomber will always get through', that bomb attacks would destroy civilian morale and undermine the enemy's will to resist and that bomber attacks would destroy the enemy's economy, destroying as well the ability to resist. All three proved false. British bombers could not survive German fighters' attacks or even hit their targets in daylight, and the British therefore shifted to night attacks, giving up all hope of hitting 'precision' targets of economic significance. The technique known previously as 'indiscriminate' bombing was rechristened 'area' bombing and became the new orthodoxy. Lord Cherwell, Churchill's scientific advisor, estimated that a 'de-housing' campaign could destroy the homes of one-third of the German population in fifteen months and 'break the spirit of the people'. 'Area' bombing was Churchill's preference in any case and was tirelessly and single-mindedly advocated by Arthur Harris, Commander in Chief of Bomber Command after early 1942.

In July–August 1943 a week of exceptional weather allowed successive raids on Hamburg. The large fires burning in the city centre joined together, heating the air to terrific temperatures, causing it to rise and sucking surrounding air inward. The resulting howling winds carried not only sparks but entire timbers and roof beams, as well as any loose object or person unfortunate enough to be in the area. This was a fire storm – those fleeing could be killed by the heat behind them, but more died from asphyxiation than burns because the fire sucked the air away from them even though they might be in shelters. Several other urban centres suffered fire storms as Harris pursued his aim of destroying two and a half German cities per month. Dresden, a previously unharmed and especially beautiful city of no military or industrial importance, its population swollen by large numbers of refugees, was destroyed by three raids in February 1945 in 'Operation Thunderclap' intended to crush civilian morale and thereby undermine any attempt at last-ditch resistance by the Nazi leaders.

The strategic bombing offensive poses both moral and military problems. The raids were clearly directed against noncombattants. The victims were not even, say, workers in armaments industries, but included the aged, mothers and children as well. To justify them as revenge for German air attacks is not an appealing argument; in any case British authorities insisted publicly that the bombers' targets were in fact military. In addition the attacks failed in their intended purpose. After the war Harris himself concluded that the attempt to break German civilian morale 'proved to be wholly unfounded'. Not only German civilian morale, but also the economies of the bombed cities proved to be remarkably resilient. The fire storm in Hamburg reduced the labour force by ten per cent, but military production was fully restored in five months. 'Area' bombing may have reduced German armaments production by about five per cent in 1943 and eight per cent in 1944, a small return for a very expensive campaign. The strategic air offensive did score one spectacular success, but it marked a return to the original strategy of 'precision' bombing. Beginning in mid-1944 American and British bombers began to raid oil fields and refineries systematically, causing a fuel shortage which hampered the movement of mechanised army units and drastically reduced the number of German fighter planes in the air. For the last year of the war the Allies had complete command of the air on all fronts. Round-the-clock strategic bombing – British by night, American by day – eventually did have an impact on German industrial output, and unimpeded tactical support could be provided for Allied ground troops, by whom the war had to be won.

The end of the Axis

Literally amid collapsing ruins, some Nazi leaders still hoped for a separate peace with the western powers as the prelude to a joint crusade against the Soviet Union, and others still hoped to restore the Nazi-Soviet pact of 1939 and thereby remove Russia from the war. Hitler hoped occasionally for rescue by new super weapons, but the jet plane arrived too late and there was no fuel even if it could have been produced in sufficient numbers. Germany did not develop the atomic bomb. Hitler's violent prejudice against 'Jewish physics' was well known. In the absence of any support from Hitler, the doubts regarding the bomb's feasibility, the immense expense of nuclear research and the destruction of Europe's only heavy water plant in 1943 by the Norwegian resistance ended German attempts to develop nuclear weapons. Without a nuclear warhead, the V-2 rocket remained merely another large bomb.

Finally, Hitler ordered that the German armies should destroy everything as they retreated. This final scorched earth directive was systematically sabotaged by Speer and others who had begun to look towards the postwar world. On 29 April 1945 Hitler learned of Mussolini's death at the hands of Italian partisans, and also learned that Himmler had attempted to negotiate a peace settlement with the

Allies. On 30 April Hitler married his longtime mistress, and then both committed suicide. Hitler's adjutant was unable to burn his body completely before Russian troops covered the final few blocks to the Reich chancellery building. A week later German armed forces surrendered unconditionally on all fronts.

Japan's fate rested on a German victory in Europe. With Germany's defeat the situation became hopeless. Even at the peak of Japanese strength, the ships necessary to deploy troops and matériel from one point to another within the far-flung maritime empire had been in short supply. Before the war the United States had been Japan's most important supplier of oil, steel and heavy machinery; Japan lagged in the new technologies as well, especially radar. After Midway the United States enjoyed supremacy on the sea and in the air. Some Japanese leaders favoured a compromise peace, but the Allied demand for unconditional surrender, and the clearly implied threat to the emperor's safety, strengthened the position of those army leaders who wanted to fight to the end. The Japanese did attempt to secure Russian mediation; they were surprised to be rebuffed, not knowing that Stalin had committed himself to a declaration of war on Japan following a German surrender.

American military planners predicted that an invasion of the Japanese home islands would cost approximately a million Allied casualties. To avoid those losses, the United States decided to use the atomic bomb. Only the United States possessed the necessary resources for the bomb's development, and the Americans in effect absorbed the British programme while benefiting from the emigration of some of Germany's best minds. The Russians also somehow found resources for nuclear research, but could not press their programme to success before the war's end. At Hiroshima on 6 August and Nagasaki on 9 August 1945 the world entered the atomic age, though even then only the personal urging of the emperor himself finally convinced the leaders of Japan to accept unconditional surrender.

2
RECONSTRUCTION

The Second World War took the lives of approximately 40 million persons, including 17 million Russians, 6 million Jews and 4 million persons uprooted and either murdered outright or worked to death. By disrupting normal delivery of food and services the war significantly increased civilian mortality rates, sometimes far from the actual battlefields; over 1 million persons died in a famine in Bengal, for instance. Across Europe the combination of aerial and ground bombardment had reduced entire cities to undifferentiated expanses of smoking rubble. Where industrial plants had escaped destruction they suffered from six years of neglected maintenance. Industrial output in Germany and the occupied territories had been declining since 1944 and now collapsed. Agricultural output had declined even more drastically due to the shortage of labour and diversion of resources into armaments. Distribution systems broke down completely and even the reduced supplies of food and industrial products were not available to those who needed them. Millions found themselves not only without food and shelter, but uprooted from their homes and forced to move.

Across Europe, military decisions congealed into political structures. American forces turned south after crossing the Rhine to prevent the Nazis from massing their remaining troops for a last stand in southern Germany. As a result Soviet armies took Berlin and pressed on to the Elbe River, and the resulting line of demarcation became the border between the new Federal Republic of Germany and the German Democratic Republic. To the east, the presence of the Soviet army ensured that the emerging postwar regimes would be friendly to the Soviet Union; to the west, American power favoured regimes friendly to the United States. In Italy, France and Scandinavia a coalition of anti-German forces cooperated with the British and American armies. Communist partisans in Albania and Yugoslavia threw off the Axis yoke through their own efforts, and received the Russians' blessing. Elsewhere in eastern Europe liberation was achieved through the work of the Soviet army; in Finland, Estonia, Latvia, Lithuania, Poland and Rumania the Russians adjusted borders in their favour and they permitted no revival of the predominantly anti-Soviet groupings which had characterised the region between the wars.

The war forced an even closer union of science and technology; the resulting array of new products and processes seemed to open the door to a world where all problems could be solved through the development and application of new technologies. The end of the war also seemed to create the conditions for a progressive restructuring of social institutions. The experience of the war demonstrated conclusively that, contrary to the received wisdom of the 1920s and 1930s, central governments could in fact control economic development effectively. Virtually every European nation introduced some form of economic planning during the postwar period. Further, planning would be based on a broader political consensus; for the first time parties representing the working class became legitimate participants in the political process. New international institutions were intended to facilitate representation and cooperation of all nations and avoid the external conflicts which had produced the economic instability of the interwar years.

If technology made a promise of abundance, it also threatened destruction; the capability of the atomic bomb to obliterate civilised existence quickly became one of the unpleasant facts with which all peoples had to live. Worse, the experience of the Holocaust proved that there were no depths to which the most civilised and cultured Europeans would not descend. No assurance could be given that some ingrained sense of restraint and decency would hold back those who might consider employing nuclear weapons to achieve their ends. And even beyond this, the Holocaust raised the suspicion of something dark and hidden within

European civilisation itself. Uncertainty and doubt shadowed even the brightest promises and the most brilliant achievements of the postwar world.

For all these reasons the Second World War marks a great divide in European and human history. Nonetheless, the war proved neither a mere interruption in Europe's social and economic life, nor a completely new beginning. The war continued certain important tendencies already well-established before the outbreak of hostilities. Conventional industrial development – textiles, iron and steel, machinery – continued its eastward march. By 1945 Poland, Hungary, Yugoslavia, Rumania and Bulgaria all possessed the foundations of basic industrial sectors, while the development of the eastern regions of the Soviet Union continued the thrust of the industrialisation drive of the 1930s. Despite the pressures of war, new developments also remained circumscribed by economic realities. For instance, the high capital intensities and long lead times for development of new weapons systems meant that most 'new' technologies rested on prewar developments and that only the most advanced economies succeeded in moving significantly beyond the techniques and designs available at the war's outbreak. Only the United States, Britain and Germany progressed in this sense with radar, aircraft, motorised vehicles and synthetic materials, and only the Americans possessed the resources necessary for the creation of an atomic bomb in addition to the prosecution of a conventional war.

Socially and politically, postwar Europe also picked up strands from the interwar period. The need to integrate the working class into political life had been widely recognised. The first labour governments had already served in Britain, France, Spain and Scandinavia; throughout Europe indeed even the most extreme right-wing movements had claimed to represent the true interests of the working class. The postwar vogue of economic planning also rested on prewar developments. Theoretically, the writings of Keynes in the west and the experience of Soviet Marxism in the east promised more effective approaches to economic management. Practically, all governments had intervened extensively in their domestic economies during the 1930s, and the League of Nations and a large number of more limited agreements foreshadowed postwar international political and economic cooperation as well.

THE PROBLEM OF GERMANY

Germany inevitably became the proving ground for competing models of postwar society. The Allies had agreed on certain basic principles. They forced Germany to surrender unconditionally on all fronts, kept Admiral Doenitz as a figurehead just long enough to place the burden of defeat and surrender clearly on the Nazis and instituted a military occupation intended to root out and destroy German 'militarism' and to 'democratise' German government and society. All Nazi organisations were abolished and 'more than nominal' participants in Nazi organisations excluded from public office. Germany was to pay reparations and to lose substantial amounts of territory, notably to Poland.

Beyond these principles, however, the Allies found little on which they could agree. Denazification and democratisation caused problems, for virtually all government officials and professionals had been Party members, and all economic leaders of course had cooperated in the Nazi war effort. The Allies found it impossible to administer their zones without the assistance of such persons, and as the split between east and west deepened, whole categories of potentially useful persons received amnesties. Soviet authorities argued that central institutions headed by reliable Germans should be re-established immediately, and set about creating centrally-controlled administrative organisations, political parties and labour unions. The Americans, British and French worried at first that there might not be any reliable Germans and permitted only local organisations in their zones. As exonerated, rehabilitated and amnestied Germans moved back into positions of power, they therefore occupied quite different institutional structures in east and west.

Economic policy also caused problems. The policy originally enunciated in 1944 by United States Secretary of the Treasury Henry Morgenthau, calling for the destruction of German military industrial capacity, would have proved impossible.

The loss of agricultural lands to Poland, the sudden increase in population through flight and expulsion of Germans from the east and the requirements of European economic integration required a high level of industrial development in Germany. In the event, the limits set on industrial production were never enforced. American policy changed, becoming a determination to press for rapid industrial development in western Europe to counter the perceived threat from the east. The Americans and British restored virtually all of the leaders of Germany's prewar financial and industrial combines to their former positions in the hope that they would rebuild the German economy. The newly-installed central authorities in the Soviet zone, in contrast, encouraged the expropriation of all firms which had cooperated with the Nazi regime and their transformation into 'people's property'. As the West German economy was being restored to private corporate control, therefore, the East German industrial and commercial sectors were reorganised under the leadership of central government agencies.

Even in the absence of ideological issues the policies of the two superpowers towards Germany and Europe would have differed. The United States emerged from the war with its industries larger and more efficient than ever, and therefore needed trading partners and investment opportunities. The Soviet Union possessed a large military industrial base located far to the east, but the basic industries constructed in western Russia during the 1920s and 1930s had been destroyed, agriculture was prostrate and appalling losses of life had been sustained. Now all that had been destroyed would somehow have to be recreated. Reparations proved a particularly intractable problem. Russia wanted large reparations of the order of ten billion dollars in both dismantled industrial plants and current production. Railways in East Germany were being torn up and the rails shipped to Russia as late as 1947. The United States and Great Britain wanted a smaller total, paid over a longer time. As the western Allies came to emphasise economic recovery, they made reparations dependent on prior German economic development and the cooperation of an all-Germany government.

The mutual suspicion of the United States and Russia, reflected in economic policy, led directly to the division of. Germany. The United States and Great Britain unified their zones in 1947, infuriating both the Russians and the French. But by 1948 the three western Allies were cooperating in planning West German economic recovery, and after the Russian boycott of the Allied control council the French merged their zone with the American and British zones. The Russians had been inflating the German currency to satisfy their reparations demands more easily. In June 1948 the western Allies announced a currency reform to apply only to their zones. In reply the Russians attempted to blockade Berlin and suffered a humiliating defeat. Soviet and East German authorities began to interfere with road and rail transport from the western zones to Berlin, ultimately cutting off all ground connections. Though not challenging the authority of the Soviet Union on the ground, on 26 June 1948 the western Allies began the famous 'airlift' which flew essential supplies into West Berlin for almost a year. The Soviet Union in turn did not challenge the right of the western Allies to fly to and from Berlin along the recognised 'air corridors'. By the time the Russians permitted the highways and railways to reopen, the division of Germany was an accomplished fact.

Through late 1948 and early 1949 the Americans forced the pace on the creation of an independent West German government. The United States, France and Britain convoked a parliamentary council to draw up a constitution for a new Federal Republic of Germany. The resulting 'basic law' (*Grundgesetz*) was not a 'constitution', as the framers hoped for the reunification of West Germany with the Soviet sector; one clause of the document said that when this occurred, the basic law 'shall cease to be in force'. Such a development seemed progressively less likely as the years passed, and the 1949 law remains the constitution of West Germany. It set up a federal system with power shared between the national government and eleven states. West Germany was to have a two-chamber parliament, the upper house elected by the state assemblies and the lower house elected by universal suffrage in a rather complex combination of majority and proportional representation. The system preserved a great deal of autonomy for local government in West Germany; for example, state governments were given control over the universities in their districts.

The status of West Berlin was peculiar. Although in the strictest legal sense not a part of the Federal Republic, it was economically and socially integrated into the new state; West Berlin's representatives to the Bundestag could vote in committees but not in plenary meetings of the chamber. Another peculiarity of West Germany during the first years of independence was the continuing role of the occupying powers in its affairs; not until 1955 was full sovereignty restored to the state, and West Germany was not allowed to establish an army until the following year. Finally, relations with East Germany were anomalous; West Germany did not recognise East Germany as a foreign country or a separate state. Under the 'Hallstein Doctrine' of 1955, the government in Bonn broke diplomatic relations with nations which officially recognised the government of the German Democratic Republic (with the exception of the Soviet Union), since Bonn claimed to be the legal successor to the previous regimes and to be the sole representative of the German people.

The major parties which emerged recruited their supporters from the old clienteles of the interwar Weimar parties. The Social Democratic Party (SPD) was the old socialist party. The new Christian Democratic Union (CDU), successor to the Catholic Centre party, was suspicious of socialism but hopeful of economic growth and parliamentarianism and found an ally in the Bavarian Christian Socialist Union (CSU). The Free Democratic Party was an unusual grouping, originally conservative but becoming more liberal; it attracted those who disliked the religious ties of the CDU/CSU and the socialism of the SPD and drew into its ranks a number of intellectuals. There was also a revived Communist Party; although it obtained more than a million votes in the first Bundestag election, it declined rapidly and was banned in 1956 as unconstitutional. Small parties were kept to a minimum by a law requiring that any party obtain at least five per cent of the total vote before it could be represented in parliament – passed in response to a sudden increase in support for right-wing organisations in the wake of an economic recession.

The first elections of 1949 gave a victory to the CDU/CSU coalition. Their leader, Konrad Adenauer, became the first federal chancellor in 1949 and retained the office until 1963, when he was succeeded by former finance minister Ludwig Erhard. The CDU/CSU governments were similar to other conservative parties in Europe; they encouraged the free market but also instituted a welfare state, and allied with the United States but also participated in European integration. West Germany became one of the first members of the Common Market in 1957. The CDU/CSU was suspicious of the Soviet Union and its allies in eastern Europe and unenthusiastic about any rapprochement with East Germany short of reunification. They oversaw West Germany's 'economic miracle', maintained the status of the ever more valuable Deutschmark and based their electoral support on the prosperous and growing middle classes.

Reconstruction in West Germany involved problems of rebuilding and resettlement. In many of the larger cities, three-quarters or more of the housing had been destroyed by Allied bombing attacks. Fully ten million refugees flooded into West Germany from the regions annexed by Poland, from East Germany, and from Czechoslovakia and the other countries of eastern Europe. Observers inside and outside West Germany expected the refugees to prove an insupportable burden to the ruined economy, but the Americans brusquely rejected the West German government's claim that the refugees were an international problem. West Germany granted the refugees full rights of citizenship and entitlements to pensions based on each individual's previous social status. Beyond that, little was done for the refugees as a group. Housing was in critically short supply for all West Germans, and the government structured the tax system and capital markets so as to provide incentives for housing construction Firms could deduct the cost of housing constructed for employees, and interest rates were strictly controlled until 1968 to ensure that funds were available to local government housing agencies. Four million housing units were constructed between 1949 and 1955, and construction continued at the rate of half a million units each year for another decade. However, housing was not constructed where the refugees were located, but rather in industrial centres; the government opted to require people to move to jobs rather than attempt to create jobs where there were people.

Instead of a burden, the refugees proved to be a crucial support of the new West German economy. Many possessed important industrial skills, notably the two million Sudeten Germans from Czechoslovakia. In many cases, entire firms reconstituted themselves in West Germany, sometimes after smuggling key pieces of equipment from their old factories in the east. Overall, the refugees felt tremendous pressure to regain their lost social position if at all possible. They proved mobile and competitive, willing to accept low-paid jobs and long hours in the hope of a better future. Their pressure undoubtedly held down wages, especially in skilled trades, making West German products more competitive in international markets. On the other hand, their demand for housing and consumer durables widened and deepened West Germany's domestic market, providing the basis for further growth.

West Germany benefited from extensive American aid under the Marshall Plan. In addition, the CDU/CSU governments granted substantial concessions to investors in the hope of stimulating savings and capital formation. In a classic study published in 1955, Henry C. Wallich concluded that West German industry had 'pulled itself up by its tax-exempt bootstraps'. The labour unions cooperated by placing their emphasis on the creation of employment opportunities and expansion of social services. Wage demands were moderate and strikes infrequent. Workers accepted large reductions in their real incomes as part of the 1948 currency reform, which put an end to the postwar inflation and channelled resources into capital formation. On the other hand, though wages remained relatively low, the government taxed overtime work at preferential rates. In 1951 West German industrial production was already 50 per cent higher than in 1936 and the West German economy was poised to become one of the major forces supporting the great western European boom.

Two weeks after the western Allies recognised the new Federal Republic of Germany, the Russian zone of occupation was recognised by the Soviet Union and other socialist countries as the German Democratic Republic. The government was under the control of the Socialist Unity Party (SED), the union of the communist and socialist parties in the Soviet sector which had been effected in 1946. By 1950 the general secretary of the SED was Walter Ulbricht, a carpenter, who had belonged to the Spartacus League after the First World War, served as a communist Reichstag deputy during the Weimar era and spent the Second World War in the Soviet Union. Ulbricht remained at the head of the party – and, thus, the effective ruler of the GDR – until his retirement in 1971.

Ulbricht established a reputation as one of the most loyal supporters of the Soviet Union, but his task was not always easy. Reconstruction was difficult in East Germany. While West Germany successfully absorbed 10 million refugees, East Germany lost 2.6 million persons who fled west between 1949 and 1961, when the 'Anti-Fascist Protective Wall' was erected along the border between East and West Berlin. In 1951 East German industrial production was still 25 per cent below its 1936 level, in part because of heavy reparations and occupation costs levied by the Soviet Union. East Germany's five-year plan announced in 1951 emphasised the expansion of heavy industrial production but had already fallen far behind schedule by the end of 1952. Religious repression, increased work norms, the introduction of Soviet-style labour relations in industry and agriculture and a severe food shortage resulted in widespread discontent. In June 1953, following Stalin's death, strikes in Berlin and other centres involved between 300,000 and 400,000 workers. After a day of protests, 21 workers had been killed; some police units proved unreliable. Rioting flared sporadically until October. An estimated 1,000 demonstrators were ultimately sent to prison for their insurrection. Ulbricht put down the rebellion with Soviet support, and East Germany has not since seen a similar outbreak of protest.

ECONOMIC RECONSTRUCTION

Western Europe

The economy of western Europe, seemingly prostrate in 1945, recovered remarkably rapidly, far more rapidly in fact than anyone, expert or layman, would have predicted. More active intervention by governments in economic life, greater cooperation among national governments and the beginning of a rapid convergence of Nordic and Mediterranean Europe towards the western European pattern of development marked the years of reconstruction. Rates of growth varied, but in every case industrial output at least had been restored to prewar levels by the early 1950s. Pursuing policies more or less parallel to those of West Germany, western European governments worked to end the inflation which marked the immediate aftermath of the war. Wages were held down, consumption restrained and resources channelled into industrial investment; in retrospect, the need to rebuild plants damaged and destroyed during the war, added to the backlog of investment opportunities remaining from the depressed 1930s, ensured the success of what in other circumstances might have proved an excessively one-sided policy.

The war accelerated Britain's decline relative to the newer industrial powers. Britain emerged from the war with substantial new investment in advanced sectors of industry such as engineering and aircraft, but also with the continuing need to modernise other important sectors, particularly mining and the railway system. The government greatly extended its role in the management of the economy but had also taken on the heavy burdens of a new comprehensive social security system. Partly as a result of the terms of the massive American Lend Lease programme during the war, British foreign debt had increased from 800 million pounds in 1938 to some 5 billion in 1946, while the value of overseas assets had declined from 4.5 to 3.4 billion pounds. Britain had become a net debtor for the first time since the eighteenth century, and the decision to quit India signalled the loss of empire as well. The decline in overseas assets and the loss of colonial possessions increased British sensitivity to short-term fluctuations in the balance of payments. The initial large postwar deficit was covered by a loan from the United States and Canada, which was conditional on the pound being made convertible as soon as possible. The attempt to restore convertibility in 1947 failed, however, as foreigners holding pounds rushed to convert them to dollars in order to cover their own deficits with the United States. Controls on foreign exchange had to be reimposed, and the government extended the wartime rationing and allocation system as well, while attempting to hold down imports and stimulate exports. Food was rationed until 1954, and periodic shortages of coal and electricity made life unpleasant. However, supported by Marshall Plan aid and general European recovery, the programme succeeded, as exports rose 60 per cent from 1947 to 1949 while imports rose only slightly.

The instability of France became legend in the postwar period. The annual and sometimes semi-annual political crises were punctuated and occasionally caused by labour unrest. Chronic inflation and periodic financial and foreign exchange crises seemed further evidence that the weak governments of the Fourth Republic lacked the ability to deal with difficult problems decisively. Behind these scenes of turmoil, however, France developed a set of institutions which worked to foster both economic growth and social stability. During the war, government officials and business executives had adopted the opinion, long held by labour leaders and widespread in the Resistance, that some form of planning was required to overcome the continual economic crises of the preceding fifteen years. As a result of nationalisation during the 1930s and the war, the state already controlled a large sector of the economy directly, but even here postwar shortages of raw materials required that clear priorities be established. The first plan was designed as an ad hoc emergency measure, but was extended to coincide with the Marshall Plan, and eventually *le plan* became a permanent institution. The first plan aimed to rebuild and modernise basic industry and to eliminate bottlenecks. Planning was 'flexible', however; no production quotas were established as in the Soviet planning system, but 'targets' were established for each sector. Decentralised discussions then established the role of each individual firm. The government had considerable leverage, but the possibilities for compulsion were limited, and on balance the plan depended on voluntary cooperation for success.

The French planning system has since aroused considerable enthusiasm among observers who either dislike the centralised compulsion of the Soviet model or are attempting to convince suspicious audiences that 'non-socialist' planning is a viable possibility. It is therefore important to note the degree to which the adoption and success of planning in France depended on specific individuals and a specific historical situation. The plan could not have succeeded without a remarkably gifted corps of administrators, notably Jean Monnet, the first administrator and later instrumental in the founding of the European Coal and Steel Community and the European Economic Community. Further, French government officials and business managers enjoyed extremely close and relatively cordial relations. They attended (and continue to attend) the same elite schools, and crossovers from government to business were common. In these circles the idea of the state's role in 'directing' economic development had a heritage dating back to the seventeenth century. More directly, Monnet and others had been influenced by the ideas of Etienne Clémentel, who had hoped to 'plan' France's reconstruction after the First World War. In addition, many of the leaders of postwar France shared the experience of the Resistance in common. The sudden turnover of top positions, as leaders discredited by their association with Vichy or tainted by collaboration with the Germans were ousted, provided a unique opportunity for younger men sharing a common vision to move from middle to upper levels in both government and business much more rapidly than would otherwise have been the case.

Of the Low Countries, Belgium had suffered the least damage to industrial plant, and after the liberation in 1944 recovery proceeded rapidly. The inflation which had marked the German occupation was halted by a currency reform and a rather restrictive monetary policy, accompanied however by increases in wages and the introduction of a comprehensive social security system. Belgium could enjoy these luxuries because of large dollar reserves, the result of American purchases of uranium from the Congo and fees paid by the Allies for the use of the port of Antwerp. Damage in Luxembourg and the Netherlands had been more extensive, and reconstruction was correspondingly more difficult. The Dutch currency reform was accompanied by controls on wages, prices and foreign exchange, though here too extensive social security measures were adopted almost immediately. The increase in the Dutch birth rate, the repatriation of former residents of the Dutch East Indies and the decline of agriculture led to an emphasis on industrial expansion under government leadership.

Drawing on a history of economic cooperation, the three countries began to plan for the postwar world before the war had ended. Already in 1922 Belgium and Luxembourg had formed an economic union, and during the International Economic Conference in Geneva in 1927 they had drawn closer to the Netherlands. In 1930 Belgium, Luxembourg and the Netherlands concluded the Oslo Agreements with the three Scandinavian countries, under which all six agreed not to increase tariffs without notification and consultation, and in 1932 Belgium, Luxembourg and the Netherlands agreed in the Ouchy Convention to reduce tariffs among themselves. The Benelux Agreement signed by the three governments-in-exile in London in 1944 provided for the elimination of tariff barriers and eventual economic integration with free movement of labour, capital and services within the new union. Internal free trade and a common external tariff were established in 1948, the three countries presented a united front in the negotiations leading to the Marshall Plan and in 1953 the three formed an economic union which realised many of the goals of the 1944 agreement.

In the context of the postwar world, the policies of these three small countries exercised an important influence on their larger neighbours. The Benelux Agreement had been intended as a defensive move, to prevent domination by larger countries, but in addition Benelux leaders began to present their union as a model for a broader union of

European peoples. Both ideas appealed to leaders elsewhere in western Europe. It was therefore no surprise when in 1955 Paul-Henri Spaak, the Belgian foreign minister and an established leader of the movement for European unity, became chairman of the study group whose proposals led to the Treaty of Rome and the establishment of the European Economic Community.

Among the Nordic countries, neutral Sweden had fared the best during the war and enjoyed a higher national income at the end of the war than at the beginning. Sweden's position as an important supplier of iron ore to Germany and of certain highly specialised manufactured goods such as ball bearings to both sides gave the Swedes enough negotiating leverage to ensure a continued minimal respect for their neutrality. In 1943 the Allies forced the Swedes to agree to reduce shipments to Germany, though as the war dragged on through 1944 Swedish firms often ignored the agreement under duress from the Germans, whose subject territories virtually surrounded Sweden. Norway and Denmark had suffered under the German occupation and Norway especially from reduced food supplies. However, the Germans had undertaken some new industrial investment, physical destruction had been relatively limited, and both therefore entered the postwar world prepared to reassert themselves in their respective fields of shipping and high-quality food production.

Finland, allied with Germany, recaptured the territory seized by the Soviet Union in 1940, only to lose it again in 1944. In addition to damage caused by the heavy fighting, most of the 450,000 Finns who had lived in the lost territory had to be resettled, and heavy reparations imposed by the Russians made recovery more difficult. In particular they demanded that Finland supply large amounts of capital goods, and the need to import machinery and raw materials to produce them resulted in large balance of payments deficits. The Finnish mark was devalued three times in 1945, twice in 1949, and again in 1956, and foreign trade was strictly regulated throughout the 1950s. In the longer run, the production of capital goods for reparations resulted in the growth of new industries, but the government's conservative agricultural policy hindered a thoroughgoing modernisation of the economy.

The wartime experiences of the countries of Mediterranean Europe demonstrated that the supposed unity of authoritarian dictatorships was not all that it seemed. Portugal and Spain preserved a canny neutrality, Greece was conquered and occupied by the Germans and even Italy, though formally allied with Germany, entered the war only with reluctance. Spain and Portugal possessed very small industrial sectors before the war, and in both countries agricultural productivity was low. Their limited export earnings had barely covered interest payments on government debt and sizeable imports of food. They therefore could not become suppliers of manufactured goods or food to the belligerents, and their poverty precluded extensive new investment to take advantage of the demand resulting from the war. Spain fared better than Portugal because of the desperate need of both sides for industrial raw materials and iron and steel, but in both countries food shortages led to the introduction of rationing schemes, new construction of all kinds stagnated and even the small industrial sectors suffered during the final two years of the war. Recovery began rather slowly, hampered by the general lack of financial and physical resources; however, in the context of the Cold War the resolute anticommunism of Salazar and Franco transformed them into prime candidates for United States aid. In 1951 the United States, France and Britain again exchanged ambassadors with Spain after a five-year lapse, and in 1953 Spain signed a defensive treaty with the United States, including lucrative leases of military bases and a package of direct aid. Portugal received military and economic aid from the North Atlantic Treaty Organisation (NATO) as well as from the United States directly, and in 1953 embarked on a six-year development plan emphasising hydroelectric power. Both remained dependent on the yearly harvest; only the end of a drought in 1952 permitted Spain to end wartime rationing.

The Greek economy declined under German occupation and in addition the guerrilla warfare waged by both communist and anticommunist resistance movements in the mountain areas further dislocated the economy. After the war, the two groups of resistance fighters turned on each other, and the ensuing civil war caused perhaps more destruction than the invasion and occupation. United States military and economic aid ensured victory for the anticommunists and laid the basis for economic recovery. In 1953 the conservative government announced a long-term programme of government investment with a fifth of the funds to be supplied by the United States, forced a series of bank mergers, froze domestic prices and devalued the drachma by 50 per cent, but also ended restrictions on imports. The next year an internal loan for the balance of the investment programme was oversubscribed by one-third in only ten days, and by early 1955 industrial production was two and a half times higher than the depressed level of 1948.

Italy's national income had declined by 60 per cent during the war, but population had risen substantially due to repatriation from the colonies and the end of emigration to the Americas. Widespread starvation at the war's end was only prevented by United Nations aid. However, wartime destruction had been largely confined to housing; agriculture and most industrial plants had escaped. An expansionary government policy helped return the large labour force to work, and by 1949 national income had risen above prewar levels. Inflation in the postwar years played a positive role of sorts, reducing the burden of government debt and redistributing income away from rentiers and into investment projects. The currency stabilisation programme of 1947–48 slowed growth and increased unemployment, but increased confidence in the financial system was reflected in a lower velocity of circulation of the money supply. Growth was impressive in part only because of the low base from which it began; in per capita terms Italy remained far behind the northwestern European average. Italian growth also depended on foreign aid to a relatively great extent. Total aid from the United Nations, the Marshall Plan and other sources totalled three billion dollars between 1945 and 1952, between three and four per cent of national income.

Structurally, Italy's problems remained the same. The shortage of raw materials, especially coal, continued to hamper industrial expansion. Fascist autarky policies had created large but overstaffed and inefficient firms in a number of areas, but attempts to close plants or lay off workers resulted in serious strikes through the early 1950s, while a shortage of capital precluded modernisation of the plants' outdated equipment. Excessive production costs reduced possible exports, but imports consisted primarily of food and essential raw materials and therefore could not be reduced significantly. The peace treaty of 1952 and Italy's entry into NATO opened the way for increased military and economic aid which covered the deficit in the balance of payments. The government had already announced a major land reform, at least in the south, and in 1955 secured a large loan from the World Bank to fund the Cassa del Mezzogiorno, an agency to stimulate economic development in the south – as the centrepiece in an ambitious ten-year plan of government investment which was to raise national product by five per cent yearly, create four million new jobs and end unemployment.

Eastern Europe

The desires and needs of the Soviet Union determined the course of reconstruction in eastern Europe. The Soviet Union's needs were formidable. The Nazi 'war of extermination' had laid waste to immense tracts of agricultural land, destroyed mines and manufacturing plant and thoroughly disrupted communications. To this disheartening task of reconstruction had been added the need to integrate the large territories acquired at the war's end into the Soviet system. The Soviet Union rejected the offer of American aid under the Marshall Plan, with its implied threat of dependence on the United States; instead, heavy reparations were exacted from 'enemy' states such as East Germany, Hungary and Finland, and highly favourable trade agreements were imposed on 'friendly' states such as Poland and Yugoslavia.

In the Soviet Union enormous movements of population dominated the period of reconstruction. Millions of survivors of the earlier eastward flight to escape the Germans now returned to their original homes, as did millions of industrial workers shifted east to operate the military plants. Millions more moved into the districts vacated by Poles who desired or were obliged to move west. The Fourth Five-Year Plan emphasised reconstruction in areas occupied by the Germans, and relied on the new industrial capacity erected in the east before and during the war. The hardships endured by all in the Great Patriotic War, the elation of the final victory and the emergence of the new technocratic elite provided the system with a solid foundation, but some of the old problems remained. By 1950 total industrial production was well above prewar levels, but the emphasis remained as before on heavy industry and the military. Consumer goods languished, and agriculture had only with difficulty been able to return to prewar levels of output. Particularly in agriculture, but in industry as well, techniques had not progressed. Productivity remained low compared to western Europe, but unrealistic and rigid directives from central agencies often hampered attempts to improve efficiency at the local level.

In east-central Europe, the coalition governments which emerged from the collapse of the Nazi regime confronted problems whose seriousness varied directly with the course of fighting during the war. Poland, Yugoslavia and Albania had ceased to exist during the war and had suffered continual military action, both regular and partisan. Yugoslavia lost 10 per cent of the total population, 50 per cent of all farm animals, 60 per cent of all buildings and 70 per cent of total industrial capacity. Poland suffered similar losses, but the westward shift in borders actually brought a net increase in industrial capacity, though coupled with the necessity of resettling nearly five million persons. Hungary suffered severely during the final six months of the war, and had to accept territorial losses as well. Czechoslovakia, Rumania and Bulgaria were somewhat better off in terms of direct destruction, but all had to endure food shortages and the nearly complete collapse of trade and distribution systems.

The coalition governments announced land reforms, whose extent depended primarily on the previous distribution of holdings. In Hungary more than one-third of the land was seized and over a quarter redistributed. In Poland land reform accompanied the population transfers. In the Balkan states, where land reform had followed the First World War, the changes were less extensive. Throughout, the land went exclusively to small peasants. Private holdings of more than fifty hectares virtually ceased to exist, while holdings of less than five hectares greatly increased both in number and as a percentage of the total. At the same time the already extensive role of the state in the industrial sector increased. The coalition governments nationalised enemy property and that owned by collaborators, which in several cases amounted to virtually the entire heavy industrial sector.

The victorious powers had agreed that the nations of east-central Europe belonged to the 'eastern' sphere, and in 1947 and 1948 the coalition governments were replaced by exclusively socialist regimes. The new governments immediately began to nationalise industry and commerce. For most large-scale industry and wholesale trade this was a formality, as those firms the government did not already own depended on government orders and finance, but for small industrial enterprises and retail trade the break with the past was abrupt and ruthless. United Nations relief aid and some loans from the western Allies had been important in the immediate postwar years, but with the rejection of the Marshall Plan western aid evaporated. Soviet trade credits were limited, and payments of reparations to the Soviet Union were heavy. Hungary and Rumania did convince the Russians to take goods rather than dismantling industrial plants, however, and gained the advantages of long production runs in certain commodities. In addition, the expropriation of German property by the Soviets led to the establishment of joint industrial ventures, whose investment activities stimulated the local economy.

The Soviet-style plans adopted by all the new governments emphasised reconstruction and the elimination of bottlenecks, and by 1949 industrial output was generally above prewar levels. As in Russia, however, light industry and consumer goods output stagnated, and a backward agricultural sector remained a drag on the economy. In 1951 and 1952 the governments revised existing plans or introduced new ones which further increased the emphasis on heavy industry, announced their intention to collectivise agriculture and tightened regulations governing workers' freedom to move and behaviour on the job. Passes prevented workers from changing jobs without permission, absenteeism and 'negligence' became punishable offences and in Czechoslovakia a currency reform effectively deprived many workers of their savings. There was some resistance; in 1952 the Czech prime minister denounced the 'capitalist prejudices and outlived views, which still exist in the ranks of our own working people' and the agricultural ministry called for 'stricter discipline' on state farms. Strikes and riots in 1953 in East Germany, Czechoslovakia and Hungary were repressed, though in the case of Hungary they did lead to a shift within the government.

SOCIAL RECONSTRUCTION

Population and labour force

Europe's population expanded substantially after the Second World War. Indeed, the war did not even prove a simple 'check' on population, despite the horrendous loss of life. In western Europe birth rates increased during the war years. Profamily policies pursued by the Vichy government in France and the stubborn optimism of the British have been advanced as possible explanations for the sudden upsurge in births. However, birth rates also rose in Norway, Denmark and the Netherlands, all occupied by Germany, and in neutral Sweden, Switzerland and Spain as well. In eastern Europe wartime birth rates continued the decline of the 1930s, though remaining well above those of western Europe. Returned soldiers and others who had been forced to delay starting families contributed to higher birth rates in the immediate postwar years. Rising population increased demand for food, clothing and consumer durables – demand which governments in both western and eastern Europe attempted to repress during the reconstruction period.

The most wrenching demographic fact in the immediate postwar world, however, was enforced migration, a shifting of entire ethnic populations. Some ten million Soviet citizens displaced eastward by the war now moved from central and eastern Russia towards the west and northwest, and 2.5 million members of various minority nationalities were forcibly resettled in the same direction. Five million Poles left western Russia and eastern Poland to resettle within the new Polish boundaries. Nearly 2,000,000 Czechs and Slovaks moved from eastern to western Czechoslovakia, 160,000 Turks were expelled from Bulgaria, and 400,000 persons moved from southern to northern Yugoslavia where they replaced some 300,000 Italians and an equal number of Germans. Everywhere in eastern and central Europe, Germans found themselves pushed westward. Between ten and twelve million Germans – four million from Poland, three million from Czechoslovakia, two million from the Baltic states and smaller numbers from Hungary, Yugoslavia, Rumania and Russia – were forced into Austria, East Germany and West Germany. Finally, approximately one million 'DPs' or displaced persons settled in France, Britain and overseas in Israel, the United States, Canada and Australia. This brutal simplification of ethnic boundaries 'solved' some of Europe's most intractable problems, although 40 years later there was still, for instance, a powerful organisation of Silesian Germans in West Germany who demanded the return of their homeland and a large, unhappy Turkish minority in Bulgaria whose existence the Bulgarian government resolutely refused to recognise.

War and reconstruction together accelerated the rise of industry and the decline of agriculture as the main employment of Europe's workers. All governments had attempted to the best of their ability to increase industrial output during the war. In the occupied territories the Nazis encouraged and sometimes forced new industrial investment. At the same time, agriculture had been seriously disrupted, whether directly by the fighting or indirectly by drafting of agricultural workers into the armed forces and the new industrial plants. At the end of the war, therefore, all nations found themselves despite the destruction with larger industrial sectors and correspondingly smaller agricultural sectors than they had possessed before the war. In addition, the main thrust of reconstruction in all countries was a conscious attempt to increase industrial investment and output.

Dislocation, industrialisation and the attendant concentration of population in urban centres had the effect of
opening new horizons for European women. During the
depression of the 1930s women had often found themselves
pushed out of industrial employment, but during the war
they were cajoled and often compelled to take jobs previously
reserved for men in industry and transportation. Women
who remained on the farms, though overworked, became
independent decision makers in the absence of fathers,
husbands and grown sons. Even when forced to flee from an
invader or ordered to move by their own governments or
occupying powers, women were forced to take on an
independent responsibility for their own survival. These
trends continued in the reconstruction period. The desperate
need for labour to clear the rubble and rebuild factories and
housing, and the need for increased numbers of industrial
workers as manufacturing output began to rise, continued to
draw unprecedented numbers of women out of traditional
part-time and unpaid employment and into full-time paid
occupations. In eastern Europe these economic factors were
reinforced by the ideology of the new socialist regimes, which
proudly emphasised the equality of the sexes as one of its
main tenets, and by the overriding desire of the new regimes
to stimulate industrial development by all possible means.

Governments, ruling elites and the working classes

The realm of government action and responsibility expanded
greatly during the war and reconstruction period. All
governments extended the range of social services available
to their citizens. In eastern Europe the new socialist regimes,
adopting Russian models, insisted that child care, education,
medical treatment and support in old age should be provided
to all equally, as a matter of individual right and public
responsibility; unemployment insurance was unnecessary
because the socialist reorganisation of the economy would
guarantee uninterrupted full employment. In fact, as in the
Soviet Union, low levels of income and the official emphasis
on investment in heavy industry meant that many of the
promised social services could not be provided; a start was

made in expanding the educational systems, but medical facilities remained inadequate and full employment was guaranteed by the legal requirement that every individual be employed or suffer unpleasant consequences. In western Europe, however, governments also began to provide a range of services previously regarded as private responsibilities. In Britain in 1942 a report prepared under the leadership of William Beveridge recommended a comprehensive system of social security benefits covering every person from before birth to after death, and a national health service to provide subsidised medical care. In addition all parties accepted Beveridge's 1944 recommendation that the government commit itself to restricting unemployment to a maximum of three per cent, and in 1946 the Beveridge Report's recommendations for social security and health services were enacted. West German social legislation drew on a tradition dating back to the 1880s; the new social security systems of the Benelux countries owed something to German and Scandinavian models; in France, a comprehensive social security system, building on the family allowances introduced by the Vichy regime and incorporating ideas from the British Beveridge report, expanded to cover nearly all French citizens.

Government control over the economy also continued to expand after the end of the war. Britain's commitment to a maximum level of unemployment entailed government management of the economy through a Keynesian manipulation of monetary and fiscal policies, while the West German system of tax incentives and French 'indicative' planning provided other models of indirect control over the economy. In eastern Europe the coalition governments and later socialist regimes eventually nationalised all economic activity, instituting a system of planning directed by central agencies modelled on those of the Soviet Union. In fact, in the industrial sector at least, the differences were more subtle than contemporary polemicists claimed. In the east, central governments had controlled much of the heavy industrial sector even before the war. In the west, France and Italy both possessed large state-owned enterprises, and the West German government inherited extensive industrial interests from the Nazi regime which it organised into two massive holding companies. In Britain the Labour government pressed through nationalisation of the Bank of England, the coal, iron and steel industries, gas and electricity, and the railways and road transportation.

The reconstruction of European society included a restructuring of social elites closely connected with the expansion of the powers and responsibilities of central governments. In both eastern and western Europe the process included the elimination of those who had been openly identified with the Axis regimes. Most dramatic were the Nürnberg Trials in Germany in 1946 in which an international court put on trial Nazi leaders accused of war crimes and 'crimes against humanity'. Nazi institutions were declared criminal organisations with their members liable for punishment. Sentences meted out to prominent Nazi leaders ranged from ten years' imprisonment to death. Similar trials were carried out elsewhere in Europe; in France, for example, the collaborationist Head of State Marshal Pétain was given a death sentence, subsequently commuted to life imprisonment because of his age. Informal justice was also meted out. Mussolini and his mistress were murdered by a mob, as were others; estimates of those killed by the victorious forces are unclear but number in the thousands. Penalties were also imposed on those who had been implicated in the Axis regimes, especially Germans; in Czechoslovakia for example all Germans were stripped of their citizenship and expelled.

The old apex of the class structure, the titled aristocracy, for all practical purposes lost its role in postwar Europe. Noble titles had been abolished in the Soviet Union with the revolution of 1917 and disappeared as a matter of course in the east-central European countries. In Austria, former nobles were forbidden to use the 'von' particule in their names, and in West Germany titles had no legal status. Elsewhere, they continued to carry a cachet of prestige but without real power. The monarchs of Europe also suffered a final decline; the kings of Greece and the east-central European countries were deposed and a referendum in Italy in 1946 rejected the monarchy in favour of a republic by a two million vote margin. The claimants to the Austrian and the Italian thrones were forbidden by law to set foot in their countries. In the Low Countries and Scandinavia, monarchs remained as figurehead chiefs of state, although even in those countries they adopted democratic manners, sometimes even dispensing with coronations. Britain was a partial exception; the monarch retained substantial legal powers and the aristocracy continued to wield considerable influence. However, the powers of the monarch were so rarely exercised that they could easily be forgotten, and the aristocracy preserved its position not through legal right but through the continued operation of an entrenched 'old boy' network of patronage and favouritism.

Military leaders played a surprisingly small role in the aftermath of the war. Charles De Gaulle became the head of the French government, but resigned in January 1946 when the new constitution failed to grant him the power he desired; no British general rose to political prominence. In the east the two victorious partisan leaders Enver Hoxha of Albania and Tito of Yugoslavia remained in power until their deaths in 1980 and 1984 respectively. Elsewhere, although the Soviet army contributed to the establishment of socialist governments and helped maintain the new order, no general dared challenge Stalin's personal authority, and the army as a whole remained firmly under the control of the Communist Party. In no country did demobilised soldiers become a political force, as they had done after the First World War. Psychologically, the Axis had been too completely defeated and discredited to provide any sort of a rallying point; socially and economically, most governments granted veterans substantial benefits and all veterans participated in the new social security systems as well.

The increased importance of economic management brought power to those who controlled economic institutions. In the west political leaders shared power with the leaders of industrial and financial corporations and with labour union leaders. The leaders of industry and commerce overwhelmingly remained the same; in France a number of Vichy supporters were encouraged to retire, but Italy's timely surrender had transformed erstwhile supporters of the fascist regime into allies against Nazi Germany. Even in Germany only a very few, such as members of the Krupp family too openly identified with German 'militarism', lost their positions. In politics too, only the senior leaders of the Nazi and collaborationist regimes disappeared, though older political leaders gradually gave way to younger men with more technical qualifications. West Germany, which experienced the greatest change, exemplified these underlying continuities. Adenauer, 'the Old Man', a Weimar politician who in the absence of war would have ended his public career as mayor of Cologne, reluctantly yielded the chancellorship to Erhard, 'Mr Wirtschaftswunder', a university-trained economist.

Positions of power in the Soviet Union increasingly fell to trained engineers, graduates of the expanded technical institutes during the 1930s, whose initial opportunities for advancement had come as replacements for the victims of the purges and whose administrative skills had brought the victory over Nazism. Combining their party membership with economic responsibilities, they were moving from posts as secretaries of provincial party organisations to the central economics ministries in Moscow. In east-central Europe, as the national communist parties came to power, their leaders became the new elite. Initially this meant older, long-term communists; the new leaders of East Germany, Poland, Hungary, Czechoslovakia, Rumania and Bulgaria all had experience in the communist underground dating back to the 1920s. In each of these countries a contest for power pitted these 'Muscovite' communists, their supporters and ideological 'purists' against a younger, technically-trained generation, whose more 'pragmatic' approach to economic problems sometimes carried nationalistic overtones.

As the war ended, workers seemed on the verge of gaining control over their destiny at last. Socialist parties contended for power in all countries, and new unions arose to replace the fraudulent institutions of the Nazi and collaborationist regimes. Where industry was not nationalised directly by socialist governments, new forms of economic democracy were imposed: in Britain a move to give more power to worker-representatives on the shop floor, and in West Germany a system of 'codetermination' with works councils to hear grievances and workers' representatives sitting on corporate boards of directors. Widespread strikes in Britain, France and Italy challenged the right of employers to dismiss workers, lower wages or arbitrarily reallocate or redefine the tasks of individual employees.

However, in western Europe the emerging definition of 'democracy' emphatically did not include a reduction of the authority of employers in industrial relations. Stalin, abiding by the agreement dividing Europe into east and west, ordered western communist parties and communist labour unions not to support the strike movement. Paradoxically, though without communist support, the strikers found themselves branded as dangerously leftist by their own governments, an accusation which cut off support among the middle classes and other workers. The strike movement collapsed; British shop-floor democracy remained a dream, and West German codetermination was narrowed in scope and the 'labour directors' became university-educated union functionaries whose outlook and policies did not differ significantly from other members of their corporate boards. Radicals tended to disappear from union leadership. Unions expanded and occasionally struck in their members' interests, but those interests were defined in terms of the existing system, not in opposition to it.

In east-central Europe labour organisations emerged with the coalition governments, sometimes for the first time. However, the imposition of Soviet-style plans by the succeeding socialist governments severely limited consumption and entailed restrictive Soviet-style labour organisation and work norms, and the new labour organisations rapidly became centrally-controlled instruments of discipline. The first steps towards agricultural collectivisation caused farmers to produce less, lowering food supplies. Stalin's death in March 1953 raised hopes of change, and triggered the strikes in East Germany in June. The East German uprising had varying consequences. In Poland the Muscovite ideological purists won the ensuing debate, and repression of potential opposition increased. In Hungary, however, Muscovite Matyas Rakosi was replaced as premier by Imre Nagy, who publicly bemoaned the lack of a better standard of living, criticised his predecessor for economic mismanagement and said that workers and peasants had been 'exploited' with long hours and discipline. He promised to rectify these 'grave mistakes', but remained at loggerheads with Rakosi, who continued as head of the party. Nagy lost his premiership in 1955, but discontent with his more orthodox successor mounted steadily. The government was uncertain whether to suppress or compromise with the demonstators.

Discontent festered in Poland, and discontent turned into demonstration in June 1956, when workers in Poznan rioted, demanding better living conditions and greater freedom from Soviet overlordship; at the end of the riots in Poznan and elsewhere, 54 were dead and hundreds wounded. The Polish disorders found an immediate echo in Hungary. A massive protest on 23 October began the Hungarian Revolution of 1956. The following day, Nagy became premier once again. On 25 October, Soviet troops fired on demonstrators in Parliament Square, killing between 300 and 800 protesters. Nagy was now seen as the defender of the Hungarians opposed to both the military intervention and the rigid ideology of the Soviets. He formed a coalition cabinet, including liberal communists, non-communists and several intellectuals. On 1 November, he removed Hungary from the Warsaw Pact and proclaimed the nation's neutrality. This was too much for the Soviets. On the morning of 3 November, Nagy announced on the radio: 'Today at daybreak Soviet forces started an attack against our capital, obviously with the intention to overthrow the legal Hungarian democratic government. Our troops are fighting. The government is in its place. This is my message to the people of our country and to the entire world'. He appealed for help from the United Nations, but no aid was forthcoming. The following day, the Soviets occupied the parliament; Nagy took refuge in the Yugoslav embassy, and the revolution was over. Some 200,000 Hungarians fled their country in the wake of the revolution. Nagy was taken into custody by the Soviets when he left the Yugoslav embassy; he was subsequently spirited to Rumania, where he lived until 1971.

POLITICAL RECONSTRUCTION

The Allied leaders had realised that the thrust of military operations was dividing Europe and had sought to solve the question before the end of the war at the Yalta and Potsdam conferences of 1945. The details and implementation of the explicit agreements made there almost immediately became matters of dispute. Nonetheless, the underlying principal of the agreements was clear enough. Britain and the United States would create a sphere of influence in western Europe and in Greece, while the Soviets would have sway in east-central Europe. To Stalin, this seemed a reasonable arrangement given that twice in the twentieth century Russia had been invaded by German armies marching through eastern Europe; for the west, the compromise was a recognition of the presence of the Soviet army in the eastern part of the continent.

In most states, the transition from war to postwar was relatively rapidly accomplished within the framework of these agreements. In France the first elections of the new Fourth Republic gave the Communist Party the largest number of seats in the Chamber of Deputies. The division of seats created a deadlock until the formation of a coalition government early in 1947; soon, however, the communist ministers were expelled from the cabinet. This left power in the hands of the socialists and conservatives who formed governments from 1947 to 1958 as a Third Force, as they called themselves, between the communists and the new party of Gaullists established with the general's benediction. In Italy elections returned a constituent assembly in which the Christian Democrats held 207 of 556 seats, followed by the socialists with 115 and the communists with 104. A multiplicity of small parties emerged, including the conservative lay parties, which opposed the close ties between the Christian Democrats and the Catholic church, and a neofascist grouping. The assembly put together a constitution for the Italian Republic which came into effect in 1948. The Christian Democrats excluded socialists and communists from the government in 1947 and maintained themselves in power with the support of the smaller centrist and conservative parties.

The Soviet Union emerged from the Second World War with its institutions intact and with greatly increased prestige. In addition to the many other talents attributed to him, Stalin was now the liberator of the motherland and a military hero. The official message of congratulation to him on his 70th birthday in 1949 praised Stalin for his 'wisdom, indomitable energy and iron will' and referred to him (among others things) as 'a fearless revolutionary, brilliant theoretician and splendid organiser . . . great commander and organiser of victory . . . great architect of Communism' and even 'great coryphaeus of science'. Nevertheless, in January 1953 the Kremlin announced that nine doctors had confessed to committing a number of murders, including that of Andrei Zhdanov, one of Stalin's lieutenants, who had died mysteriously in 1948. The 'confessions' were questionable, and charges that the 'Doctors' Plot' was funded by American and Jewish sources (since many of the physicians were Jewish) hardly believable. Stalin may have been planning a new purge of his advisers and comrades, but his death in March put an end to this possibility. Although the speeches made at his funeral praised the leader, evidence suggests that his colleagues viewed his death with relief. The head of the secret police, Lavrenti Beria, was arrested and executed. A struggle for Stalin's succession took place, though now on the tacit assumption that losers would be demoted but not shot. Nikita Khrushchev became secretary of the party in September. Khrushchev was the son of a coal miner and himself the former head of the Ukraine party organisation; he had worked his way up the ranks, being given Politburo membership after his success in conducting a purge in the Ukraine in 1938. Khrushchev spent the next several years consolidating his power and in 1958 became premier as well as head of the party.

In east-central Europe, antifascist coalitions were formed which included communists, socialists, liberals, centrists and representatives of peasant parties. The communists nowhere formed a majority in the first parliaments, but they did secure key positions in government, generally in the ministries of the interior or justice, and could rely on the support of the Soviet Union and the Soviet army. Gradually noncommunist elements were eliminated from the governments through the gerrymandering of electoral districts, disqualification of noncommunist candidates and intimidation. A coup left the Communist Party in control of the Czech government in 1948. By 1949 communists were in control of all of the east-central European governments with the exception of Austria and Greece.

Austria, defined by the Allies as 'liberated' rather than 'defeated', was divided into four occupation zones as Germany had been. In 1945 a provisional government under the last president of the Austrian parliament before 1933, a socialist, was supported by the Soviet Union and, less willingly, by the other three powers which occupied Austria. Elections at the end of the year gave 85 seats to the centrist People's Party, 76 to the socialists and only 4 to the communists. Thus began a coalition between the People's Party (whose leader took the chancellorship) and the socialists (whose leader became vice-chancellor) which lasted until 1966. Caught, geographically and figuratively, between east and west, Austria was in a delicate position. The influence of socialists in the 1940s had perturbed the west, while the acceptance of Marshall Plan aid from the United States had infuriated the Soviets. The Russians claimed all the industrial plants in their zone were due to them as 'German' property, and those firms were accordingly boycotted by all Austrians except members of the Communist Party. The deadlock hampered recovery, and there were serious riots in 1950 over increases in prices and rents, but in 1955 the Russians suddenly agreed to a compromise and a peace treaty. Austria should remain disarmed and unaligned; the treaty brought to an end the four-power occupation of the country, and eventually opened the way for Austrian membership in the European Free Trade Association and association with the European Community.

In Greece opposition to the Nazi occupation forces had solidified into communist and noncommunist groups. The return of the king and the establishment of a prowestern government (with Stalin's approval) was contested by the communists, who received arms from across the Yugoslav border. Brutal fighting between the two forces was marked by torture, summary executions and the rounding up of children who were sent by the communists to homes in eastern Europe. Simultaneous Russian pressure on Turkey suggested the Soviet Union might be attempting to expand its sphere. In 1947, the American president Harry Truman proclaimed that the United States had the right to intervene in the affairs of another country to contain the spread of communism and dispatched large amounts of money and military aid to Greece and Turkey. Then in 1948 Yugoslavia's communist president Tito broke relations with Stalin and closed the border to aid for the communist forces in Greece. These two actions assured their defeat, and by 1949 prowesterners were in control of the government and Greece was left with the bitterness and recriminations of the civil war.

The civil war in Greece foreshadowed the Cold War, and the Berlin Blockade in 1948 inaugurated it, while leading to the creation of separate states for the united western sectors of Germany and the Soviet sector. The end of the war had left the United States and the Soviet Union dominant in Europe, but the difficulties to be faced in holding together the alliance were obviously too great to be overcome. The two countries represented two different ideologies, socialism versus capitalism, representative democracy versus the dictatorship of the proletariat. Their past experiences were different: in the United States, a revolution which had taken place well over a century before and that had resulted in the establishment of a strongly Protestant middle-class society with the legend of the self-made man, and in the Soviet Union, a new revolution followed by a civil war and the status of international pariah, accompanied internally by the elimination of the monarchy, aristocracy and bourgeoisie and the collectivisation of the peasantry. Strategically, they saw their security lying in different approaches and dangers coming from different directions. Russia had been invaded by Germany twice through Poland; the United States had never suffered invasion and had come into the war because of the Japanese attack in the Pacific. Economically, the United States stood poised on the verge of a consumer durables boom, while Russia faced the arduous task of reconstruction.

Europe was in the middle of the debate between the Soviet Union and the United States, and each stage in the establishment of the postwar system was accompanied by the most intense and bitter controversy. Yet the framework hammered out on the ground by the armies and in conference by their leaders remained solid. The western powers did not intervene in the east, and the Soviet Union did not intervene in the west. Neither pushed the other too far; during the Berlin crisis, the Americans did not challenge the Russians on the ground, and the Russians did not challenge the Americans in the air. Along the border, each side might try their chances. Where there was an indigenous communist movement with a good chance of gaining power, as in Greece, Stalin was ready to give support, but when the chance faded or the risks increased, he cut off aid. Where local communists were weak, as in Austria or Finland, they received no Soviet support. Similarly, when émigrés offered to spy on or subvert eastern regimes, western authorities accepted the offer as long as it entailed no risk. For instance, the landings of anticommunist guerrillas in Albania in 1950 and 1951 were disavowed by their British and American sponsors when they failed.

Given the disasters of the war, the uncertain situation which obtained in the years directly following and a heritage of dictatorship in many states going back to the 1920s, the speed with which the new order emerged was remarkable. If economic recovery was well underway by the early 1950s, social and political stability had also been achieved by that time. Political fragmentation did take place in the west, while the eastern European nations were governed by authoritarian regimes which restricted and denied basic liberties. But in both parts of Europe, these regimes displayed noteworthy stability, most indeed lasting from the immediate postwar period to the present.

3
EUROPE'S CHANGING PLACE IN THE WORLD

INTERNATIONAL RECONSTRUCTION

International organisations

Planning for the postwar international order began before the war ended, indeed before anyone could be absolutely certain of its outcome. In the Atlantic Charter of 1942 the United States and Britain pledged themselves 'to bring about the fullest collaboration between all nations'. In their 1942 Mutual Aid Agreement, they committed themselves not only to wartime cooperation, but to postwar reconstruction and cooperation as well. They declared themselves ready to give mutual support, to reduce restrictions on trade and to pursue policies to maintain full employment after the conclusion of the war. Other meetings followed, notably the Yalta and Potsdam conferences at which the United States, Britain and the Soviet Union agreed to cooperate in the reconstruction of Germany and the other nations of Europe. Finally in 1945 the United Nations came into being, an association of sovereign states whose 51 founding members pledged themselves 'to save succeeding generations from the scourge of war, which twice in our lifetime has brought untold sorrow to mankind'.

The United Nations was a direct successor to the League of Nations of the interwar years. The League had failed to prevent the Axis aggression which had led to the war, and Allied leaders hoped the new United Nations would have the power to restrain potential future aggressors. Further, the rise of the Axis regimes had resulted from the depression, and the depression in turn from the failure of nations to cooperate in the economic sphere. Allied leaders therefore also hoped that new international organisations would enforce economic cooperation among nations and avoid the problems of war debts, reparations, trade discrimination and unemployment which had marked the 1920s and 1930s.

The formation of powerful organisations for economic, political and military cooperation represented a new development in the international system. In a world of nation-states, and especially for Europe, the home of the nation-state, such organisations added a new dimension to diplomacy, since member nations had to give up at least some of their sovereignty to the new groupings. Absorbing a number of existing international bodies and adding new ones, the United Nations rapidly developed into a huge complex of specialised organisations dealing with the entire range of human activity. Regional associations also emerged, the most ambitious of which was the European Economic Community (EEC), many of whose founders aimed at nothing less than a unification of the states of Europe.

Great power politics and international rivalries did not disappear. Churchill did not intend to oversee the dissolution of the British empire, and Roosevelt and Stalin worked to preserve American and Soviet interests in their respective spheres as well. Decisions of the United Nations General Assembly, in which each member state had a single vote, were made subject to the veto power exercised by the permanent members of the Security Council. Not coincidentally, the Security Council's five permanent members were the victorious great powers: the United States, the Soviet Union, Britain, France and China. With the Cold War, 'defensive alliances' emerged once again, the North Atlantic Treaty Organisation (NATO) in 1949 and the Warsaw Pact in 1955. The United Nations reflected the mutual hostility of the two superpowers, as each relied on its client states for support, bid for additional votes from 'non-aligned' nations and used its veto when outmanoeuvred by the other side. Membership in the EEC remained restricted, and its governing commission was often paralysed by the necessity for unanimous approval of any measure considered important by one of the members.

Nevertheless, as in the case of the domestic reconstruction of virtually all countries, the new international system proved not only durable but also capable of absorbing significant change. This was most dramatically true in the case of decolonisation, the rapid movement of Europe's colonies towards independence. Independence movements could use the United Nations as a sounding board to gain attention and support for their cause, and UN peacekeeping missions in several cases prevented armed confrontations from spreading and possibly triggering a war between the superpowers. If these new international organisations were less than totally successful, they provided forums for cooperation and, to some extent, replaced the bilateral arrangements and strictly military alliances which marked the period before the Second World War. They also provided a third layer of politics to supplement the traditional local and national arenas, and their very existence posed new questions for political debate.

Bretton Woods

The decisions reached during the war, especially the agreements between Roosevelt and Churchill, became the framework of the new international economic system. However, the course of the detailed negotiations was determined by the fact that the United States would be the dominant economic power in the postwar world. The United States accounted for a very large share of world trade, which however made up a relatively small share of the immense American national product. The position of other countries was much weaker. Britain's smaller share of world trade made up a much larger fraction of British national product; the economies of Continental Europe would need years of reconstruction before their wishes would have to be considered, the Soviet Union played a small role in the international economy and the possible role of Japan in the postwar world was ignored. Therefore, American prejudices dominated. British negotiators would have preferred broad agreements embodying general principles, and would have preferred to leave a large amount of discretion to responsible authorities. Those authorities, in the view of John Maynard Keynes and other British leaders, would be technical experts, not subject to 'political' influence and preferably working only part-time for the new international agencies. American leaders in turn were hostile to 'big money' and 'bankers', and they instinctively distrusted individual experts with discretionary powers. They preferred decentralised institutions with carefully defined and limited powers, detailed agreements covering all possible contingencies, and officials who were full-time employees appointed by and therefore dependent upon national governments, who would therefore be 'political' in precisely the sense the British wished to avoid.

In July 1944 representatives of 44 nations met in the United States, at Bretton Woods, New Hampshire, to erect the institutions which would provide the framework for the postwar economy. Again, the views of the Americans and British carried the most weight, and the American voice proved the preponderant one. There were, however, broad areas of ageement. All favoured stable exchange rates, controlled by the intervention of a new international agency. All favoured reducing restrictions on trade. All wished to encourage international investment, but all also wished to avoid destabilising short-term capital movements. All had compared the interwar period with the period before the First World War, and were seeking some way in which the world could gain the benefits of the pre-1914 gold standard system without excessive rigidity, while at the same time avoiding the instability of the interwar exchange standard system.

The structure of both the new International Monetary Fund (IMF) and International Bank for Reconstruction and Development (IBRD, better known as the World Bank) conformed to American rather than British hopes. The purpose of the IMF was to guarantee stable rates of exchange among currencies, but to avoid the direct controls over foreign exchange characteristic of the 1930s and also to avoid the wide fluctuations in exchange rates characteristic of the 1920s. Keynes proposed an 'international currency' without any connection to the stock of gold, whose amount would be controlled by the IMF to maintain an appropriate level of effective demand for the entire world. The Americans rejected this visionary scheme. Instead there was to be no new currency, but a pool of funds made up of contributions from member countries based on the size of their national income and their role in international trade. The contributions would be one-quarter gold and United States dollars, and three-quarters in the members' own currencies. Each member country agreed to establish a 'par' value for its currency in terms of gold or United States dollars and to maintain the actual value of the currency within one per cent of par. To meet 'short-term' deficits in the balance of payments and to deal with 'temporary' fluctuations in exchange rates, members could borrow from the common pool.

Complex regulations governed the conditions of borrowing from the IMF pool by debtor nations, the management of the 'scarce' currencies of creditor nations, and the supply of gold and United States dollars. In theory, balance of payments surpluses were as undesirable as deficits, because either could place excessive pressure on the fixed exchange rates which the system was intended to maintain. In fact, however, members with persistent deficits in their balance of payments were subjected to increasingly punitive conditions for further loans, intended to force them to 'correct' the deficit by introducing deflationary domestic policies. Increased interest rates and decreased government budgets were to stimulate capital imports while decreasing imports of commodities; eventually, the resulting lower domestic prices would raise exports and restore the balance of payments to equilibrium. In short, the 'rules of the game' under which the old gold standard had theoretically operated were introduced in a new, more explicit and rigorous fashion. The obvious alternative, devaluation of the currency, was discouraged – indeed American authorities came to regard devaluation as a kind of sin. Changes in the par value of a member's currency were only permitted to correct a 'fundamental' disequilibrium, and required the prior approval of the IMF if they exceeded ten per cent. IMF members thus committed themselves to avoid the competitive devaluations of the depression years; however, the system discriminated against countries likely to be debtors, most of which were poor, and in favour of those likely to be creditors, most of which were rich.

The World Bank was intended to provide long-term loans for projects to stimulate economic development. Again, the experience of the interwar years lay in the background; because private firms seemed to have failed to undertake sufficient investment during the 1920s and 1930s, a new agency seemed necessary to supplement the flow of private capital. As with the IMF, the World's Bank's capital was to come from members' contributions, though with only ten per cent of the original subscriptions required in gold and United States dollars. Loans were originally intended for members only, most of which were more or less highly-developed. Over time, however, the World Bank extended its field of operations to include loans to 'developing' countries. At the same time, the Bank tended increasingly to raise its funds in international capital markets and relend them. It also lent only when private capital was unavailable, and could impose requirements which 'tied' loans to purchases from specified countries. It did not, therefore, become a simple channel for funds from rich to poor countries.

British and American planners hoped that increased trade would become the third pillar of the new system. In 1947–48 a conference was held in Havana to establish an International Trade Organisation (ITO), and both the United States and Britain hoped the new institution would have sufficient power to eliminate the quantitative restrictions on trade which had worsened the depression and hampered recovery in the late 1930s. Negotiations beginning in 1943 had revealed potentially serious disagreements between the Americans and British, but these seemed minor compared to the gap which appeared between the developed industrial countries on the one hand, and exporters of primary products and underdeveloped countries on the other. The latter demanded that the proposed ITO explicitly adopt 'economic development' as one of its major aims. They pressed for controls on international investment, a system of preferences to aid the exports of developing countries and the introduction of quantitative restrictions on trade to promote development in poor countries. This was not at all what the wealthy manufacturing nations had in mind. A compromise formula embodied in the Havana Charter was signed by 53 of the 56 delegations, but ratified by only one country, and both the Havana Charter and the ITO were abandoned.

Before the Havana Conference, an 'interim' General Agreement on Tariffs and Trade (GATT) had been signed in October 1947. The GATT provided for mutual bilateral concessions only, but did specify that each agreement would include a most-favoured-nation clause, so that every concession would apply to all GATT members. This very limited agreement became the only possible avenue for trade liberalisation following the failure of the Havana Conference. The first GATT 'round' at Geneva in 1947 in fact proved extremely successful. The 23 countries participating signed 123 agreements covering 45,000 tariff items affecting half of total world trade. By 1951 GATT included 37 countries which among them accounted for four-fifths of world trade. Though limited, GATT did lessen restrictions on trade. Tariffs were substantially reduced – United States tariffs by approximately half – and many quotas and other non-tariff barriers were eliminated as well. However, neither the goal of a strong agency with power to force trade liberalisation nor that of one which would use trade policy to stimulate development was realised.

In the background of the failure of the Havana Conference was the failure of the first attempt to put the new international monetary system into operation. In 1945 the United States and Canada made a large loan to Britain to cover the deficit in the British balance of payments caused by the end of the Lend Lease programme. In return, Britain agreed to make sterling freely convertible, including the sterling balances held by all other countries. This would pose a problem, for most British earnings in third countries would still not be convertible into United States dollars, though those countries' sterling earnings would be. In addition, very large amounts of sterling earned during the war, for instance in India, would also become convertible. The United States had foreseen at least this latter problem and offered to help in negotiating reductions and delays of these commitments, but the British had refused because these balances were a 'British' problem. In February 1947 sterling became convertible, and countries with pounds rushed to convert them into United States dollars to meet their own needs for imports from America. Attempts to distinguish between current earnings and wartime balances proved unsuccessful. By July two-thirds of the 3.75 billion dollars lent by the United States had already gone and the rate of conversion was accelerating. Britain suspended convertibility in August.

The Marshall Plan and the CMEA

American policy now began to shift from a reliance on trade and financial arrangements towards the granting of direct aid for reconstruction. An influential State Department report on European conditions emphasised the weakness of the European nations' economies, especially that of Britain, and emphasised as well the strength of communist parties, particularly in France and Italy. It pictured a power vacuum in Europe, which might be filled either by the United States or by the Soviet Union. A severe winter in 1947–48 and the civil war in Greece stalled European recovery and seemed to confirm aggressive Soviet intentions. Immediate aid was offered to Greece and Turkey, and American Secretary of State George Marshall offered all European countries the financial aid they required to cover imports needed for reconstruction. The resulting European Recovery Programme is better known as the Marshall Plan.

Emergency aid had been flowing from the United States since 1945 through the United Nations Relief and Rehabilitation Administration (UNRRA) to most of the nations of Europe. The Marshall Plan, which replaced UNRRA aid, imposed more stringent requirements in the administration of aid by recipient countries. The Marshall Plan also aimed at long-term reconstruction and development rather than the immediate satisfaction of consumer needs. Nations accepting Marshall Plan aid and its conditions formed the Organisation for European Economic Cooperation (OEEC, the forerunner of the Organisation for Economic Cooperation and Development or OECD) to identify projects and to administer the funds. Also, in 1950 a new European

Payments Union (EPU) provided for monthly clearing of surpluses and deficits among members. The overdraft system introduced by the EPU resembled Keynes' 'international currency', and the administration of the EPU by non-political experts reflected his ideas as well. The EPU made possible continued controls on foreign exchange and limits on convertibility without restrictive bilateral agreements. The goal of convertible currencies was postponed; in fact Marshall Plan aid recipients were forbidden to borrow from the IMF, which receded into the background.

United States aid to Europe under the Marshall Plan was substantial, over thirteen billion dollars. Aid was focused on Britain, France, Italy, West Germany and the Netherlands, which together received three-quarters of the total. For all recipients, Marshall Plan aid paid for about a quarter of total imports and perhaps two-thirds of commodity imports from the 'dollar area' (those countries whose currencies were convertible into United States dollars) between 1947 and 1950. The genuine enthusiasm of contemporaries glows in accounts of the period. Nonetheless, the direct economic significance of the Marshall Plan has sometimes been overrated. It is not known, for example, what fraction of imports were 'essential' or exactly how they were used. Recovery had already begun in many countries before Marshall Plan aid began to arrive, and the Marshall Plan did not eliminate the balance of payments deficit of western Europe with the United States. In some areas, aid made an important addition to western European resources and worked to make recovery smoother than it would have been otherwise. Certain potentially serious bottlenecks were overcome, for instance in the coal, iron and electric power industries of West Germany. Perhaps most important, the Marshall Plan permitted planning without the pressure of immediately pressing crises, especially in Britain, which was still intended to take a leading role in the international economy.

The Marshall Plan was also connected to the division of Europe. In two famous speeches in 1946 Churchill had called for the creation of a 'United States of Europe' but also asserted that an 'iron curtain' was descending and separating east from west. The Marshall Plan itself was inextricably bound up with the anticommunist Truman Doctrine of aid intended to prevent Soviet expansion. Marshall Plan aid was explicitly offered to all European countries, but the Soviet Union, Poland and Czechoslovakia rejected the proposal because, they said, the conditions of aid would entail excessive interference in their domestic economies. The other emerging socialist governments also rejected Marshall Plan aid. In 1949 most of the socialist states joined together under Russian leadership to form the Council for Mutual Economic Assistance (CMEA or Comecon).

While the United States gave aid to stimulate European-American trade and economic recovery to forestall the threat of communism, the Soviet Union insisted on reparations from enemy countries to pay for reconstruction, and for defence against what Soviet leaders saw as aggression by the capitalist powers. Russia extracted net payments of fifteen to twenty billion dollars from eastern Europe during the reconstruction period. Some two-thirds of the total came from East Germany alone. Large numbers of industrial plants were appropriated in Poland, Hungary and Rumania. Eastern European countries delivered large amounts of manufactured goods and raw materials to the Soviet Union at prices well below world levels. Poland sold coal to Russia at only one-tenth the world price, Rumania agreed to deliver 1.7 million tons of petroleum a year for six years at about half the world price, and the joint Yugoslav-Russian navigation company charged Yugoslav customers twice the rates paid by Russians.

The CMEA proved ineffective in stimulating the growth of trade, but in the Soviet view that was not its primary purpose. It had been formed in part to impose an economic boycott on Yugoslavia, whose independence had angered Stalin. In addition, international trade was not held by socialist theorists to play an especially important part in socialist economic development, though a certain amount of cooperation among socialist nations was certainly regarded as desirable. Eastern European trade was drastically reoriented; trade among CMEA members made up only 15 per cent of their total trade in 1947–48, but 80 per cent in 1953. Certain cooperative undertakings, such as the processing of Russian iron ore in Polish, Czech and Hungarian coal-mining districts, the production of electric power and the standardisation of some industrial products to Soviet specifications, represented an improvement on the competitive nationalism of the interwar period. However, as part of the Soviet-style planning they were adopting, all eastern European countries attempted to achieve the highest possible degree of self-sufficiency, which had the effect of limiting trade among them. Within the CMEA, moreover, all trade relations were balanced on a bilateral basis, further reducing the amount of possible trade. Bilateral balancing worked to the advantage of the Soviet Union as well; some eastern European countries, especially Hungary and Czechoslovakia, earned large surpluses in their trade with Russia, but their positive balances were blocked. Russia could not supply sufficient goods in return, but because all CMEA currencies remained inconvertible their balances could not be used in other countries. Russia did extend some aid to eastern Europe in the form of trade credits worth about one billion dollars, but this did not solve the problem.

The European Community and Britain

Many saw nationalism as the underlying cause of the disasters which had befallen Europe, and hoped that a united Europe could avoid the mistakes committed by a Europe divided into rival national states. With the advent of the Cold War, it was clear that two blocs existed, each under the domination of one of the superpowers. Still, in western Europe support for supranational organisations came from persons who envisaged them as the first step towards a united Europe, possibly more independent of the United States and possibly able to act as a counterweight to both the United States and the Soviet Union. Thus the founders of the European Coal and Steel Community (ECSC) in 1952 noted optimistically that the new institution included all the regions formerly part of the empire of Charlemagne. The ECSC's more prosaic task was to ensure free trade and the free flow of capital and labour in the coal, iron and steel industries of West Germany, Belgium, Luxembourg, the Netherlands, France and Italy.

The new organisation hoped to avoid the negative aspects of the policies pursued by international cartels in these same industries between the wars; however, it also hoped to modernise and rationalise production in the member countries, and ultimately to ease the difficulties of a shift out of these 'declining' industries. A High Authority with real power pursued these tasks with determination and considerable success. The coordination of investment programmes led to the rapid modernisation of the steel industry in particular, and success bred confidence and encouraged large amounts of new capital to flow into enterprises under the control of the ECSC.

The success of the ECSC provided an important impetus behind the six members' agreement to join a common market; from a slightly different direction the Benelux customs union was also important in demonstrating the possibilities and benefits of the more ambitious project. The six agreed in the Treaty of Rome in 1957 to the establishment of the European Economic Community (EEC or Common Market) the following year. The EEC was intended to eliminate tariffs, quotas and subsidies affecting trade. Members committed themselves to encourage the free movement of capital, labour and services throughout the community, and to coordinate their monetary, fiscal and agricultural policies. The EEC was to be responsible for establishing consistent economic relations with outsiders, most importantly in setting a common external tariff. Supporters of the EEC looked forward with some optimism to the realisation of their dream – the eventual political unification of member states.

Britain had rejected membership in the ECSC. This was unfortunate from the standpoint of the ECSC's goals, since Britain produced around half as much coal and perhaps one-third as much steel as the six ECSC members combined. Politically, however, the British refusal seemed inevitable. The Labour Party condemned 'a system by which important fields of national policy were surrendered to a supranational European representative authority, since such an authority would have a permanent anti-Socialist majority'. Conservatives on the other hand feared that to join in the attempt of Continental Europeans to build a 'third force' between the United States and the Soviet Union would drive America back into isolation and open western Europe and Britain to communist aggression. Above all, British politicians agreed with Harold Macmillan: 'One thing is certain, and we may as well face it. Our people will not hand over to any supra-national Authority the right to close down our pits and our steel-mills'.

Having declined to join the ECSC, Britain was unlikely to join the even more intimate union of the EEC. Instead the British proposed mutual reductions of tariffs by OEEC members. Even these proposals excluded raw materials and agricultural products, however; Britain wanted access to western European markets for manufactured goods, but also wanted to preserve the system of Imperial Preference which favoured the primary products of Commonwealth countries in the British market (and ensured British consumers lower prices than their Continental cousins). The negotiations continued until 1959, but reached an impasse. Britain thereupon took the lead in the formation of the European Free Trade Association (EFTA), joined by Austria, Denmark, Norway, Portugal, Sweden and Switzerland.

Britain was also centrally involved in the question of currency convertibility, the intended foundation stone of the entire system. Successive British governments had been hesitant to risk repeating the failure of 1947, and successive British balance of payments crises suggested that in fact the pound was not strong enough relative to the United States dollar to play its intended role. Britain's earnings from 'invisibles' more than offset a consistently negative trade balance, but not by enough to cover the continued outflow of long-term capital investment, and the overall balance was therefore negative in most years. The EPU permitted limited exchange of European currencies, and Britain's membership in the EPU allowed European currencies to exchange with sterling-area currencies, but nothing bridged this large group of currencies and the United States dollar. Beginning in the mid-1950s British authorities undertook a series of very gradual moves to allow limited conversion of pounds to dollars. By 1958 convertibility had been largely achieved, but the system remained complex and hedged with restrictions.

Then in 1959 France declared the franc convertible into dollars. At a stroke this ended the EPU and forced the convertibility of all other OEEC currencies as well, including sterling. Fifteen years after Bretton Woods, the system finally came into operation.

DECOLONISATION

Perhaps the only thing more remarkable than the rapidity with which Europeans established their colonial empires in the late nineteenth century was the even greater rapidity with which they relinquished their grip in the mid-twentieth century. In 1945 Europe still ruled the world; a decade and a half later, virtually all the former European colonies had become independent states. The suddenness of the loss of empire has seemed simply inexplicable to some; others – mostly Europeans – have attributed it to a 'loss of confidence' or 'failure of nerve' on the part of colonial administrators, while still others – mostly non-Europeans – see it as the inevitable victory of nationalist movements arising within the colonies themselves. In evaluating the tenacity of the Europeans and the strength of indigenous nationalisms, some points about the history of colonisation need to be noted. First, the colonies had been acquired at relatively minor cost; second, colonial administrations always operated under the strictest injunction to finance themselves, if at all possible, and never to cause embarrassing increases in the 'home' country's budget; third, since the First World War the system of 'mandates' had assumed that some former colonies would some day become independent, a principle which logically had to apply to the rest as well; and fourth, significant numbers of Europeans had settled in only a few of Europe's colonial possessions.

The history of European colonisation suggests that when it became expensive to hold colonial possessions, Europeans would give them up. Conscription to fight in colonial wars had already provoked violent protest in Italy and Spain before the First World War. Ordinary Europeans demonstrated a similar allergy to sacrifice in the name of colonial glory after the Second World War. Though it was not impossible in all cases to send conscripts to repress colonial revolts, the financial and political costs of doing so almost always strained the 'home' government to the breaking point.

The movements of national liberation which succeeded in making colonial rule intolerably expensive for Europeans had a history which also reached back before the Second World War. Education provided by missionaries and colonial administrations, though grossly inadequate, had nonetheless had the effect of proving that the 'natives' were intellectually capable, undermining the case for continued paternalistic control by Europeans. In addition education created small but influential native elites. Indignant over continued social, political and economic discrimination, these groups moved to more or less radical opposition to colonialism. They drew on a diverse range of sources of inspiration. In Asia the examples of Japan and the Chinese revolution led by Sun Yat-sen provided models of the way in which military and intellectual weapons could be trained on the Europeans. In the Middle East and North Africa the new Islamic intellectual movement admired the administrative reforms pressed through in Turkey by Atatürk but disliked his secularism, and hoped instead to combine western economic development with revivified Islamic religious and social values. In sub-Saharan Africa the influence of freed slaves in the Americas played an important role, and the idea of racial equality possessed particular resonance.

All independence movements looked back to the history of resistance to European conquest and further back to history before the conquest, seeking models, inspiration and myth. The medieval state of Ghana, a mercantile and gold-mining empire at its peak around the year 1000 A.D., was located some 800 kilometres northwest of the nearest border of its present-day namesake, for instance, but provided a powerful inspiration for west African independence movements. In addition all nationalists took note of the Russian Revolution, many committed themselves to one or another form of 'socialist' economic organisation, and a minority sought aid from the Soviet Union – though such aid was never allowed to interfere with the overriding goal of national independence.

During the depression, potential supporters of these incipient nationalist movements could not have failed to notice that as export markets collapsed, colonial administrations had cut social services drastically while attempting to hold taxes high, and 'home' governments had offered little or no aid. The outbreak of war brought a sudden increase in demand for food, industrial raw materials and manufactured goods. Exports from northern Rhodesia rose ninefold during the war and reconstruction years and exports from the Congo fourteenfold. Employment increased, but so did prices, and again the bias in favour of Europeans was obvious. Wartime developments uprooted masses of people, breaking down traditional local social structures and creating a broader audience for nationalist appeals.

The announced policies, and more fundamentally the attitudes of the imperialist powers, had also continued to change. The Atlantic Charter proclaimed 'the right of all peoples to choose the form of government under which they live'. Roosevelt and especially Churchill intended the statement to apply to the European countries conquered by Nazi Germany, but the principle had obvious application to colonial possessions. The French constitution of 1946 announced that the period of colonial 'exploitation' was coming to an end, and that French colonies henceforth would move toward 'maturity' and eventual self-government. The Dutch announced plans for a parliament in the Dutch East Indies with an indigenous majority. British leaders expressed a pragmatic concern for the interests of white settlers, but they also gave clear notice of their intent to grant independence to the colonies – though no time was specified.

India

India was crucial because of its size and role in the British imperial system. In the late 1930s divisions within the nationalist movement set Hindus who advocated a socialist reorganisation of economic and social life as well as immediate independence against Gandhi and the more moderate Hindus, while Muslims became progressively less enthusiastic about an independent India in which they would be a minority.

With the outbreak of war first in Europe and then in the Pacific, India again supported Britain but with notably less enthusiasm than in the First World War. Significant numbers of Indian troops captured by the Japanese defected, in the hope that a Japanese victory would bring Indian independence. Meanwhile, in 1942 nationalist leaders rejected a British offer to grant India autonomous government 'after the war' – their memories of a similar offer made in 1917 were still fresh – and demanded immediate independence instead. Widespread demonstrations and rioting followed, but the British once again suppressed the disorders and arrested Gandhi and Muslim leaders as well.

Wartime demand led to an inflationary industrial boom; tens of thousands of workers shifted into the expanding urban industrial centres in response to the high wages offered. Merchants and industrialists profited, not only increasing their wealth but also their assurance and self-confidence. Landowners in the countryside also profited from rising food prices, and these two classes of entrepreneurs were prominent supporters of the nationalist movement.

Because of the low level of per capita consumption, inflation had pernicious effects on food supplies. In some areas rising prices led peasants to market less food than before, leading to hunger in urban centres. In others, rising prices in the towns drew food from the countryside, leading to hunger among labourers in the countryside who depended upon food purchases. Because only between a quarter and a third of all food produced in India was marketed, rationing would have been difficult to administer in any case; in fact British authorities opted for 'unrestricted free trade' in food, and since supplies were barely adequate for subsistence this policy led to widespread famine. Most tragically, in Bengal the Japanese invasion of Burma had cut off supplies of rice on which Bengal depended, while refugees now had to be fed as well. Other provinces refused to supply food out of their already inadequate stocks, and even emergency relief proved largely impossible because the government had requisitioned most boats for use against the Japanese. Estimates indicate that over one million persons perished in Bengal during 1943. Acute food shortages continued into 1946, leading to rioting between Hindus and Muslims as the backdrop to the final withdrawal of the British.

In late 1945 the new British labour government offered to reopen discussion of Indian autonomy on the basis of the 1942 proposals. An All-India Congress flatly rejected the offer and called on the British to 'quit India'. In the meantime Muslims had begun to demand an independent Muslim state. Hindu leaders rejected the idea of anything but a single united India, and the resulting stalemate in the ensuing three-cornered negotiations was broken only by a British declaration in February 1947 that power would be transferred to the Indians no later than June 1948. On 15 August 1947 India and Pakistan both became independent. An extraordinary outburst of mob violence accompanied partition. Estimates of the dead range from 200,000 to 1,000,000. Some five million Hindus fled Pakistan, and an even greater number of Muslims fled India – a total of over ten million refugees, most of whom were systematically deprived of their property before leaving their former homes. Gandhi, the apostle of non-violence, was himself murdered by a Hindu who held him responsible for India's partition.

Southeast Asia

In Southeast Asia the defeat of the American and European imperial powers by the Japanese stimulated native nationalist movements. The Japanese demonstrated conclusively that the imperialist powers could be beaten; in addition they attempted to undermine colonial authority by recruiting captured native troops to fight against the imperialist powers and by establishing native governments. It developed soon enough that the 'Greater East Asia Co-Prosperity Sphere' was a euphemism for Japanese imperialism, and that the native governments were puppet agencies subservient to Japanese wishes. Resistance movements opposed to the Japanese emerged and cooperated with the Allies in the later stages of the war. However, anti-Japanese resistance emphatically did not imply a willingness to return to colonial status.

Developments in Indonesia established a paradigm for

events elsewhere in the region. The Dutch underestimated the strength of nationalist sentiment. A communist-led revolt in 1926–27 had been serious enough, and in 1937 a unanimous petition from the local parliament signed by both Dutch and native representatives had demanded dominion status. Nationalist feelings crystallised during the three-year Japanese occupation, and when the Japanese surrendered in 1945 Indonesian leaders declared their independence. The Netherlands, humiliated by defeat and occupation by both Germans and Japanese and hoping to utilise colonial revenues for reconstruction, refused to recognise the new government. Aided by British troops, a Dutch army recruited mainly from the Christian districts in the eastern portions of the Indonesian archipelago succeeded in capturing the main urban centres, but could not hold the countryside or destroy the 'Indonesian People's Army' which opposed them. British troops withdrew, the United States advised the Dutch to yield, and after a series of attempted compromises and much-violated cease-fire agreements, in 1949 the Dutch finally accepted a United Nations plan for Indonesian independence. Still they could not surrender everything; they insisted on retaining western New Guinea, which had become a haven for die-hards and émigrés, in order to placate public opinion in the Netherlands and permit the bill granting Indonesian independence to pass the Dutch parliament. In return, Indonesia expelled most remaining Dutch citizens, sequestered Dutch property, repudiated the large debt owed to the Netherlands and eventually annexed the disputed territory.

In Burma the Japanese had promoted Burmese to high positions, then granted formal independence and helped organise the first Burmese national army. By the end of the war, however, a number of resistance movements had emerged, the most powerful of which were communist. The British, with inadequate resources to control a rapidly deteriorating situation, decided to grant independence in June 1947, partly out of concern that further delay would cause the communists to gain complete control over the nationalist movement. In Malaya the British had granted a constitution in 1946, which was opposed by the quasi-independent Malay sultans because it reduced their power and by Malays in general because it granted full citizenship to the Chinese and Indians, who together outnumbered Malays. In 1948 another grant from the British restored the sultans' sovereignty, separated Singapore and its Chinese population and placed restrictions on Chinese and Indians. A communist movement arose which demanded complete independence; while British troops combatted and eventually defeated the communists militarily, aristocratic Malay political leaders began to demand independence in order to pre-empt the communists' main political appeal. Despite the Malays' intent to restrict the rights of Chinese and Indians, the wealthier segments of both communities supported independence as the lesser of two evils, and the British granted full self-government in 1957.

The relatively large French community in Indo-China supported the Vichy regime after the fall of France, and surrendered to the Japanese. The Japanese in turn left local administration in French hands. When the French turned their backs on the losing Vichy cause and declared their support for de Gaulle and the Allies, the Japanese replaced them with puppet regimes in Vietnam, Laos and Cambodia. French collaboration and the dislocation caused by the subsequent imposition of the puppet regimes together eased the task of Vietnamese nationalists, the Viet Minh. The Viet Minh also enjoyed the support of the Nationalist Chinese, and by the end of the war controlled most of the northern region of Tonkin. Like independence movements elsewhere, they declared their independence following the Japanese surrender. The French, many of them retired army and civil service personnel who owned land in the Tonkin region, opposed Vietnamese independence and were supported virtually unanimously by public opinion in France. Even the French Communist Party did not proclaim itself in favour of Vietnamese independence until after it had been expelled from the government in 1947. However, actual hostilities against the new Vietnamese republic were begun by local military commanders, and the war was fought almost exclusively by professional forces. French intransigence led to the ascendency of the communists within the Vietnamese nationalist movement; the United States had initially opposed the reimposition of French colonial rule, but the victory of the communists in China and the Korean War convinced United States policy-makers that communism must be combatted in Southeast Asia as well. Massive American aid to the French did not prevent their defeat, however, and in 1954 Laos and Cambodia became independent states, while Vietnam was divided along a military cease-fire line pending elections to determine a national government. A new Vietnamese government emerged in the south with American support, and in attempting to maintain this regime the United States became ever more deeply involved; only after the American withdrawal twenty years later was the country finally unified.

China

In 1945 1.2 million Japanese soldiers were fighting in China, out of a total of 2.3 million; the China war had absorbed one-third of all Japanese military expenditure and cost 400,000 Japanese lives. Chinese military units had suffered 1.3 million deaths. Japanese attacks on civilians, reprisals for guerrilla raids, forced labour drafts, food confiscations and the general dislocation of economic life had caused the deaths of millions of civilians. Resistance to the Japanese invasion and occupation had created a new, widespread nationalism in China but had not unified the nationalist movement. Both the nationalists and the communists, no matter how desperate the struggle against the Japanese, continued to look beyond the war to the resumption of their contest for domination over China. The best nationalist troops never faced the Japanese, but were used instead to maintain the blockade of the communist base areas, and the communists never placed their forces at the disposal of the nationalist government.

   The Soviet Union occupied Manchuria following the Japanese surrender, turned over captured Japanese equipment to the communists and then evacuated the province before nationalist forces could arrive from the south. However, Soviet forces also dismantled and carried off some two billion dollars' worth of industrial equipment, depriving the future People's Republic of its only major centre of heavy industry.

Stalin in fact did not consider the communists capable of defeating the nationalists, and had signed a treaty recognising the nationalists as the only forces to whom Japanese could surrender.

The United States transported nationalist troops by sea and air to Manchuria and gave the nationalists limited amounts of arms and money, while attempting at the same time to play a 'neutral' role in the negotiations between them and the communists. George Marshall, later famous as the architect of European recovery, saw his carefully-balanced agreement blown away in an escalating series of clashes which by mid-1946 had become a full-scale civil war. Marshall left China embittered, and American policy drifted: 'When I came back, I was hard put to find a long-view conclusion in the matter'. Later, when the tide had begun to run against the nationalists, the United States gave more arms and money, which ensured that the nationalists would be labelled American puppets and earned the hostility of the communists, but which did not alter the outcome.

For a year, the nationalists enjoyed a series of victories. However, Chiang insisted on occupying as much territory as he could as rapidly as he could. The Nationalist Party thereby placed itself in the same strategic position as the Japanese, occupying cities, towns and isolated strongholds in a countryside controlled by communist guerrillas. The nationalists also failed to press through the sort of social reforms which might have won popular support away from the communists. There was no land reform in nationalist regions, and in districts captured from the communists, social and economic reforms were reversed. In the cities, Chiang's rigidity alienated intellectuals, inflation injured the middle class and private industrialists suffered from the favouritism shown by government agencies to those with inside connections. Throughout, Chiang continued to rely on old, trusted members of his personal clique, most of whom were both corrupt and incompetent.

The communists were everything the nationalists were not. They aimed to include the largest possible fraction of the rural population in the revolution and therefore did not abolish property but redistributed existing property and encouraged the peasants to form associations to administer it cooperatively. Socially, the peasants were encouraged to overthrow the authority of the clan organisations and ancestral temples, the system of sacrifices to the myriads of deities and the system of patriarchal authority. This last deserves emphasis, for in the liberation of women the communists discovered a powerful and reliable revolutionary force. The subjection of women in traditional China had been total, but Mao argued the authority of the husband 'has always been comparatively weak among the poor peasants, because the poor peasant women, compelled for financial reasons to take more part in manual work than women of the wealthier classes, have obtained more right to speak and more power to make decisions in family affairs'. The promise of improving the economic lot of all poor peasants, combined with the promise of improving the social lot of rich and poor women alike, proved irresistible. Finally, taxes paid to the communists did not disappear into the pockets of local officials or the coffers of a distant central government, but supported local improvements and local guerrilla units dedicated to the defence of the revolution.

In mid-1947 the communists launched an offensive against the overextended nationalist troops, and as success followed on success, the guerrilla units began to coalesce into armies. The battle of Huai-Hai, near the coast of central China, pitted 550,000 communist troops against 400,000 nationalists along a front of over 300 kilometres. Chiang insisted on the location over the objections of his advisors. The communists surrounded the main nationalist force, and when Chiang ordered a relief army to the rescue, they surrounded that as well. Learning that Chiang planned to bomb his surrounded force in order to prevent the heavy equipment being captured, the commander of the relief army surrendered. After a fruitless attempt to reach a negotiated settlement, Chiang abandoned China for Taiwan, and the People's Republic of China was proclaimed in Peking on 1 October 1949.

The great size of China and the completeness of the communist victory virtually assured great prestige for the Chinese 'model' of revolution and Mao's version of Marxism. In flat contradiction to Soviet orthodoxy, Mao had emphasised the revolutionary potential of the entire peasantry, not some arbitrarily defined segment of peasant society. Instead of proletarian internationalism – which under Stalin had become a cloak for the protection of the interests of the Soviet Union – Mao emphasised an indigenous nationalist reaction to foreign imperialism, whether European, Japanese or American. Mao was pragmatic above all; though he argued on orthodox Marxist lines that 'every kind of thinking, without exception, is stamped with the brand of a class', he also asserted flatly that 'whoever sides with the revolutionary people is a revolutionary'. Mao was and remained a Marxist; Marxism's secularism and antitraditionalism served as an important aspect of a new integrative nationalism, and provided justification for an industrialisation programme which would raise China's status in the world. However, after their victory, the communists continued to emphasise local enthusiasm and initiative. China did not suffer the mass collectivisation and forced exactions from the peasantry which had marked the Soviet Union between the wars. All these things recommended 'Maoism' to would-be revolutionaries everywhere. Nationalist leaders in colonial areas looked to rural revolt as a possible source of revolution. In advanced industrial countries, as the organised industrial proletariat appeared to be losing its revolutionary potential, intellectuals looked hopefully to classes still 'outside' the ruling hierarchy, such as peasants in the Third World, racial minorities and the 'underclass' of chronically unemployed who might be mobilised to achieve genuinely revolutionary change.

North Africa and the Middle East

Italy's possessions in northern Africa were the first to gain independence. The Allies restored the independence of Ethiopia immediately following their victory; however, each would have liked to retain some portion of the remainder for themselves. The French coveted the portion of Libya which they occupied, the British showed little disposition to leave the areas they had occupied, the Americans wanted guarantees that their Libyan air base would remain under their control, the Russians proposed a joint administration of the territories which would have ensured them a voice at least equal to the others and even the Italians, now restored to international respectability, demanded some voice in the disposal of their former possessions. These divisions among the powers and the new forum for international public opinion provided by the United Nations played a role perhaps equal to that of indigenous movements in securing independence. A British-Italian plan for a ten-year joint trusteeship which would have divided Libya into French, British and Italian spheres provoked widespread hostile demonstrations and was defeated in the United Nations General Assembly. Instead a United Nations resolution prescribed that Libya should become independent with a constitution produced by the Libyans themselves. The leader of the Muslim sect which led opposition to the Italians became ruler of the new United Kingdom of Libya in 1951. In the east, Eritrea was annexed to Ethiopia, and the United Nations placed Somalia under Italian administration for a ten-year period – in 1960 the district was merged with British Somalia and became independent.

Libyan independence placed pressure on the British in Egypt and even more extreme pressure on the French in Tunisia, Algeria and Morocco. The British had intervened freely in Egypt during the war to secure their base of operations, but the corruption and incompetence of the government they had installed led in 1952–53 to its replacement by a group of young army officers led by Gamel Abdel Nasser. Even the Suez Canal passed out of British control, and the failure of an armed intervention in Egypt by Britain and France in 1956 only confirmed their inability to affect the course of events in the region. The United States, loudly denouncing the Soviet invasion of Hungary, felt compelled to denounce the Suez invasion as well, and a United Nations resolution called on Britain and France to withdraw. The Sudan, coveted by Egypt but under British administration, was placed under international supervision in 1953 and in 1956 voted to become independent.

Tunisia and Morocco were French protectorates. In theory France administered them on behalf of native rulers; in reality even the 400,000 Europeans in Morocco and 250,000 in Tunisia, and much less the natives, possessed no political rights. The French had outlawed the Tunisian nationalist party and imprisoned its leader in 1938. Freed by the Germans, he moved to Egypt after the restoration of French rule by the Allies, and used Egypt as a base for propaganda and resistance. The French government negotiated a compromise settlement with the nationalists, but the local French community sabotaged the agreement. After two years of guerrilla warfare, France granted Tunisia local autonomy in 1954, and in 1957 the traditional ruler was deposed in favour of a new Tunisian republic. In Morocco the sultan had himself become the leader of the independence movement. The local French commander deposed him in 1953, a move sanctioned after the fact by the French government, but the new French-sponsored sultan commanded no support. Urban terrorism became endemic, and in the countryside an 'army of liberation' arose, which drew support from Spanish Morocco as well. In 1956 the French government consented to the sultan's restoration and to complete independence. The Spanish government likewise conceded independence to its zone, and the two regions were merged.

The relatively conciliatory policy adopted by the French in Tunisia and Morocco resulted in large part from the outbreak of the war of independence in Algeria in 1954. Legally, Algeria was a part of metropolitan France, and the one million European residents exercised an important influence in domestic French politics. They dominated the eight million Algerians through a system of parallel voting and representation which effectively disfranchised all who were not French citizens. Native Algerians could only apply for French citizenship after renouncing Muslim law, a difficult decision which might result in marriage annulment and confiscation of property. Many French families had been established in Algeria for three or four generations, and considered the country theirs by hereditary right. Algerian nationalism meanwhile developed somewhat more slowly than the movements elsewhere in northern Africa. The indigenous tribal elites had been defeated far back in the nineteenth century, and limited educational and economic opportunities had hampered the growth of a native middle class. The small Algerian elite in fact admired and identified with French culture, and protests against French rule were largely confined to demands for equality within the existing system. The French community in Algeria opposed any such reform, and the government was quick to repress any movement which hinted at the desirability of independence.

Demographic and economic trends provided fuel for a new Muslim nationalism. The Algerian population increased far more rapidly than the French, but French farmers monopolised the land; pressed towards the cities, Algerians were forced into overcrowded native quarters in the old city centres or shanty towns on the outskirts. During the Second World War Algerian leaders increasingly abandoned their previous policy of assimilation and moved toward a forthright demand for independence. In May 1945 a confused series of demonstrations led to violence against Europeans, followed by a series of savage reprisals; nearly a hundred Frenchmen died, but in return Frenchmen slaughtered thousands of Algerians. The massacres – and the news of independence movements elsewhere in the Arab world – broke the old habit of deference to the French. A number of organisations appeared and came together in 1954 under the title Front de Libération Nationale (FLN). The demand for independence solidified the mounting feelings of resentment among all groups within the Algerian population; though the government survived the initial outburst of guerrilla attacks and had rounded up virtually all the leaders within a few months, the FLN did not disappear. Attacks on French interests continued, and reprisals and punitive raids in the countryside only made new recruits for the nationalists. The French government's attempts to combine military repression with some kind of reform short of independence were vehemently rejected by the French community in Algeria, and the spreading violence reinforced the intransigence of the nationalists.

From late 1956 through to 1958 the French scored a series of tactical successes against the FLN which looked as though they might foreshadow victory. French troops dominated the Algerian countryside, and the systematic use of torture and summary executions intimidated the population. In February 1958 a local commander ordered an FLN base in Tunisia destroyed by an air strike, an event whose consequences seemed to solidify the position of the French in Algeria by bringing De Gaulle back to power in France. Tunisia protested to the United Nations, and the United States and Britain offered their 'good offices' as mediators. Fearing that the French government would yield, the army seized power in Algeria and some officers at least planned an invasion of France. It was this crisis which created the conditions for De Gaulle's return and the formation of the Fifth Republic.

Still the FLN was not beaten. Guerrilla activities were increasingly difficult within Algeria – only 7,000 guerrillas were active by the end of the war – but the 40,000 FLN troops stationed in Tunisia and Morocco pinned down much larger French units along the border. A new FLN 'provisional government' utilised the United Nations as an effective forum. De Gaulle meanwhile introduced a series of reforms improving the economic and political position of Algerians, amnestied a large number of prisoners and in 1959 announced that Algerians would be given a choice of independence, unification with France or a federal organisation of all ethnic groups. The outraged Algerian French community demonstrated and army leaders planned another coup, but De Gaulle repressed both challenges, and when Algerian self-determination was ratified by a referendum in France in 1961 public opinion had clearly swung against the intransigent settlers and the army. Finally in 1962 De Gaulle and the leaders of the FLN ended the war and independent Algeria joined the other north African states.

In the Middle East, the United States and Britain forced France to relinquish the mandate over Syria in 1946. The French were not pleased; De Gaulle said their actions 'stank of oil'. In 1948 the British withdrew their troops from Palestine, and the United Nations recommended the creation of both a Jewish state of Israel and an Arab Palestinian state as well as the internationalisation of Jerusalem. The neighbouring Arab states attacked the Israelis, but superior organisation led not only to an Israeli victory over their more numerous opponents, but also to enlargement of the new state to include part of the city of Jerusalem, a corridor to the Mediterranean coast and the portion of Galilee which the United Nations had allotted to the Arab Palestinians. Nearly one million Palestinian refugees fled Israel; they were never assimilated by the neighbouring Arab states, but remained housed in makeshift camps, a permanent source of discontent in the region. The humiliation of defeat led to calls for social and economic reform in the Arab states, to attempted military revolts in Syria and Jordan and to the successful coup and rise to power of Nasser in Egypt.

Sub-Saharan Africa

In Britain's west African territories the war had created boom conditions, many west Africans had served with British forces and the Atlantic Charter and the creation of the United Nations had raised expectations. The continued domination of Europeans in economic life, delays in promised development projects, shortages of consumer goods and the evident reluctance of the British to move towards granting independence caused mounting frustration. In the Gold Coast the new constitution of 1946 actually granted Africans a majority in the legislative council, but nevertheless in 1948 a boycott of European traders was followed by widespread rioting in the larger towns. An inquiry into the riots concluded that the constitution had been 'outmoded at birth', and the attempt to devise a satisfactory replacement which still withheld full independence was pre-empted by the rapidly expanding nationalist party which won a crushing victory in the elections of 1951. In 1957 the Gold Coast became independent Ghana. The precedent thus established made it impossible for British authorities not to accede to the demands of nationalists for independence in neighbouring territories, and by 1965 all of Britain's west African colonies were independent.

The success of the independence movement in British west Africa exerted heavy pressure on colonial regimes throughout the sub-Saharan region. In 1956 the French government introduced an outline law under which considerable powers of self-government could be granted to each of its sub-

Saharan African territories, and in 1958 De Gaulle dramatically offered each of these territories the choice of independence or autonomy within a French 'community'. In a referendum all but one territory accepted continued membership in the community. In Guinea, however, the nationalists won a nearly unanimous vote, and their rejection of membership in the community led to the failure of the entire scheme. In the following year some countries asked for complete independence within the community, others then demanded independence outside the community as a preparation for negotiations about the community's final structure, and by 1960 the entire vast area ruled by the French in western and central Africa had become independent. In 1955 the Belgians began for the first time to permit limited political activity by Africans in the Congo, and by 1960 spreading violence had convinced them that only by granting independence could they save their economic interests.

In southern and eastern Africa the attainment of independence was more problematical, primarily because of the larger number of white settlers. In South Africa the voting rights which non-whites retained in Cape Province were gradually reduced and finally abolished, and from 1948 onwards ever-greater majorities of the all-white electorate voted for the extension of the system of apartheid, the legal and physical separation of the races. In 1961 South Africa left the Commonwealth to become an independent republic; despite the South African government's commitment to the establishment of 'homelands' for the African population, this clearly was independence for the white minority only. Similarly in Southern Rhodesia the white settlers had instituted a system of racial segregation, but not wanting to come under the domination of South Africa they persuaded the British colonial administration to unify their territory with Northern Rhodesia and Nyasaland in 1953. The new Federation of Rhodesia and Nyasaland reserved a minority of seats in its parliament for Africans, but this and other 'guarantees' of African rights only stimulated nationalist sentiment. In Kenya, to the north of the new federation, the Mau Mau revolt had broken out in 1952; though the British largely succeeded in containing the insurrection over the next four years, by the late 1950s the government had accepted that all of its African colonies would become independent, and Kenya, Uganda and Tanzania did so in 1961–63. African opposition to the structure of the federation became so open and obvious that Nyasaland and Northern Rhodesia were permitted to secede, and in 1964 they became independent under the names Malawi and Zambia. The intransigent whites of Southern Rhodesia in turn demanded independence under a constitution which would guarantee their continued domination, and when the British government refused, they declared their independence unilaterally in 1965, though as in South Africa this meant independence for whites alone. Black majority rule was finally achieved in 1980 and the country renamed Zimbabwe.

Finally, in 1961 a rebellion against Portuguese rule broke out in Angola and spread to Moçambique. For the next thirteen years, the Portuguese government regularly announced that the rebels had been defeated. In the meantime the expense of the ever-larger campaigns absorbed Portugal's limited economic resources, and increasing conscription drove young Portuguese men to migrate in large numbers. Following Salazar's death, the debate within the army and government over the best way to end the conflict contributed to the revolutionary situation in Portugal. The revolt and its ultimate success are of broader interest in explaining the decolonisation movement. Portugal came closer than any other European nation to realising its imperial rhetoric; the colonies were ruled as integral parts of Portugal, there was virtually no racial discrimination and the Catholic church was strong and active. Though colonial government was certainly authoritarian, there was no damning contrast with the 'home' government as there was in the British, French and Belgian possessions. Portugal in fact gave the colonies all it had to give – except independence.

4
THE GREAT BOOM

THE ORIGINS OF THE GREAT BOOM

Western Europe slipped from the period of reconstruction into an unprecedented boom, but observers adjusted to the new situation rather slowly. By 1948 or 1949 industrial output in all countries already exceeded its prewar level, but growth rates were expected to drop once the 'recovery phase' ended. In 1950 and 1951 the Korean War created a sudden worldwide increase in demand for raw materials and machinery, but this was regarded as a temporary phenomenon. American pressure for rearmament further stimulated demand, but in the absence of cuts in consumption the continued boom was generally seen merely as dangerously inflationary. By the late 1950s the boom showed no sign of ending, and economists began to turn to their shelves for copies of works offering explanations of long periods of economic growth. The boom persisted through the 1960s. It was interrupted on four occasions, in 1952, 1956–58, 1963 and 1967. However, these interruptions were not traditional 'depressions', but 'recessions', years in which output continued to grow, but at rates somewhat lower than those which Europeans came to see as 'normal'. In 1958 total output declined in Belgium, Eire and Norway; these were the only three cases in which output declined in any western European country during any of the four recessions. By the end of the decade some economists had concluded that advanced economies would no longer suffer depressions, but would experience 'growth cycles', alternating periods of relatively rapid and relatively slow growth. Others disputed the statistical evidence, but most agreed that the title of a collaborative volume published in 1969, *Is the Business Cycle Obsolete?*, posed a legitimate question.

Eastern Europe shared in the great boom, though again recognition of the facts spread rather slowly. Recovery was somewhat slower in the Soviet Union and east-central Europe than in the west, but even in those countries which had suffered the greatest wartime destruction industrial output had risen above prewar levels by the early 1950s. In the meantime socialist regimes had replaced the postwar coalition governments and embarked on Soviet-style industrialisation programmes while beginning to collectivise agriculture. Statistics became weapons in the Cold War. Eastern European governments calculated output in ways which maximised their growth rates, and western economists regularly recalculated the official figures to reveal much lower 'true' growth rates. Socialist governments cited their figures as evidence of the success of their system, while western commentators belittled the successes and emphasised socialism's failures. By the late 1960s, however, it had become clear that the eastern European economies had grown extraordinarily rapidly, and that the boom in the east shared important characteristics with the boom in the west.

In balancing possible explanations of this sustained boom, certain factors can be seen to have been relatively fortuitous and others to have been more subject to direction and control. Technological advance and much of the flow of capital, for instance, can be seen to have been relatively lucky developments with important consequences for Europe. Technological discovery had continued during the interwar period, but the comparatively low levels of investment had slowed the rate at which new developments could be introduced. The rebuilding of industrial plants damaged or destroyed during the war provided an opportunity to exploit this backlog of improvements, and the creation of new capacity as the boom continued created a more or less automatic tendency for European industrial efficiency to increase. In western Europe, the technology embodied in the new plants was often American, and so too was the capital which financed their construction. In the case of steel, new techniques introduced in European plants were superior to those still in use in the United States, and by the 1970s had reversed the competitive positions of the two industries.

Eastern Europe had begun from a low base, and the available backlog of technologies was therefore even greater than in western Europe. Despite an official American embargo on exports which might increase the military potential of the socialist countries, technology and capital flowed from west to east in increasing amounts – first to Yugoslavia and Rumania in the hopes of loosening their ties with the Soviet Union, then in response to more narrowly economic motives as in the cases of plants constructed by Fiat and other western European firms in the Soviet Union and elsewhere. In addition, the Soviet Union ceased to extract reparations payments from east-central Europe, and began instead to grant subsidies in the form of large trade credits and low prices charged for Soviet petroleum and mineral exports.

Internally Europe benefited from the opportunity to shift workers out of agriculture into industry. Observers noted the decline in employment in agriculture in West Germany from 5.1 million in 1950 to 3.6 million in 1961 and ascribed it to the 'economic miracle'. However, in France the decline was equally dramatic, from 5.2 million in 1954 to 3.9 million in 1962, and it was actually Italy which experienced the most substantial structural change, as agricultural employment fell from 8.3 to 5.6 million and industrial employment rose from 6.3 to 7.9 million between 1951 and 1961. The smaller countries kept pace in percentage terms, and during the 1960s Spain began to follow along the same path. In eastern Europe the rapid increases in industrial employment caused the share of agriculture in total employment to decline rapidly, and by the 1960s the number of workers in agriculture was declining absolutely as well. In percentage terms the structural transformation of East Germany nearly matched that of West Germany, and in Bulgaria the share of agriculture in the labour force declined from 80 per cent in 1950 to 40 per cent in 1970.

Because in all countries output per worker in agriculture remained substantially lower than output per worker in industry, the increasing share of industry in employment raised average productivity and increased the rate of growth of national product. In western Europe, the increasing share of highly-paid industrial workers in the labour force increased the size of the domestic market. Further, contrary to the predictions of population experts in the 1930s, birth rates increased and population rose rapidly. High and rising real incomes and the formation of new families led to vastly increased demand for consumer durables: better quality housing, automobiles, domestic appliances, radios and television sets. In the east, governments taxed away most of the increased income and channelled resources into further industrial investment. In both east and west the result was a tendency for the boom to reinforce itself, each round of investment paving the way for another.

Foreign markets, notably the United States, were large, buoyant and relatively open, and European exporters were quick to take advantage of the opportunities they provided. Western European labour costs were low compared to the United States, initially because of low wages, particularly those of skilled workers, and later because of generally improved technology, increased productivity and the flow of migrant workers. Eastern Europe stood in a roughly analogous position to western Europe, and the boom in the west provided highly profitable opportunities for the state export corporations of the east. Yugoslavia and Rumania benefited from trade concessions which accompanied western loans, and East Germany gained access to the Common Market because of preferential trading arrangements with West Germany.

Europe also benefited from the relatively abundant supply and consequently low costs of imported food, raw materials and especially energy. Prices of food and raw materials rose much less rapidly than prices of manufactured products in world markets, which improved Europe's terms of trade and raised income from exports. Western European energy consumption increased more than 70 per cent during the 1960s, the share of petroleum in total energy consumption rose from 30 to 60 per cent and over fourth-fifths of the petroleum consumed was imported from the Middle East and north Africa; as long as prices remained low and the sources of supply seemed politically stable these figures caused little concern. In any event, Europeans confidently expected nuclear power to replace fossil fuel and provide limitless power for the foreseeable future.

PLANNING AND GROWTH IN WESTERN EUROPE

Much of western Europe's economic success was attributed to government policy, and indeed economic 'planning' became an undoubted fad in the mid-1960s. George J. Stigler told his American colleagues in 1965 that economics stood on the 'threshold of its golden age', because economists seemed not only to have uncovered the secrets of growth, but also to have the ear of sympathetic and responsive governments. The phrase 'the new Europe' became a cliché, and a generation of 'Eurocrats' exemplified by Walter Hallstein, president of the Commission of the European Economic Community (EEC), became semi-legendary figures who according to press accounts drove themselves twelve hours a day, six days a week, and whose efforts had ushered in a new era of economic growth. The 'French model' of 'indicative planning' was discovered and popularised, and Robert Marjolin, the French representative on the EEC Executive, produced an influential paper calling for coordinated planning by all EEC members, rather than 'isolated national efforts'. Keynesian macroeconomic theory provided the tools of monetary and fiscal policy which central governments could use to ensure levels of demand corresponding to full employment, while investment in the private sector adjusted to targets outlined by government planners – so ran the popularised version of planning in the western literature.

Actually, planning on a supranational basis never became possible, and national economic policy makers in fact performed rather unimpressively during the 1950s and 1960s. Under the unsympathetic eye of the International Monetary Fund (IMF), each government struggled to maintain both a positive balance of payments and a 'strong' currency. Under the even less sympathetic eye of its finance ministry, each government also sought to balance its budget and to hold prices constant. Although growth depended as much on domestic markets as on exports, most governments' primary concern was to depress domestic prices in the hope of stimulating exports. In doing so they resisted wage increases and extension of social security programmes and caused the periods of recession and unemployment which marred the overall picture of economic advance. In the 1970s, when the positive factors which had aided growth in the 1950s and 1960s weakened or disappeared entirely, these predispositions persisted, often with disastrous consequences.

The failure of Britain to participate fully in the boom of the 1950s and 1960s was widely noted, commented upon and debated. After the success of the postwar recovery plan, British growth rates slumped and did not recover. Industrial output had risen 50 per cent to 1969, only half of the western European average. Slow British growth was blamed on the government, the labour unions and even the entrepreneurial middle classes, who were accused of harbouring a deep cultural antipathy towards industry. It is therefore worth noting that a portion of Britain's 'decline' was merely relative to the stunning and unprecedented growth of the other countries of western Europe. Though Britain could have made more of the opportunities of the 1950s and 1960s, the fortuitous factors accelerating growth in those other countries were absent or much weaker. Because of the overriding need for maximum output, Britain had not undertaken new investment or modernised existing industrial plants during the war. In addition, Britain suffered relatively little damage during the war, and consequently did not benefit from the modernisation of reconstructed plants or from direct American aid to the same extent as other western European countries. Because British exports, industrial output and national income were already large, they could not in general increase at the same rates as those of countries beginning from lower bases. Some 200,000 workers shifted out of agriculture during the 1950s, but the small size of the sector (3.3 per cent of total employment in 1961) precluded the sort of gains in income and productivity available to countries with larger reserves of agricultural labour. The initial 'consumer durables revolution' had already passed in Britain; though British consumers might extend and upgrade their possessions, the rates of increase could not match those of countries whose citizens were enjoying the fruits of widespread affluence for the first time.

Britain's 'stop-go' economic policies probably worsened the problems which promoted them. Each period of expansion brought increased imports, leading to a negative balance of payments, an exchange 'crisis' and loans from the IMF and other governments. The British government in turn restricted credit, cut government spending and attempted to freeze wages, as in 1955, 1960–61 and 1964–69, in the hope of lowering export prices. However, these 'austerity' policies reduced domestic demand, causing unemployment and widespread labour unrest. The government's response was to ease credit and increase spending, as in 1958–59, 1962 and 1971. Unfortunately, the resulting expansion brought renewed balance of payments problems, and the cycle then repeated. Further, the delayed impact of changes in the supply of credit and government spending accentuated the fluctuations by creating inflationary tendencies during expansions and choking off recovery from contractions. Workers perceived restrictions on wages as an attempt to force them to bear the burden of adjustment, and the long series of bitter strikes in fact resulted in wage increases well in excess of increases in prices, since no government possessed the power to impose really effective wage controls. Sometimes policy was merely confused, as in the erratic course of nationalisation, denationalisation and renationalisation in the steel industry or the combination of increased taxes and expanded credit in 1968–69. The resulting insecurity worked to depress investment, lowered possible increases in productivity and income and slowed the adaptation of labour to new processes.

Weaknesses in British policies were of course as widely discussed as the notoriously slow rate of British growth; the fact that they were merely an extreme example of a general tendency largely escaped notice. Variations in rates of growth could be explained largely by variations in the strength of exogenous or fortuitous factors; the luckier countries grew faster. The British stop-go pattern of government policy repeated itself in most countries, though not always with the same frequency or regularity; the luckier countries were not so often compelled by foreign exchange crises to introduce the restrictive 'stop' policies, and the subsequent resumptions of the boom did not require the expansionary 'go' policies.

France, West Germany and the smaller nations of western Europe were the luckiest countries during the boom. France enjoyed unprecedented rates of growth during the 1950s and 1960s. Industrial output increased eight to nine per cent each year; even more significantly, total output rose at an average rate of five per cent yearly. Somewhat paradoxically, the roots of French growth can be found in the defeat and humiliation of the Vichy years. Profamily policies encouraged a higher birth rate, resulting in the highest rate of growth of population seen in France in over a century. The German occupation authorities and the Vichy bureaucracy broke up organisations of both workers and employers. Both Vichy and the Resistance movement favoured an increased role for government in the economy. Rising population resulted in increased demand, and investment increased in response to demand. There had been very little new investment in France during the interwar years, but from 1950 to 1960 an average of nineteen per cent of each year's gross national product was devoted to new investment. This new investment was accompanied by new technologies and extensive business reorganisation.

Most importantly, these changes affected agriculture as well as industry. The government provided greatly increased numbers of technical consultants and lent money to farmers for new equipment. There were 46,000 tractors in France in 1946, 200,000 in 1953 and 600,000 in 1960. The state in the late 1950s also started a programme of land redistribution, which consolidated less productive small parcels into larger estates where the new machinery was cost-effective. The resulting increase in agricultural productivity released labour which flowed into industrial occupations. Behind these aggregate measures, a complex social and political transformation was taking place. For the first time, a majority of French peasants were becoming farmers, integrated into and responsive to a market economy. They now insisted that the government provide them with the necessary resources for agricultural modernisation. They also demanded remunerative prices and guaranteed markets for their products; during the early 1960s demonstrations spread across the country, with blocked roads, stopped trains and destroyed products attesting to the farmers' determination. During the boom, this aspect of the farmers' new attitude was less important than their receptivity to technical improvements.

The cross-fertilisation of talent between the public and private sectors continued, and a generation of new administrators rose to senior positions in these organisations, such as Pierre Massé, head of the government electricity corporation and later director of economic planning. These leaders received much of the credit for the expansion and efficiency of government enterprises in France, with which the nationalised sector in Britain was often unfavourably compared. In industry, the state sector now included some large manufacturing firms such as Renault, mines, banks and public utilities. In the 1960s the government also encouraged a decentralisation of industry and the build-up of new industrial centres, such as aircraft construction in Toulouse and heavy industry and shipping in La Ciotat.

However, the French enjoyed the advantages of new technologies particularly appropriate to their situation, such as hydroelectric techniques and the backlog of innovations in coal mining. Exploitation of the important deposits of natural gas discovered at Lacq in 1956 would have been impossible without a newly-developed technique to separate sulphur from the gas. When economic performance depended more on skill and judgement than on good fortune, results were less than brilliant. In France during the 1950s it was safe to predict inflationary policies during election years and restrictive policies thereafter. The advent of the Fifth Republic in 1958 led to a monetary stabilisation programme, but inflation continued nonetheless. In 1963 the austerity programme of the treasury minister and later president Valéry Giscard d'Estaing created the conditions for the serious recession of 1965–67.

Total output in West Germany rose 6.2 per cent yearly from 1950 to 1970; manufacturing output rose at 8 per cent yearly, and had trebled by the end of the great boom. The

Allied occupation authorities, especially the Americans, had planned to break up Germany's cartel organisations, but in general large firms remained large and in a number of cases cartels reconstituted themselves as loosely-organised 'groups'. I.G. Farben was broken up, but the three successor firms (Hoechst, Bayer and BASF) remained three of the largest chemical firms in the world and appeared to allocate markets and production among themselves on an informal basis. The large banks, notably the Deutsche Bank, not only escaped dissolution but also continued under the control of the same managers. The government passed an 'anti-cartel law' in 1957 and strengthened it in 1965; however, despite an ideology which advocated 'prosperity through competition', the government remained very lenient towards cartel arrangements, especially in export industries or where such agreements would improve Germany's position in the European Community.

Political and social stability received much of the credit for this remarkable performance. As in France, close connections between government and large industrial firms contributed to policies favouring growth, while the unions continued to make only moderate wage demands. Both the banks and the government had large holdings in major corporations; the banks cooperated in financing major new investments, and the government held interest rates low and continued the tax incentives which had stimulated investment during the reconstruction period. The results were dramatic; German investment had averaged only 14 per cent of gross national product from 1914 to 1949, but the average rate of investment rose to 27 per cent from 1950 to 1970, while the total capital stock of West Germany's manufacturing sector doubled during the 1950s and doubled again during the 1960s. West Germany seemed the true home of the great boom, but even here government policy sometimes interfered with the smooth upward course of growth. Government and business leaders believed the West German economy depended on exports and therefore feared that inflation would reduce competitiveness in foreign markets. The response to any increase in prices was apt to be drastic. The government reacted to a 4 per cent increase in prices during 1965 with an abrupt tightening of credit and cuts in spending, and by 1967 some 700,000 persons were unemployed, not including additional thousands of *Gastarbeiter* ('guest' workers) dismissed and sent home. Similarly, a seven per cent price rise in 1970 occasioned a new series of restrictions, worsening the recessions of 1970–71 and 1975.

In the Low Countries, Switzerland and Austria the same broad factors worked to stimulate growth as in France and West Germany. Total output increased rapidly from 1950 to 1970 at 3.5 per cent each year in Belgium, 4.2 per cent in Switzerland and 5 per cent in Austria and the Netherlands. A rapidly modernising agricultural sector provided a reservoir of labour, supplemented by 'guest' workers from southern Europe. (In Switzerland migrants made up over a third of the labour force by the early 1970s.) The portion of the economy controlled directly by the government expanded. Government ownership of manufacturing plants was greatest in Austria, where in 1955 the government purchased firms originally confiscated by the Russians as part of the peace settlement. In 1960 the nationalised sector of the Austrian economy employed 30 per cent of the labour force and produced nearly a third of total exports. In the Low Countries and Switzerland governments tended to confine themselves more to public utilities and housing, but in those fields they controlled massive flows of investment and therefore exercised a substantial influence on other sectors as well. In 1957 the Dutch central government assumed the debts of local governments, mostly for housing, and embarked on a large housing construction programme of 80–100,000 homes a year. All governments electrified their railways and extended and improved highways for the rapidly increasing numbers of automobiles.

Close cooperation among government agencies, labour organisations and representatives of private industry produced policies favouring rapid growth. The integration of representatives of the working class reduced social conflict and also generally restrained demands for rapid wage increases. In Belgium the loss of the Congo in 1960 caused a substantial decline in government revenue, and the government planned to cut welfare expenditures while undertaking new investment to create jobs; a series of strikes and riots by workers was ended by the moderating action of the socialist party, which entered a coalition cabinet pledged to increased state planning combined with fiscal reform. Governments used tax systems and subsidies to stimulate savings and investment. Savings in the Netherlands rose from 12 to 20 per cent of gross national product from 1950 to 1959 and averaged 26 per cent from 1950 to 1970. Governments channelled these increased flows of savings quite deliberately. The Dutch held interest rates low to favour housing construction, and the Dutch government went into partnership with Shell and Esso to exploit the natural gas discoveries at Groningen and Slochteren. Austria controlled private firms through the nationalised banks; in 1964 the Swiss federal government imposed controls over bank credit as an 'emergency' measure, confirmed the next year in a referendum.

The Nordic countries grew rapidly from the late 1950s to the late 1960s, but the boom did not extend over as long a period, and the interruptions tended to be more severe than in the fortunate nations of western Europe. All were relatively small countries, all depended on exports and despite two generations of industrial development primary products continued to make up a large proportion of those exports. Fluctuations in international demand therefore resulted in alternating periods of inflationary expansion, broken by relatively severe recessions. Surges in demand for primary products forced their prices upward, raising incomes and employment in those sectors, but also placing severe upward pressure on wages and other domestic prices, especially those of manufactured exports. A boom in the primary sector therefore could be followed closely by a depression in the manufacturing sector. In addition, all four governments attempted to contain inflationary pressures by restricting credit and imposing controls on investment, which had the effect of spreading the depression to the construction industry in particular.

Through the mid-1950s the Nordic countries struggled with inflation and persistent deficits in their balance of payments. The United States provided aid to Norway to cover the deficit, but imposed a quota on cheese imports and dumped butter on the West German market, hurting Denmark, while restricting imports of Swedish timber products because of alleged Swedish dumping. Reparations due to the Soviet Union imposed similar burdens on the Finnish economy. Then the superpowers apparently began to see the benefits of more supportive policies. In 1954 the Russians agreed to begin paying for Finnish products in convertible currency, returned a former military base and industrial plants seized at the end of the war and agreed to supply oil if Finland built a refinery. The World Bank in turn granted large development loans to Finland and Norway in 1955, and the United States made direct loans to Norway in 1955 and to Denmark in 1958. All four countries enjoyed substantial increases in exports in the opening years of the 1960s, but Denmark's exports to the newly-formed EEC declined after 1961 and Sweden and Finland suffered recessions in 1962–63 and 1963–64 respectively. Sweden boomed for two years after 1964, slumped for a year and then boomed again from 1968 to 1971. Denmark's manufacturing industry boomed through the mid-1960s, but in 1967 growth suddenly stopped, choked off by the British devaluation of the pound and the protectionism of the EEC. Finland struggled with a negative balance of payments and persistent inflationary pressures through the later 1960s, though without a major interruption in the rate of growth. Norwegian shipping and manufacturing enjoyed high rates of growth through the 1960s, but in 1969 here too imports and prices suddenly began to rise. .

The socialist governments of the Nordic countries, and Sweden in particular, were widely held to have discovered a 'middle road' between west and east. A high degree of government involvement in the economy, combined with widespread democratic participation in decison making, theoretically allowed more rapid and stable growth than in the west while permitting far higher levels of consumption and greater personal freedom than in the east. Even here the record was mixed, however. For example, in Sweden a large increase in military spending in 1958 was followed by rising prices in 1959. Fearing inflation and wanting to balance its budget, the government increased taxes and raised interest rates in 1960 and 1961; the resulting decline in demand and investment led to the recession of 1962–63. Similarly, the boom conditions of the mid-1960s renewed the government's fear of inflation, and restrictive fiscal and monetary policies imposed through 1965, 1966 and 1967 led to declining investment and a new recession in 1969–72.

The southern perimeter also enjoyed unprecedented prosperity during the 1950s and 1960s. The southern countries were poor in 1955 compared to their northern neighbours; they remained so fifteen years later, but the growth of the modern industrial and service sectors had reached the point at which they, and not the traditional agricultural and artisan sectors, dominated economic and social life. In Portugal when one of the first major hydroelectric plants went into operation in 1955, the price of power dropped 40 per cent in the Lisbon region. New rounds of investment in 1956 and 1965, supported by further loans from the United States and the World Bank, extended the power and transportation systems and raised industrial output. In Spain government investment in housing led the boom of the late 1950s; the monetary stabilisation following 1959 was accompanied by loans from the United States and western European countries for long-term development projects, especially power. Industrial output, notably shipbuilding and automobiles, began to rise rapidly in the mid-1960s – a 'Spanish miracle' to match those occurring elsewhere. Italian industry grew extremely rapidly from the mid-1950s to the early 1960s; by 1961 unemployment had declined to less than one million nationally and northern industrial districts were experiencing a shortage of labour. New highways encouraged migration from south to north, and higher wages increased the size of the domestic market; the resulting demand for housing and consumer durables seemed to provide the basis for long-term prosperity. Greece seemed another variation on the same optimistic theme. Large loans and grants from the United States and western Europe provided capital for investment in infrastructure, and association with the EEC and trade agreements with eastern European countries opened export markets.

As in the north, however, interruptions of the upward

trend were severe compared to western Europe. In addition the boom in the south remained confined to the industrial sector; agriculture did not progress as rapidly as for instance in France. In Spain in 1964 and in Portugal in 1966 agricultural output declined sharply; large numbers of small farms remained without irrigation or capital for mechanisation. There was no famine, but in both countries food prices shot upward and large amounts of food had to be imported. Imports had to be paid for, but rising prices led to demands for wage increases, making exports more expensive, and the resulting decline in the balance of payments increased the difficulty of paying the foreign loans which had financed development. In Italy increasing wages raised domestic prices; higher incomes and lower tariffs on goods from the European Community resulted in increasing imports and therefore in periodic crises in the balance of payments which hampered growth through the mid and late 1960s.

The boom in the southern countries also depended directly on the boom in western Europe. All depended heavily on capital imports, and although the markets of western Europe absorbed large amounts of processed agricultural products and manufactured goods from the south, commodity exports would not as yet have sufficed to pay interest and principal on foreign loans. The difference was made up from two sources. Hundreds of thousands of workers from the south found jobs in western Europe, and the remittances of these 'guest' workers helped their 'home' countries' balance of payments. In addition, millions of newly-affluent workers from northern and western Europe began to take holidays in the south, and this explosive increase in tourism provided another large source of foreign exchange. However, when the boom in western Europe was interrupted, export markets, jobs for 'guest' workers and tourism all declined and therefore so did the southern economies.

Politics could hamper growth as well. The Italian economy boomed from 1959 to 1962, but a deficit in the balance of payments and the nationalisation of the electricity industry in 1962 led to a widely reported 'crisis of confidence' and a flight of Italian capital. Swiss banks at one point refused to accept lire. A rescue operation mounted by the IMF, with participation by the United States and EEC countries, 'saved' the lira by providing loans to cover Italy's payments deficit, but the cost was high. The Italian government embarked on an austerity programme to reduce imports, creating widespread unemployment. Exports revived as other countries began to recover from the 1967 recession and Italy recorded a positive balance of payments, but total output stagnated until the end of the decade.

Portugal, Spain and Greece had all embarked on development plans dependent on foreign aid and loans supplied by the United States and northwestern European countries. The plans all emphasised large industrial projects but neglected the rural sector, and the periodic need to import food as well as expensive machinery led to recurrent balance of payments crises, followed by further loans and government austerity programmes. Portugal's attempt to prosecute the war in Angola and Moçambique while continuing the heavy domestic investment programme exacerbated inflationary pressures through the early 1970s, and the revolution in 1974 and subsequent land seizures accelerated inflation, caused a decline in tourism and created a food shortage. The coup in Greece in 1967 cut off the flows of tourists and foreign capital, causing a downturn in the balance of payments and slower growth until United States aid was resumed three years later. In 1959 Spain was granted 375 million dollars in aid and permission for a single devaluation of the peso, having agreed in return to a programme of monetary 'stabilisation' and domestic austerity – which resulted in a sharp recession. Spain's 1964–67 *Plan de Desarollo* disappointed foreign observers, who considered Spanish statistics inadequate, the 'poles' of growth poorly chosen and subject to overly restrictive regulations and the state sector too small and diverse for effective management. Spanish industrial production more than doubled between 1958 and 1966, but observers lamented the inflation which accompanied growth. A balance of payments deficit caused by food imports led the government to restrict credit, which slowed growth but not inflation, and Spain entered the 1970s lurching along much the same 'stop-go' path as Britain.

PLANNING AND GROWTH IN EASTERN EUROPE

In the Soviet Union and east-central Europe during the early 1950s all governments attempted to replicate the Soviet model of economic development inherited from the 1930s. Comprehensive, centralised economic planning funnelled resources into a complete range of heavy industries. Agriculture was organised into collectives and state farms intended to operate on the same principles as industrial factories. Production of consumer goods was restricted, and the standard of living held low by conscious intent. However, the attempt failed, though tergiversations from orthodoxy were concealed in various face-saving ways. Planning was decentralised, more resources devoted to consumer goods and real incomes increased. Incentives to farmers were increased and the system of collective agriculture modified in various ways. The attempt to isolate the socialist economies from the international economy also ended, and eastern European countries began to look to the west for trade, technology and capital not available closer to home.

In 1953 the deaths of Stalin and Beria ushered in a period of 'collective leadership' and a 'new course' in the Soviet Union which promised increased incentives to farmers, more consumer goods and lower prices. In 1955 the leadership officially returned to Soviet orthodoxy, restoring the emphasis on heavy industry and investing 20–30 per cent of national income. However, the central planning agencies were reorganised and a new agency created to study the problems of labour scarcity and the relatively low levels of productivity in Russian industry. During Nikita Khrushchev's rise to leadership from 1956 to 1958, the government admitted its current plan was impossible and revised its targets downward, and several central planning agencies were abolished and replaced by 105 regional economic units (*sovnarkhozy*). Khrushchev's seven-year plan for 1959–65 emphasised the chemical industry and industrial development in the eastern territories but also envisaged shorter working hours, higher wages and improved living standards. Khrushchev promised to 'overtake' the west by 1970 at the latest.

Economist Yevsei G. Liberman's critique of Soviet planning

and his proposals for its improvement emerged into the arena of public discussion in 1962. Liberman argued that the high costs of Russian output resulted from overly rigid planning and the fixing of production targets in terms of physical quantities. To improve productivity he suggested direct incentives, in particular bonuses linked to the profitability of each enterprise. To allocate resources more efficiently he recommended a central bank to channel investment to priority sectors. Enterprise managers would be made responsible for investment, staffing, production and marketing decisions, and resources therefore would flow to the most efficient enterprises in each sector. In 1963 and 1964 planning institutions were again reorganised, the regional economic units reduced to 47 and nearly 300,000 factory managers given relative freedom to make decisions regarding staffing, wages and investment. The Bolshevichka clothing plant operated as a pilot project in pricing and profits, and its success led to the decision to allow enterprise managers to base production on orders from retail outlets rather than central directives. Khrushchev fell from power and was replaced by Leonid I. Brezhnev in 1963, but the reform continued and was extended in the new five-year plan beginning in 1965. The discretionary powers of enterprise managers were further widened, and enterprises now were to be evaluated on the basis of the 'quality' (the cost of production) as well as on the physical quantity of their output. Trade agreements with France and Britain reflected Russia's desire for foreign exchange earnings and imported western technologies.

In 1966, 704 Russian enterprises operated under 'direct links' of producer to consumer. They accounted for 10–12 per cent of total industrial production, and according to Liberman's figures increased their sales 10 per cent (compared to the national average of 8.6 per cent), their profits by 25 per cent (compared to the national average of 10 per cent) and their productivity by 8 per cent (compared to the national average of 5.2 per cent). Their success led to the extension of the programme and to more freedom for all enterprise managers to set prices. In 1967 some 3,600 enterprises operated under the new system, and by the end of

1968 the number had risen to 25,000 enterprises, concentrated in the high quality metal and machinery industries and producing about half of total industrial output.

In 1968, parallel to the increased repression of political dissidents, came a sudden outburst of public criticism of the new system and of Liberman, who defended himself vigorously and rejected the accusation that he had ever opposed central planning. The economy seemed to falter; the goals of the series of one-year plans in 1968, 1969 and 1970 could not be met, and the increased wages and bonus payments brought little real benefit since there were virtually no consumer goods to purchase. Opponents of the new system continued to press for a return to tighter central control. The remaining regional economic units were downgraded, but Brezhnev focused his personal criticisms on the transportation and distribution systems. Under the new five-year plan for 1971–75, 44,000 enterprises producing 95 per cent of industrial profits operated under largely autonomous management.

Apostate Yugoslavia often revealed trends in eastern European economic policy and performance before they appeared elsewhere. In 1951 Boris Kidric, head of the planning agency, announced the end to regular five-year plans. Unremunerative attempts to create a complete range of industry were also ended. Control over planning was decentralised, and central investment focused on the provision of basic requirements, particularly electric power. The United States, Great Britain and West Germany replaced Russia and Czechoslovakia as Yugoslavia's most important trading partners, and western capital was actively sought to promote development. Yugoslav successes were undeniable: a rapid increase in aggregate income and industrial production, a thirteenfold rise in electrical power output from 1950 to 1970 and several showpiece projects such as the Zagreb chemical plant constructed with an American loan. Nevertheless, despite devaluations, loans from the IMF and western countries and remittances from Yugoslavs working in the European Economic Community, Yugoslavia suffered from periodic deficits in the balance of payments, shortages and unrest, and remained in many respects chronically backward.

Rumania (officially spelt Romania since 1966) followed

Yugoslavia's independent nationalist orientation. In 1957 the industrial plan was admitted to have failed, but by focusing on certain branches such as railway, electrical and drilling equipment, Rumania achieved very high rates of industrial growth over the next five years. The Rumanians therefore were disturbed that the Soviet Union continued to view them merely as producers of agricultural and industrial raw materials. In 1963 Nicholae Ceausescu, secretary of the Rumanian Central Committee, delivered a speech to a visiting Russian trade delegation, during which he reminded them forcefully of Lenin's assertion that a heavy industrial base was essential to every socialist country. Rumania refused to abandon its industrialisation plans and looked to the west for trade and capital, though without breaking relations with other socialist countries. Industrial output rose 120 per cent from 1963 to 1970, and Ceausescu utilised his advocacy of industrial independence in his successful bid for absolute leadership.

Poland and Hungary travelled less peaceful paths. In Poland, strikes, riots and an uprising in Poznan in 1956 led to the rise of a more moderate leadership and the enunciation of a 'Polish road to socialism' which included freedom of religion and speech as well as greater flexibility in economic planning. Khrushchev accepted the new Polish regime, and the Soviet Union agreed to supply 1.7 million tons of grain and long-term trade credits in 1957, as well as to begin paying world prices for Polish exports. The United States contributed 250 million dollars in loans from 1957 to 1959 alone, and in the early 1960s Poland signed trade agreements with the United States, Great Britain, West Germany and France. Industrial output increased 78 per cent between 1963 and 1970, but low productivity and high costs led to recurrent balance of payments problems. In Hungary in 1956 demonstrations of sympathy with the Polish rioters escalated into a full-scale revolt directed against Russian domination. Russian forces crushed the revolt, but the new regime still required some basis for a *modus vivendi* with its disaffected subjects. Industrial plan targets were lowered and living standards raised, implicitly in return for political quiescence. In 1963 the planning mechanism was reorganised and more emphasis placed on the technical qualifications of industrial managers, and proposals for an incentive system came under discussion. In 1968 the Hungarians introduced their 'new economic model' based in part on similar reforms in Czechoslovakia. Industrial managers were given more freedom as in the Liberman reforms in Russia, evaluated on the basis of the profits made by their enterprises and subjected to increased foreign competition in the hope that they would increase productivity. Industrial output and exports did in fact rise dramatically through the early 1970s, and the regime rewarded Hungarians with substantial increases in living standards.

In East Germany and Czechoslovakia, the weather played a role in changing economic structures. Through the late 1950s heavy industrial output rose rapidly in both countries, though substantial evidence suggested that all was not well. In Czechoslovakia in 1961, after an accident in a coal mine which cost 108 lives, the government admitted that increased output had been achieved partly at the expense of lower safety standards. Consumer goods gradually became more abundant than elsewhere in eastern Europe, but both countries suffered from very high turnover rates among dissatisfied workers. The severe winter of 1963–64 clearly revealed the shortcomings of rigid centralised planning. In Czechoslovakia industrial production increased by only one per cent, and agricultural output, already stagnant, declined precipitously. A coal shortage led to power cuts and unpaid overtime. In East Germany the ambitious seven-year plan announced in 1959 was abandoned, an admitted failure.

Following the 1963 crisis East Germany reorganised industrial planning agencies to give greater flexibility, and industrial output rose rapidly through the remainder of the 1960s. East Germans came to enjoy the highest standard of living in eastern Europe. West German insistence on the existence of a single Germany in effect eased East German entry to the EEC market, and foreign trade expanded. The increasing share of the west in East German trade caused concern in Berlin and Moscow, and in 1965 an extensive new trade agreement was signed with Russia. At the same time, however, slow population growth led to fears of a labour shortage and an emphasis on productivity, and in 1967 planning was officially decentralised, with a much greater role given to the ministries for each individual industry.

Similarly in Czechoslovakia, the 1963 economic crisis led to decentralised planning and increased trade with the west, but the Czech 'new economic system' broke with the past much more completely than the East German reforms did. A rapid turnover among senior government officials brought younger, more liberal men to power, notably Alexander Dubcek, who had been influenced by the ideas of the economist Ota Sik. Sik noted that Czechoslovakia had been a highly developed industrial country before the establishment of a socialist government, that the people had been promised tangible gains and that they were therefore justifiably dissatisfied. Czechoslovakia required capital to modernise the industrial sector, which had largely escaped destruction during the war, but trade with socialist countries was of little help because Czechoslovakia's generally positive trade balances were frozen in inconvertible currencies by the east's bilateral trading structure. In 1968 the Czechs applied to the Russians for a loan of 500 million dollars to cover a portion of their positive trade balance, and were refused. Rumours that the Czechs were attempting to raise the money from the United States and West Germany, and the failure of Dubcek to gain the confidence of Russian leaders, may have prompted the Russian invasion, the replacement of Dubcek by Gustav Husak in 1969 and the reimposition of central control.

Agriculture was the crucial weak spot in the eastern European economies. Inefficient by western European standards, yet still very large (a third of total employment in Russia in 1971, for instance), the agricultural sector dragged down aggregate rates of growth and posed severe social and political problems. Western observers attributed eastern agricultural inefficiency to collectivisation. Only private ownership could motivate farmers to increase productivity, they argued. However, agriculture in eastern Europe had always been less efficient than in the west. Further, eastern European governments intended that agriculture would supply the resources for their industrialisation programmes, and therefore allocated relatively little capital to agricultural investment. This historically low base and limited capital may have been as important in producing low productivity as collectivisation. In addition, 'collectivisation' itself requires closer examination. Formally, most eastern European agriculture was organised into large units under central control, but in fact small plots persisted, and extensive private trading also existed alongside official government channels.

In Russia the very low agricultural output of the early 1950s led Khrushchev to espouse expansion into Russia's 'virgin lands'. The plan announced in 1954 called for the creation of 124 state farms in Kazakhstan and Siberia, employing 150,000 workers. Thirty million hectares of new cropland were to be developed, much of it devoted to maize. In addition, between 1957 and 1962 the government liberalised the regulations governing all collectives, in the hope of stimulating production. First compulsory deliveries to state agencies were made more flexible and quotas based on land quality, then quotas were abolished and collectives allowed to sell to the state on a contract basis and sell their surpluses privately in local markets. In 1962 Khrushchev announced further increases in incentives to farmers and price increases of 25–30 per cent. Khrushchev's policies aroused opposition, first muted and then more strident. Early results on the virgin lands were disappointing. Except for 1958, the weather was poor or worse, and in 1963–65 crop failures led to food shortages, which contributed to Khrushchev's fall from power.

During the late 1960s the general Russian concern for productivity affected agriculture as well as industry. Fear of a general labour shortage led the government to increase investment in agriculture, and in the 1971–75 plan called for a massive rise in agricultural investment in order to permit the reduction of the agricultural labour force by 12 per cent. Russia suffered the worst weather in a century in 1972, but the weather was excellent in 1973, and the record harvest surpassed even the traditionally optimistic expectations of the planning bureau statisticians. The best results were achieved in Kazakhstan, where tree planting and new techniques of shallow ploughing had reduced erosion, and provided at least partial vindication for Khrushchev's policies. Poor weather in 1974 reduced the harvest, with the poorest results in the north-central portion of European Russia. Here output had averaged less than in the first decade of the twentieth century, and the 1976–80 plan accordingly called for a further massive increase in agricultural investment, much of it concentrated in this region.

During the 1950s and 1960s the other governments of eastern Europe moved to collectivise agriculture in imitation of Russia. However, the land reforms previously carried through had given land to individual small farmers, who resisted expropriation and assimilation into large enterprises. Sometimes the resistance was violent, as in East Germany in 1953, but more often it took a passive form and resulted in a bad harvest and food shortages, as in Bulgaria in 1951, Hungary in 1953 and 1961, Rumania in 1953, Czechoslovakia in 1954 and 1960 and East Germany in 1961 and 1962. Sometimes only the agriculture minister lost his job, as in Bulgaria in 1952, Czechoslovakia in 1961 or East Germany in 1963, but more commonly the result was a more extensive shift among government factions, a pause in the collectivisation campaign and increased incentives to farmers. The desire to achieve uniform collectivisation remained, however, and governments always returned to the offensive.

The results varied considerably from country to country. Bulgaria completed collectivisation in 1958 and embarked on a large programme of rural investment, including electrification, hospitals and schools along with tractors and mechanical harvesters. Yields doubled and the share of agriculture in the Bulgarian labour force dropped by half in two decades. Rumania pressed to complete collectivisation in 1965, but most collectives in fact operated as loose associations with farmers working the land they previously owned. In Hungary, collectivisation was officially completed in 1961, but much of the country's food was grown on private 'family plots' and the more successful collectives organised the production of cash crops on a sharecropping (*nadudvar*) basis after 1964. In Czechoslovakia after 1968 the market orientation which the government permitted collectives in the mid-1960s disappeared. Central control was reimposed, and grain production stagnated and cattle and poultry populations declined. The East Germans completed collectivisation in 1960, when 45 per cent of all agricultural land was pressed into collectives in a few months, but some 70 per cent of all collectives in fact leased land to their members and most farmers worked the same land they had owned. All high-quality food in East Germany came to be produced privately by so-called 'amateur gardeners' working in their 'spare time'. In Poland, full collectives and state farms occupied only 18 per cent of all agricultural land in 1959, the balance remaining in the possession of 3.6 million farmers, of whom 2.3 million owned 5 hectares or less. Productivity was higher than in neighbouring Russia, but far behind the government's hopes and plans, and Poland became a regular importer of food.

Despite their difficulties, on balance the nations of east-central Europe enjoyed spectacular economic success. In Bulgaria, for example, per capita product increased over fivefold from 1950 to 1970. Further, the eastern economies maintained their high rates of growth through the early 1970s; Polish and Rumanian rates were even higher than in the 1960s, and even the Czech rate remained nearly constant despite the obvious unpopularity of tighter central control. In the east as in the west planners happily took credit for rapid growth and failed to notice the extent to which the boom depended on a fortunate conjunction of factors, none of which could persist indefinitely. When circumstances did change it became more difficult for planners in both east and west to achieve the same sort of success.

5

EUROPE IN A MULTICENTRED WORLD

THE GROWTH AND TRANSFORMATION OF THE INTERNATIONAL ECONOMY

Trade and growth in western Europe

From 1946 to 1948 western Europe's trade deficit had averaged a massive five billion United States dollars per year. Most of Europe's imports came from the United States, and because Europe was unable to export sufficient amounts of goods to the United States, the deficit had to be met by sale of assets, use of reserves and credits advanced by the Americans. Europe's earnings from 'invisibles' had been permanently reduced by the decline in foreign assets during the war and by the substantial decline in Europe's share of world shipping. Therefore, the deficit with the United States would have to be balanced by commodity exports, but European leaders noted with foreboding that during the war markets had been lost to the United States and other competitors, that independence movements might spell the end to favourable colonial markets and finally that prices of European imports of food and raw materials were rising sharply while prices of European manufactured exports were relatively stagnant. Most governments therefore introduced strict economic controls. They restricted domestic consumption, imposed quotas on imports and channelled investment into export industries. Imports did fall and exports did rise, but a second glance at the figures only restored the gloom. The decline in imports reflected the decline in trade with some non-dollar areas, especially eastern Europe, and the increase in exports had gone mainly to other non-dollar areas and was in any case not large enough to cover the loss of invisible earnings. The trade deficit and the 'dollar shortage' played a key role in convincing American leaders that only active intervention by the United States could save western Europe.

Then, beginning in the early 1950s, growth triggered by high and sustained levels of demand led to an explosive growth of exports from all western European countries. Total exports from western Europe increased by eight per cent per year through the 1950s, and the rate of increase accelerated during the 1960s. All western European nations shared in the gains. In every country except Britain exports rose at more than five per cent per year, and in some, such as West Germany, Italy and the Nordic states the rate was well over ten per cent. In all countries, exports rose more rapidly than total output. Further, exports of manufactured goods increased more rapidly than total exports. Finally, trade among western European nations increased substantially more rapidly than total world trade. The largest increase in trade, therefore, occurred in the exchange of manufactured goods among countries with similar industrial structures and levels of income. As before the First World War, it was the supposedly 'rival' industrial nations which became each others' best customers. The theory of comparative advantage predicts that each nation will concentrate on the products it produces most efficiently, which led contemporaries to predict – either cheerfully or nervously – that the European market would come to be dominated by the early leader in each field. In fact, the opposite occurred, and the distribution of exports by commodity groups converged, with each country tending to do 'best' in precisely those areas where it had been 'behind'. Obviously, many more firms than had been thought possible were able to step over the threshold of the newly expanded markets, profit from increasing returns to scale and diversify their output in ways not clearly revealed by the available statistics and indeed not clearly predicted by economic theory.

A number of factors contributed to the increase in trade. First, intra-European trade in 1950 was at about the same level as in 1913. The depression and the Second World War had pressed trade down far below 'normal' levels, and therefore a surging 'recovery' phase could possibly have been predicted. In addition, the policies adopted to stimulate exports in order to balance accounts with the dollar area remained in place for several years, and did achieve some success, notably in Britain. Aid from the United States played a role. Growth itself stimulated demand and encouraged investment in larger and more productive plants, further stimulating trade.

Most important was the great increase in international cooperation, and in particular policies of trade liberalisation. The larger markets created by the general lowering of trade barriers played the crucial role. In the early 1950s the Organisation for European Economic Cooperation (OEEC), with encouragement from the United States, reduced quantitative restrictions on trade among its members, and the General Agreement on Tariffs and Trade (GATT) agreements worked in the same direction. The phased tariff reductions of the European Economic Community (EEC) and the European Free Trade Association (EFTA) were even more significant. Both organisations expanded; in 1961 Finland became an associate member of the EFTA and Greece became an associate member of the EEC. Further, the EEC and EFTA cooperated in some areas, notably by coordinating tariff reductions.

During the 1960s the EEC and EFTA seemed rivals whose existence might actually work to restrict trade. In 1961 Britain applied for membership in the EEC, only to be rejected by De Gaulle, and western Europe remained divided into two trading blocs for the remainder of the decade. Some wondered whether *Europe at Sixes and Sevens* (a contemporary title) could long survive, and economists debated the relative merits of the two groupings. The EEC began from a higher base, with a population of 165 million and internal trade amounting to 560 million dollars a month, compared to the EFTA's population of 80 million and internal trade of 230 million dollars a month, a third of which was accounted for by Britain alone. The trade of the EEC grew more rapidly than that of the EFTA. However, the trade of all European nations grew extraordinarily rapidly; in fact EFTA members' trade increased at the same rate as EEC trade, with two exceptions, Britain, whose large size and poor performance brought down the EFTA average, and Denmark, whose agricultural exports suffered from tariffs imposed by the EEC. Further, the EEC and EFTA did not redirect trade away from other potential partners; the trade diversion effects of the two unions were approximately balanced by the creation of new trade with non-members.

One area where the movement for trade liberalisation failed was the trade of the EEC in agricultural products. While the EFTA could fulfil its purpose of phased reductions in tariffs relatively easily, the far more ambitious plans of the EEC's supporters proved more difficult to realise, especially in the intractable area of agricultural policy. France and the Netherlands, with relatively efficient agricultural sectors and large surpluses, favoured free trade within the EEC, while West Germany and Italy, with relatively high price supports, feared excessive competition. The deadline for agreement on agricultural trade and price supports of 31 December 1961 was postponed for fourteen days by stopping the official clock. EEC negotiators, under the leadership of Sicco L. Mansholt of the Netherlands and over the opposition of virtually all organised farming interests, sat in continuous session served by staff working eighteen and twenty-hour days. At the reported cost of three heart attacks and one nervous breakdown, an extremely complex compromise agreement was pieced together. However, the Common Agricultural Policy (CAP), implemented in stages during the 1960s, was closely tailored to the specific requirements of the 'six' and rested on the premise that the agricultural sectors of all members would remain intact. It therefore placed a difficult barrier in the path of future applicants for membership, and eventually became one of the most contentious issues within the EEC itself.

The question of national sovereignty and of power within the EEC of course lay behind many of the debates over policy. Benelux backed Great Britain's 1961 application for membership partly in the hopes of imposing a check on French ambitions, and De Gaulle's brusque veto shook the morale of the EEC badly. In 1965 France blocked agreement on the financing of EEC agricultural supports, denounced the imposition of supranational authority in any form, withdrew its ambassador to the EEC, and demanded revision of the Treaty of Rome. The French boycott of the EEC council ended the following year. The obvious advantages to French farmers from the large market and high prices offered by the EEC and the extensive restructuring of French industry predicated on continued development of the EEC had already created a firm alliance of interests which even De Gaulle could not ignore. The other member nations, afraid or perhaps merely weary of French pretensions, tended to back the 'Eurocrats' of the EEC in their plans for a common external tariff, accelerated elimination of internal tariffs, administration of price supports and subsidies by the EEC Executive and admission of new members. Internal tariffs disappeared and a new common external tariff was imposed in 1967; in 1970 formal negotiations began on a new application for membership by Great Britain, as well as on applications by Denmark, Eire and Norway. If the EEC had become less ambitious in concentrating on carefully balanced economic agreements, it seemed nonetheless an overwhelming success and to be standing on the verge of substantial expansion.

The EEC did not fulfil the promise of the 1970s. Norway rejected membership in the EEC in a referendum. Britain, Eire and Denmark joined in 1971, Greece in 1981 and Spain and Portugal in 1985; however, domestic opposition to membership remained strong within all the countries which joined. The problems of integration within the European Communities (EC), as the EEC now styled itself, led to periodic calls for a 'two-speed' or 'two-tiered' community, within which those members (usually identified as the original six) which wished to pursue a closer union could do so. The most hotly debated issue remained the Common Agricultural Policy (CAP). Subsidies to farmers resulted in large net payments by Britain to the EC budget, leading to periodic crises in relations between Britain and the other members. In 1979–80 the new European Parliament rejected the EC budget because no cuts had been made in agricultural supports to match those in other areas, and only reversed itself after bitter debate and the threatened collapse of the entire CAP. If EC agricultural policy was expensive, inefficient and contentious, industrial and energy policies were simply non-existent, each national government pursuing its own goals in isolation. Symbolically, Jean Monnet – the father of the EC – disbanded his Action Committee for a United States of Europe in 1975. The EC Commission seemed on the one hand to be ineffective and incapable of developing strong, independent policies, and on the other to have become rigid and unresponsive. In 1980 a scandal erupted over the lavish salaries and expenses of the rapidly increasing number of 'Eurocrats', and in early 1982 an auditor's report revealed large discrepancies in various EC financial accounts. The energy and idealism of an earlier generation seemed to have waned, and celebrations of the twenty-fifth anniversary of the Treaty of Rome were muted, to put it no more unkindly.

Trade and growth in eastern Europe

The major exception to the movement towards trade liberalisation was the trade of western Europe with eastern Europe and the Soviet Union. The Cold War greatly restricted trade between the two blocs. In 1949 the United States imposed severe restrictions and outright embargoes on all exports to socialist countries of goods which might increase their military power, and imposed the restrictions on western European countries as well. These restrictions substantially reduced potential exports of machinery from western to eastern Europe. In addition, the imposition of very high levels of protection under the CAP closed much of the western European market for eastern European agricultural products. The Soviet Union and eastern European socialist governments continued to show little interest in trade, except insofar as it could contribute directly to their planned goals. Each national plan still aimed to create the highest possible degree of self-sufficiency, and bilateral balancing continued to be the socialist countries' ideal in trade relations.

Trade among socialist countries and between socialist countries and the west did not cease entirely. In 1955 the

CMEA announced an elaborate scheme of specialisation in export production, intended to coordinate the economic development of member countries and achieve the benefits of increased economies of scale. However, the revolts in Poland and Hungary in 1956 and the Rumanians' objections to the planned reduction in their industrial sector prevented the scheme's adoption. The creation of the International Bank for Economic Cooperation (IBEC) in 1964 and the introduction of a 'transferable ruble' allowed limited multilateral clearing of balances among CMEA members. Though trade among CMEA members increased gradually, it remained bilateral and concentrated on the purchase of raw materials which could not be produced locally. The Soviet Union continued to supply raw materials such as chrome and manganese ore to the west even during the most bitter period of the Cold War, as well as luxuries such as furs, diamonds and vodka. During the late 1960s the trade of eastern Europe with the west began to grow more rapidly as eastern European governments came to see the west as a source of capital goods embodying the latest industrial technologies. The share of the west in CMEA trade increased from about a fifth to about a third from the mid-1960s to the mid-1970s. On balance, however, the total trade of CMEA countries remained a small proportion of their national product compared to western Europe, and there remained relatively little trading contact between east and west. The main axes of trade continued to lie within western Europe and between western Europe and the United States.

The CMEA established a new International Investment Bank in 1970 to promote long-term investment in projects contributing to 'socialist division of labour' and introduced an elaborate procedure for increased trade and integration of national plans, but most trade remained tied to bilateral agreements and planning remained isolated. Calls for coordination of national plans were repeated periodically at CMEA conferences, with Russia insisting on joint funding of exploration and exploitation of Soviet central Asian mineral resources, and other members, especially Rumania and Hungary, insisting the projects would be too costly for them and detract from their own development. The five 'target areas' for cooperation announced in 1977 were reduced to three in 1978 (energy and raw materials, machinery, and agriculture and food), but no general agreement could be reached. The Soviet Union generally maintained the prices of its raw material exports to eastern Europe at low levels. Though Soviet petroleum prices increased, they remained far below western levels. The Russians also began to subsidise the eastern European economies by consistently exporting more to them than they received in return. Between 1975 and 1985 eastern European countries accumulated a total negative balance of between fourteen and eighteen billion dollars in their trade with the Soviet Union. As before, however, the Soviet Union proved unable to supply capital in sufficient amounts, and eastern European governments turned to the west for funds to modernise their industrial sectors. Total western loans to eastern Europe had reached 80 billion dollars by 1980, 23 billion to Poland alone. Trade between eastern and western Europe, which had risen rapidly during the early 1970s, declined when the depression in western Europe reduced the market for eastern exports. Servicing their large western loans therefore imposed an extremely heavy burden on eastern European countries. In addition the Soviet Union began to insist on closer trade links and a reduction of the trade deficit in return for future supplies of raw materials, especially petroleum, though as before the annual CMEA conferences did not produce specific programmes to meet the problems.

The United States and multinationals

The United States in the 1950s and 1960s played much the same role in the world economy as Britain in the generation before the First World War. A massive American trade surplus was balanced first by American aid, and then by large investments by private corporations. Attracted by differences in labour costs, the rapidly expanding European market and the desire to circumvent EEC tariffs, United States investors turned away from their traditional emphasis on Latin American farms and mines towards European manufacturing plants. United States private long-term investment in Europe rose from 3.1 billion dollars in 1950 to 6.9 billion in 1959, then jumped to 19.6 billion in 1965 and 29.6 billion in 1970, by which time investments in Europe made up 41 per cent of total United States foreign investment.

Because American investment in Europe often took the form of construction of manufacturing plants, it was highly visible. The abbreviated trademarks of the major American corporations – Ford, General Motors, IBM – seemed to be sprouting everywhere. American 'control' over advanced sectors of European manufacturing worried Europeans. Books such as *The American Challenge* exhorted Europeans to combat the Americans on their own terms, by organising larger corporations and seeking out new technologies. However, American dominance in some fields was not a new development. Subsidiaries of Ford and General Motors had numbered among the British 'Big Six' and the German 'Big Three' automobile producers during the 1930s. In the case of newer fields such as computers, the rapid introduction of new technologies resulting from the flow of investment went far to outweigh any possible negative effects. American firms intended their European investments to be profitable, of course, but the new plants tended to be located in regions with high unemployment, for instance Scotland, southern Wales and the less prosperous districts of West Germany and Belgium. In Britain, approximately one-third of United States direct investment was located in depressed areas, where it had created 150,000 new jobs by 1974.

Many observers saw the activities of American multinationals – or transnationals, as they were also labelled – as the defining feature of the postwar international economy, and a number of theories were advanced to explain their growth and behaviour. First, the general increase in the size of firms inevitably meant that the largest would break out of their national boundaries. Second, the division between ownership and control in the modern corporation may have resulted in large firms treating profit as a secondary goal next to growth, reinforcing the tendency to increasing size. Third, improvements in transportation and communication made the control of very large corporations, and especially foreign branches, easier than formerly. In particular, the development of computerised record keeping helped large firms overcome the disadvantages of excessive size. Finally, the tax systems of most western countries since 1945 encouraged retention of profits, leading to the accumulation of large reserves, which the largest firms invested by acquiring foreign as well as domestic interests.

However, a closer look at the largest multinational corporations reveals that Europe's role remained at least as important as America's, continuing tendencies reaching back before the First World War. In 1980, 430 of the world's 500 largest corporations were multinational, and between them they accounted for 80 per cent of direct foreign investment. All had their headquarters in developed countries; 53 per cent were American and 12 per cent Japanese. However, 33 per cent were European, and 45 of the companies were located in the London area alone. Further, two-thirds of the 430 firms had been founded before the First World War, and a large number of the remainder, founded in the interwar or postwar years, actually were mergers of already large firms founded before 1914. For example, the three largest chemical firms, Bayer, BASF and Hoechst, all were founded in the 1860s; they were the major participants in the merger which created I.G. Farben in 1926, but became independent and assumed their present corporate form in 1951 as part of the attempt of Allied occupation authorities to break up German cartels. In 1980 IRI, descendent of a company established by the Italian fascist government in 1933 to consolidate its holdings in banks and industrial firms it had rescued from collapse during the depression, employed approximately 500,000 persons, carried out one-third of all research and development undertaken by Italian industry and owned 6 per cent of all Italy's assets. Finally, among multinationals, age was highly correlated with size and with the role of international operations; the older a firm, the larger it was likely to be and the higher the percentage of foreign sales in its total. Despite the growth of the United States and Japan, and despite the vicissitudes of war, reconstruction and decolonisation, Europe's initial lead and tradition of international contacts remained significant in what at first glance seemed a recent and typically 'American' phenomenon.

Spreading development and the pervasive influence of large corporations had important effects in the postwar world. Capital flows became larger than ever before, and the share of direct foreign investment rose dramatically. Before 1914 over 90 per cent of foreign investment was 'portfolio' purchases of foreign securities. In 1970 in contrast, the share of portfolio investment had declined to just 25 per cent. The remaining 75 per cent was direct investment, most of it by multinational corporations, typically the construction of manufacturing plants by their foreign subsidiaries. This kind of investment played a significant role in spreading new technologies widely and rapidly. However, some of its other effects were less beneficial. The increasing number and size of subsidiaries led to a massive increase in intrafirm trade. In 1968 an estimate suggested that one-quarter of all British exports of manufactured goods were being exchanged between subsidiaries of multinational firms; by the late 1970s intrafirm trade may have constituted as much as half of total world trade. Such trade was largely unaffected by traditional policies such as devaluation. The prices charged by one subsidiary to another were of course 'administered' prices set arbitrarily by the firm; large firms could set 'transfer' prices in such a way that they reduced the income of their subsidiaries in countries with high tax rates and increased the income of those in 'tax havens'. Holding extremely large reserves in many different currencies, multinationals speculated and hedged in foreign exchange markets, and delayed or accelerated payments among subsidiaries in anticipation of changes in exchange rates. The resulting 'leads' and 'lags' could cause sharp fluctuations in the balance of payments or interest rates in exporting countries. This loss of control over their economies reinforced the hostility towards multinationals caused by the export of profits from nations and regions where multinationals invested.

Japan

In 1945 Japan was prostrate, with 25 per cent of its housing destroyed, agricultural and industrial output depressed to less than half prewar levels and shipping and financial reserves reduced virtually to nothing, yet with a population actually larger than the prewar total because of the forced repatriation of five million Japanese from Manchuria, Korea and Taiwan. The Americans, determined to root out Japanese 'militarism' and 'fascism', imposed a military occupation, threatened a purge of those held responsible for Japan's wartime policies and spoke occasionally of dismantling the entire Japanese industrial sector and transferring the factories to other Asian nations as reparations. Yet Japan arose from the ashes; beginning in the early 1950s the Japanese economy grew at a rate of nearly ten per cent per year, and by the end of the decade Japan had not only emerged once again onto the world stage, but had become the major new force with which the economies of western Europe and the United States had to contend. Beginning in the 1960s Japan began to export rapidly increasing amounts of manufactured goods to Europe, while European producers largely failed to penetrate the Japanese domestic market. In addition Japanese goods drove Europe out of traditional markets throughout the world. The United States suffered as well, and protectionist sentiment in both America and western Europe resulted in the imposition of technical restrictions, 'voluntary' restraints and other non-tariff barriers which undermined the principle of multilateralism and non-discrimination which had supported the immense increase in trade of the boom years.

Japanese growth and competition seemed mysterious, but in many respects Japan resembled western Europe, and especially West Germany, in slightly exaggerated form. As in western Europe the apparent disadvantages of wartime destruction and massive forced immigration actually contributed to the subsequent boom. Reconstruction had the effect of modernising the industrial sector, while the initial abundance of labour kept wages low. The Americans feared above all the communist uprising which might result in the absence of economic recovery. There was no dismantling of industry, and there was no purge. As in western Europe, American influence contributed to the creation of a conservative political consensus and an overriding commitment to economic growth. Savings rose from 16 to 28 per cent of national income, and government monetary and fiscal policies ensured that most of this very large pool of savings flowed towards investment in manufacturing. Non-residential investment rose at 9.2 per cent a year and manufacturing output at 14 per cent a year. Employment in agriculture declined from 36 per cent of the total in 1953 to 15 per cent in 1971, and 6.5 million agricultural workers were added to the industrial labour force. Also as in western Europe, Japanese households outfitted themselves with consumer durables for the first time, and the explosive growth in these branches fuelled the boom. Output of motorcycles rose nearly 1,000 times from 1950 to 1966, and output of automobiles rose 155 times from 1955 to 1970. In these and other areas such as electronics, Japan's large domestic market provided the initial field for new industries which later became important exporters, and again as was the case in western Europe the Japanese market was highly protected.

Japan's experience did diverge from that of western Europe in one important respect. In western Europe migrant workers provided a very important pool of labour during the boom period. From the 1950s until the early 1970s migrant workers filled unskilled and semi-skilled positions in the mining, manufacturing and service sectors of the host countries, the 'unwanted' jobs scorned by native workers. In doing so, they accepted low wages, permitting rapid expansion and holding costs low. In the short and medium term, western Europe benefited from this relative abundance of labour. In contrast, Japan, despite the large repatriations following the war and the flow of labour out of agriculture, experienced a shortage of labour during much of the 25 years of the great boom. As in western Europe, the birth rate in Japan declined, but Japan virtually prohibited immigration and naturalisation. The Japanese response to the labour shortage was a new, higher level of mechanisation, culminating in the early and extensive introduction of computer-controlled industrial robots. To remain competitive European producers needed to move in the same direction, but their previous reliance on inexpensive labour had placed them at a severe disadvantage.

From fixed to floating exchange rates

The international financial system, which seemed so securely established in the 1950s and 1960s, transformed itself into something perhaps less secure and certainly more complex. The relative decline of the United States undermined international financial stability, as had the relative decline of Great Britain 50 years before. The outflow of capital had already caused the United States to show a deficit in its balance of payments during the late 1950s, but experts considered this a temporary and beneficial phenomenon, which would increase international liquidity and encourage trade. As American deficits continued and increased in the early 1960s, the experts became less enthusiastic and more worried. In the late 1960s, the American balance of trade declined and then turned negative; as capital exports continued, the overall deficits became very large, and the experts became very worried.

The United States and the IMF defended the principles of fixed exchange rates and convertibility of all currencies into gold as natural, desirable and even moral. However, as Robert Triffen and others noted, when foreign exchange reserves are held partly in gold and partly in currency, as world trade grows the share of gold in total reserves will decline. Eventually doubts will arise as to the ability of the nation whose currency serves as an exchange reserve to meet its obligation to convert currency into gold at existing rates. Triffen noted the persistently negative balance of payments of the United States, predicted increased doubts and recommended that a strengthened and enlarged IMF create credit reserves to replace both gold and dollars as the basis for clearing international trade balances.

The major powers still had no desire to increase the power of the IMF over their financial policies. Instead they attempted to deal with the 'dollar overhang' – the excess of dollars over American gold holdings – in an informal, ad hoc manner which would preserve their independence. Central banks in western Europe and Japan agreed to hold dollars and not to attempt to exchange them for gold. Also, beginning in 1961 the major powers participated in a 'gold pool'; using the Bank of England as their agent in the London gold market, they intervened to hold the market price of gold as close as possible to its official price of 32 American dollars an ounce. Despite these measures, the American payments deficit continued to increase, and doubts about the dollar grew stronger; in 1965 De Gaulle ordered the conversion of a fraction of France's dollar holdings into gold. By 1966 most central banks were adding gold to their reserves, and the official price was coming under increasing pressure.

However, it was the British pound which proved the weakest link in the system. The deficits in the British balance of payments which caused so much concern during the 1960s actually averaged less than one per cent of Britain's gross domestic product, but because the value of the pound would never be increased but might be decreased, speculators enjoyed a situation where they could not lose and might gain by selling pounds. To prevent a devaluation of the pound, the IMF and other major financial powers made large loans to Britain in 1961, 1964 and 1965. Another deficit led to a new wave of speculation in 1966, however, and in 1967 the unthinkable finally happened; the pound was devalued from 2.80 to 2.40 United States dollars.

The devaluation of the pound did not foreshadow the end of the world, but it did mark a major step along the road to a new international financial system. What could happen to the pound could happen to other currencies as well; consequently the demand for gold rose, and the Bank of England had to sell three billion dollars' worth of gold from the gold pool to hold the official price steady. In 1968 France withdrew from the gold pool, increasing the pressure, and the Bank of England ceased to intervene in the gold market. In an attempt to prevent fluctuations in the value of the official reserves, a 'two-tiered' price system was adopted, with the 'market' price of gold set by supply and demand but the 'official' price maintained in transactions between governments. Ongoing discussions, punctuated by a series of spectacular crises in foreign exchange markets, resulted in 1968–69 in the creation of a pool of Special Drawing Rights (SDRs) by the IMF, referred to by some as 'paper gold' and by some of the wittier English-speaking experts as MANNA

('man-made assets not necessarily available'). Members of
the IMF could draw from the pool of SDRs on roughly the
same terms as they had from the previous pool of national
currencies to cover temporary deficits in their balance of
payments. SDRs provided another source of credit in addition
to gold and dollars, a situation which disturbed theoretical
purists but was probably the best attainable solution. The
fixed price of the dollar in terms of gold, the supposed
'cornerstone' of the system, disappeared in 1971 when the
United States first suspended convertibility of the dollar and
then raised the official gold price to 38 dollars an ounce
without promising to purchase gold even at that price.

In 1973 another severe monetary crisis dealt a final blow
to the system of fixed exchange rates. Britain had already
allowed the pound to 'float' or fluctuate freely against the
dollar in 1972. In January 1973 holders of Italian lire began
to exchange them for United States dollars, intending to
convert the dollars into Swiss francs. Switzerland refused to
accept dollars because of the danger of inflation, and both
Italy and Switzerland floated their currencies against the
dollar. The flight from the dollar became general, and
exchange markets were closed in February. They opened
briefly after a 10 per cent devaluation of the dollar in terms
of SDRs and an increase in the official gold price to 42
dollars an ounce, and then closed again in March. When
they opened again, most of the world's currencies were
fluctuating freely, a theoretically satisfying situation but one
fraught with insecurity, and in July it was announced that
governments would intervene as necessary to preserve
'orderly' markets. In 1974 SDRs were revalued in terms of a
sixteen-currency 'basket' rather than in terms of dollars
alone, and in 1975 the official gold price was abolished and
the obligation to use gold in IMF transactions ended. The
IMF sold its stock of gold and placed the profits in a fund to
aid underdeveloped countries. All currencies were to float,
subject to intervention under guidelines established in a
series of IMF agreements.

Hoping to preserve fixed exchange rates at least among
themselves, in 1971 members of the EEC agreed to tie their
currencies together in a common European Monetary Union

(EMU), permitting only narrow fluctuations between member currencies, establishing a common relationship with outside currencies, providing for medium-term credit to cover imbalances, and promising greater coordination of economic policies. The European 'snake', wriggling within the confines of its 'tunnel' of permissible exchange rate fluctuations, came into operation in 1972. The problems of the snake remained the same as those of fixed but adjustable exchange rates generally; as long as members' monetary and fiscal policies were not coordinated, speculative pressure was inevitable because speculation itself would force changes in the rates and speculators therefore could not lose. In 1969 the Barre Plan called for cooperation among EEC members in formulating their medium-range macroeconomic policies, and in 1970 the Werner Plan proposed a timetable for monetary and economic union to be achieved by 1980; the first stage was to be convertibility at fixed rates and a single EEC currency. However, although non-EEC members Norway and Sweden later joined the snake, both Italy and new members Britain, Denmark and Eire remained outside. Denmark later decided to join, but Sweden left in 1977 and Norway in 1978. France left the snake in 1974, rejoined in 1975, and left again in 1976. The new European Monetary System (EMS) came into force in 1979; except for the formation of a new European Monetary Cooperation Fund to support official exchange rates and the creation of a European Currency Unit (ECU) based on a 'basket' of participating currencies, the EMS did not differ from the snake. France was cajoled into joining in return for changes in agricultural price supports under which (according to the French) German farmers had benefited unduly. Britain, however, dissatisfied with the changes in agricultural policy, declined to join the EMS. Greece also refused to join the EMS after becoming a member of the EEC in 1981. Because rates of inflation differed widely, it proved impossible to maintain fixed exchange rates among the eight currencies; seven revaluations had to be carried out during the first four years of the system's operation, most involving an upward revaluation of the perennially strong West German mark and all involving acrimonious debate.

Eurodollars

The so-called 'Eurodollar' or 'Eurocurrency' market sprang into being in late 1958 in anticipation of the restoration of convertibility of European currencies. It was centred in London rather than New York to avoid restrictions on interest rates imposed by the American Federal Reserve System, and because some large depositors such as the Soviet Union preferred to keep their funds outside of the United States. Funds flowed into the Eurocurrency market from three main sources: the chronic United States balance of payments deficit, the rise in the world money supply implicit in borrowing by all national governments and funds of primary producers which could not be absorbed into their domestic economies, of which the 'petrodollars' of small oil-producing countries were the most significant. The market increased dramatically in size and importance. In principle, its operation was simple. Individuals with excess cash placed it in banks, which then made loans to other individuals. Because all banks hold only a small fraction of their deposits as reserves, any sudden increase in deposits results in a much larger increase in the total supply of money in a banking system. In the Eurocurrency market, because the 'individuals' involved were often independent governments or their agencies, and because of the unprecedented sums involved, Eurocurrency transactions could have additional effects. If the price of a commodity increased, the exporting country could place its earnings as short-term deposits in a Eurobank instead of changing them into its own currency and increasing its exchange rate. These deposits were counted as increases in the exporting country's reserves. In turn, an importing country could borrow those same short-term deposits to avoid a decline in its reserves or a fall in its exchange rate, but such borrowings were not subtracted from its official reserves. Therefore total international reserves increased very rapidly after 1970, and the total world money supply rose explosively.

The Eurocurrency system was subject to certain dangers, of which the potential insolvency of the borrowers was perhaps the best known. Many countries contracted loans which seemed large in comparison to their ability to pay. In 1982, for instance, Portugal was reported to owe foreign lenders 13 billion dollars, with short-term loans making up 30 per cent of the total. Interest payments in 1982 totalled approximately 1 billion dollars, an amount equal to 27 per cent of Portugal's total exports or nearly 5 per cent of the nation's gross domestic product. In eastern Europe, austerity measures intended to aid in the repayment of international loans were an important cause of political instability, as in Poland in the late 1970s. Eastern European nations were heavily burdened but bankers could console themselves with the assurance of Janos Fekete, first deputy president of the Hungarian National Bank, that it was 'a first priority' of the socialist countries' monetary policy to pay their debts to western banks. Statements from borrowers in the Third World tended to be much less reassuring. The outright default of any very large debtor, especially Argentina, Brazil or Mexico, the three largest, would be a shock to the system, though professional economists were divided into those who predicted that the result would be a collapse of world financial markets and those who thought the system flexible enough to absorb the losses while continuing to function.

In addition, the need to pay interest and principal on Eurocurrency loans in the denominated currency could lead to changes in exchange rates which were unrelated to the monetary and fiscal policies of the government theoretically 'responsible' for the denominated currency. In particular, the United States government no longer directly controlled the total number of dollars in the world and did not 'guarantee' them in any meaningful sense. Wealth holders therefore attempted to maintain the value of their holdings by shifting among currencies and between currencies and commodities. These pressures added to those emanating from the loan market, and both were exacerbated by the high and volatile interest rates which prevailed during the 1970s and early 1980s. In certain situations these conditions could lead to violent fluctuations in exchange rates and commodity prices which were only tenuously connected to real economic factors. In addition, unlucky, incompetent and very occasionally dishonest dealing in rapidly changing financial markets could lead to large, sudden losses and further instability. In 1973 the Yom Kippur War and sudden increase in oil prices provided the background for large losses by the Union Bank of Switzerland, the Lugano branch of Lloyds Bank and the Herstatt Bank, and the beginnings of a spectacular increase in the price of gold seemed to reflect a failure of confidence in all 'paper' currencies.

Despite these dangers, the system functioned more smoothly and effectively than one would expect if one read only the more pessimistic observers. Fluctuating exchange rates and the rapid flow of information created the most open and free market in currencies that had ever existed. As always in a competitive market, speculation and hedging worked to stabilise the relation between supply and demand. In the 1920s and again in the 1950s, rumours that legally 'fixed' exchange rates might be altered led to speculation against 'weak' currencies which destabilised the market and often forced governments into undesired changes in the rates. In the 1980s a decrease in international demand for any country's currency (for instance because of domestic inflation) should – ideally – lead to a decline in the exchange rate, which in turn should lower the country's export prices and lead to a rise in exports and to an increase in demand for the country's currency – which should raise the exchange rate. In addition, forward speculation should cause an increase in demand for the currency in anticipation of rising exports even before the 'real' economic effects of the drop in the exchange rate begin to operate.

Despite recurrent crises, overall the adjustment of the world economy to the new financial situation was relatively rapid. The banking losses sustained in 1974 were in fact quite small compared with the sudden huge increase in lending activity. The price of gold declined substantially after its initial surge; gold retained a 'quasi-monetary' character, but it appeared that wealth holders had not lost their faith in paper currencies after all. The IMF cooperated with private and national banks in a series of 'rescue' operations to prevent the default of large international borrowers. In 1983, for example, a loan of 5 billion dollars to Mexico was underwritten by several international agencies and a consortium of over 500 private banks. In effect such operations lowered the rates of interest on the original loan and postponed payments on the principal. These actions contrasted dramatically with the insistence by international lenders in the 1930s that debtors fulfil the letter of their original contract. The new system and the persons responsible for it were not infallible, of course. In particular, the IMF continued its attempts to force countries with balance of payments deficits to lower prices by restricting demand and credit, and therefore bore a portion of the blame for the continuing depression of the late 1970s and 1980s. Much of the borrowing by governments from private banks which created problems was in fact a consequence of the desire of governments to avoid the conditions which the IMF typically imposed on borrowers.

TRADE, AID AND GROWTH IN THE THIRD WORLD

The need for more broadly based economic development of countries dependent on exports of primary products remained obvious throughout the postwar period. Except for the United States and the former British dominions of Australia, New Zealand, South Africa and Canada, countries exporting primary products remained dependent on a very narrow range of commodities. Again with the exception of these five, and certain districts in India, Asia and Latin America, there was little domestic manufacturing industry. On balance the Third World continued to suffer from low income, lack of infrastructure and a shortage of skilled labour. Efforts to improve the position of these countries were substantial in aggregate terms and achieved some notable successes; however, such efforts were always conditioned and restrained by international and domestic political considerations, and consequently fell far short of what could and should have been accomplished.

Little was done at the end of the Second World War. Most observers expected that the gluts which had depressed raw materials markets in the 1930s would reappear but did not see aid to the dependent economies as the highest priority;

some wartime emergency programmes were continued, but most of the aid granted under the Marshall Plan went to western Europe. Then, increasing nationalist agitation in the colonies and the Cold War together changed the attitudes of United States and western European leaders. The danger of communists gaining control of nationalist movements led to economic aid being viewed as a weapon in the Cold War. Aid might preserve politically secure sources of raw materials and markets for western manufactures; in addition it was argued that aid could increase the income of poor countries, resulting in increased trade and advantages for rich countries as well.

Through the 1950s most aid from the United States and western Europe went to countries in the Middle and Far East bordering on the Soviet Union and the new Peoples' Republic of China, and very little to Latin America or Africa. In the 1960s the amount of aid increased dramatically, and it was spread more evenly among regions. Proportionately less aid was in the form of outright grants or loans, and more was directed into specific development projects. Aid itself became big business – huge amounts of money administered by growing bureaucracies in international agencies. Total aid increased from 8.4 billion United States dollars per year in 1960–62 to 16.6 billion per year in 1969–71. Most came from the United States and western Europe; the Soviet Union made lavish promises, but they remained largely unfulfilled. The Soviet Union and eastern Europe supplied four per cent of all aid in 1960–62 and only two per cent in 1969–71. Most newly independent countries suppressed domestic communist movements as a threat to stability, including some such as Egypt which had received significant amounts of Soviet aid.

The flow of aid led to dissatisfaction on both sides. Recipients argued that the total amount of aid was an unimpressively small share of the rich countries' total product, and remained very small relative to the needs of poor countries. Total aid represented only 0.88 per cent of the developed countries' gross national product in 1960–62, and delined to 0.76 per cent in 1969–71, when the total equalled 4.4 United States dollars per year for each inhabitant of the recipient countries. In addition, the official figures for 'total' aid included private foreign investment, which occurred in response to opportunities for profit, not in response to either humanitarian concerns or the requirements of long-term development. Private investment made up 40 per cent of 'aid' in the late 1960s. Many loans to poor countries were made on normal commercial terms but were also counted as 'aid', and even 'soft' loans were only partly genuine aid. The official total of genuine assistance also included aid to European countries which the OECD considered 'underdeveloped': Spain, Yugoslavia, Greece and Turkey. Furthermore, most genuine aid was 'tied' to agreements requiring the purchase of products from suppliers in the donor country and thereby became a way of subsidising producers in rich countries. Western European nations confined their aid largely to their former colonies, and the implicit threat of withdrawal maintained their continued economic and political influence. Finally, most of the aid was actually paid to academics, technical experts and administrators from the rich countries – for example, there were more French nationals working in the former French colonies of Africa in the late 1960s than before independence, a large fraction of whom were employed in various 'technical assistance' programmes.

International agencies proved willing to sponsor only certain kinds of projects. The World Bank, one of the most important, remained convinced that private capital would and should finance export industries in the Third World, and opposed government-owned manufacturing plants. It also developed a reluctance to sponsor sanitation, education, health and agricultural training projects because of the great difficulty in measuring the 'output' of such investments and because of their unpopularity with the investors in the bond markets where the bank came to raise most of its funds. The bank also preferred to lend to countries which pursued 'sound' – that is, restrictive – financial policies, again because of the interests of the bondholders. The bank developed a sort of ideology focused on public utility investments, especially central power plants, railways and highways, as the most desirable 'path' to economic development and in the view of recipient countries became unwilling to consider other and possibly more appropriate strategies.

Poor countries were even more dissatisfied with investments by private corporations. During the 1960s, 40 per cent of all private investment went into the petroleum industry, 30 per cent into public utilities, 9 per cent into mining and most of the rest into other raw materials such as vegetable oils to satisfy the rich countries' insatiable demand for soap and margarine. Very little investment went into manufacturing industry in Third World countries, and that little often did not employ many workers. New, highly-automated plants often seemed only a way of evading the stronger unions, expensive labour regulations and more stringent safety requirements of the rich countries. Multinational corporations were often large compared to the countries in which their branches operated. They tended to operate in the former colonies of their home countries, and usually enjoyed the support of their governments in disputes with local governments. The independence of Third World countries in many cases seemed something of a sham, a system of 'neo-colonialism' and continued dependence, within which 'development' programmes operated for the benefit of the rich countries.

However, the aid givers were disillusioned as well. In the newly-independent nations, local elites were small (a consequence of previous history), but also tended to be highly restrictive and interested primarily in preserving the status quo. They showed little interest in genuine social reform which might undermine their position. High rates of population growth were the most obvious and economically debilitating results of the generally 'traditional' values and social structures of the new nations. Most showed a tendency towards authoritarianism in their attempts to retain control over dissatisfied minority groups and to compensate for an absence of underlying social and political consensus. Few enjoyed political stability. All had problems employing both their own small domestic savings and foreign aid efficiently. Unrestricted grants were often misused, consumed by endemic corruption, nepotism, clientelism and patronage similar to southern and eastern European practices of a generation before, or channelled into 'show' projects such as large international airports with little impact on the economy. On balance, development programmes pursued by Third World countries were nationalistic and competitive; governments favoured import substitution and autarky, and discouraged exchange and trade either with their neighbours or with the rich nations.

Responding to criticisms of private investment, the donor countries noted that the markets in poor countries were extremely limited, but the small profitable areas were often reserved for native firms. Investment by multinationals was often encouraged, but then subjected to arbitrary political interference or expropriation with very little chance for adequate compensation. The French Total group's oil fields in Algeria were nationalised after the country gained independence, as were foreign interests in the petroleum industries of Libya, Iraq and Iran. Unilever's branches in Egypt and Burma were nationalised, and pressure by the Indian government forced the sale of ten per cent of Unilever's Indian holdings on unfavourable terms in 1954 and the appointment of an Indian chairman and the creation of an Indian majority on the board of directors in 1961. Unilever's pretax profits from its Indian operations increased substantially, but high taxes reduced net profits to eight per cent in the early 1960s, compared to eighteen per cent in the 1930s.

The results of trade and aid through the 1960s were actually mixed. Contrary to expert predictions, raw material prices rose strongly from 1946 to 1952, because of strong demand in the United States, political instability in Southeast Asia, low prices paid to producers by the Argentine government's marketing agency which reduced supplies of wheat, maize and wool and finally the boom resulting from the Korean War. During the 1950s and 1960s absolute prices of raw materials rose, especially during the Vietnam War. However, they declined relative to the prices of manufactured goods, worsening the terms of trade of the exporting countries. The total gross domestic product of the Third World countries rose at an average rate of 4.8 per cent per year from 1950 to 1967. This was a high rate; in fact it was unprecedented in these regions, and compared favourably with Britain, Germany or the United States during the booms of the nineteenth century. However, the gap between the Third World and the developed countries increased, as this was the peak of the great postwar boom in the United States, Japan and western Europe. Although the total gross national product of the Third World countries rose 2.4 times, that of the developed countries rose 2.7 times. In addition, because the population of the developed countries rose much less rapidly than that of the Third World, per capita product in the developed countries increased from 5.2 times that of the Third World in 1950 to 7.2 in 1970. Worse still, some especially poor countries grew even more slowly; in 1950 the richest countries enjoyed a per capita product 18 times higher than the poorest countries, but in 1970 their per capita product was 26 times higher.

International agencies attempted to address the problems of the Third World. In 1958 the Haberler Report of the United Nations pointed out that the GATT agreements benefited rich countries almost exclusively because they reduced tariffs and eliminated quotas only on manufactured goods. In those manufacturing branches where the Third World could compete, such as textiles, the rich countries in fact had maintained quotas; in the most important area, that of agricultural exports, nothing had been done. Rich countries still imposed tariffs, quotas and consumption taxes on agricultural imports and subsidised agricultural exports. The United States, Japan and the EC were all serious offenders in this regard, though the EC became the most notorious because of the open and controversial nature of the CAP within the community itself. Unable to obtain satisfaction directly, Third World nations turned to the United Nations and attempted to use their voting power (increasing rapidly as a result of decolonisation) to obtain a hearing and force change. The first United Nations Conference for Trade and Development (UNCTAD), a three-month meeting in Geneva in 1964, heard a report by Raul Prébisch in which he argued that trade could become an engine for growth in the Third World if it were properly managed. Prébisch thought developing nations would inevitably fall into debt because of the need for loans and imports of capital goods, but the resulting negative balance of payments could be corrected by international agreements to control commodity prices and discriminatory tariffs imposed by rich countries to favour manufactured goods from poor countries. The second UNCTAD conference in New Delhi in 1968 called on rich countries to devote one per cent of their gross national product to aid for poor countries. Succeeding UNCTAD meetings continued to recommend commodity control schemes and increased aid, and in 1976–77 a marathon eighteen-month conference in Paris, the Conference on International Economic Cooperation (CIEC or North-South Conference), repeated all the previous demands and emphasised the need for international control of development programmes – a 'New Economic Order' to overcome the gap between the rich 'north' and the poor 'south'.

The result of the impressive number of meetings and conferences was minimal. In 1964 GATT members amended their rules to include a Generalised System of Preferences, permitting limited discrimination by individual rich countries in favour of specific products from poor countries. Some further preferences were extended following the New Delhi conference. A fund for aid to the poorest nations and a small fund devoted to commodity price stabilisation were established after the North-South Conference. However, the rich countries never agreed to a minimum level of aid, and the preferences extended did not affect the most important products.

The European Community's efforts ran along the same general lines as the United Nations. In 1958 the European Development Fund was created to assist 'associated territories' of the EC – the former colonies of France, Belgium and Italy. The Yaoundé Convention in 1963 granted 'association' status to these territories, giving their exports preferential treatment. However, the adoption of the Generalised System of Preferences, though increasing the number of territories receiving preferences, reduced their level. In 1975 the Lomé Convention extended the sphere of EC aid to all former colonies. Former British possessions were included, but this meant the end of the system of Imperial Preference dating from 1931. Most important, British agricultural imports were now subject to EC tariffs and quotas. This created grave difficulties for all Commonwealth exporters who had depended on the British market, and near disaster for some, such as New Zealand. Preferences extended under the Lomé Convention were small. The 'Stabex' programme financed from the European Development Fund granted some compensation to the exporting countries for any 'shortfall' in their earnings on exports to the EC, but the funds were limited, the scheme applied only to certain products and EC markets remained firmly closed to the products of greatest potential importance for the Third World.

Europe's role in the new world economy continued to be highly significant. Many independent Third World nations remained in fact clients of western European nations or of the Soviet Union. Outright colonialism had not disappeared; both France and Britain retained outposts in all the major oceans, and some had considerable economic significance. For instance, Hong Kong was a major commercial and manufacturing centre, and tiny New Caledonia was the location of some two-fifths of the world's richest nickel reserves. Western Europe was the home of one-third of the largest multinational corporations and continued to be the home of the world's most significant financial markets as well. If the definitions were expanded to include the state trading corporations of eastern Europe, the totals would have been even more impressive.

Europe's position in the new world system was not entirely comfortable. Relations with client states became more difficult as the Third World became more assertive in its demands. Colonialism proved expensive; France paid 40 per cent of the expenses of the government of New Caledonia, and the costs of recapturing and defending the Falkland Islands imposed a heavy burden on the British budget. Colonial possessions remained insecure; the British lease on Hong Kong was due to expire in 1997, and an independence movement destabilised New Caledonia. European producers had to contend with the continued pressure of Japanese competition. Western Europe experienced great difficulty in adapting its monetary system to the new situation of floating exchange rates and remained subject to occasional arbitrary intervention by the United

States. Eastern Europe remained caught between the conditions of economic contact with the west and the problems of political dependence on the Soviet Union. Developments in the EC and CMEA provided scant grounds for optimism.

However, given the very difficult conditions of the late 1970s and 1980s, the new system did not perform badly; certainly the fears that the international economy would collapse if currencies ceased to be exchangeable for gold were unfounded. The faith in the gold standard was in any case based on a misreading of the historical evidence; before the First World War and again after the Second World War it was not gold itself but the commitment of the single dominant financial power to gold which ensured the system's smooth operation. The system of fluctuating exchange rates and SDRs managed to cope with the unprecedented western European balance of payments deficits occasioned by rising energy costs. The Eurocurrency market provided funds not only for immediate needs arising out of the very large fluctuations in balances caused by unprecedented volumes of trade, but also to alleviate some of the major underlying structural problems, such as the development of energy resources and the need to modernise eastern European industry. If they seemed less stable than before the First World War, international institutions appeared more flexible and more responsive than between the wars.

6

EUROPEAN SOCIETY

Madère and Cessac are two European villages described by the French economist Jean Fourastié. Madère is a village of 534 residents, three-quarters of whom were born in the village or less than 20 kilometres away. A total of 279 of the residents are in the work force; the rest are made up of housewives, children or retired people. Of those employed, 208 are peasant farmers, 27 are artisans (such as masons and carpenters, farriers and tailors), 12 are shopkeepers, 19 are salaried white-collar workers (including 5 teachers, a postmaster and his assistant, the mayor's secretary and a policeman) and 12 are workers in manufacturing not connected with agriculture; in Madère there is also a doctor and a priest. The 208 farmers work on 92 farms, which average 5 hectares each. Their method of farming is still basically non-mechanised; there are only two tractors, little artificial fertiliser is used and yields are low. Social mobility in Madère is limited; of 4,000 children born since 1821, only 50 have finished secondary school. The standard of living is modest. Three-quarters of a resident's income is spent on food, and the staples are bread and soup. The peasants eat meat only once a week, and the meat is of an inferior quality; the one butcher in the village works only part-time and sells only mutton, which is available in the shop only two days a week. The residents eat no local variety of cheese. Housing conditions are as modest as food. Only 3 houses in Madère are less than 20 years old; 150 of the 163 houses are heated with wood fires, which are used also for cooking, while 10 have coal stoves and 3 have gas or electric stoves. Five houses have refrigerators, ten have indoor toilets, two have central heating, five have automobiles and none has a washing machine. There are 50 radios in the village, but only 2 televisions.

Cessac is an only slightly larger village with 670 residents. But only a third of the residents, 210, were born there or nearby; the rest have moved into the village from other places. A total of 215 are in the work force, but only 53 are farmers. The service sector accounts for 102 jobs in offices, banks and the government. There are 25 artisans in Cessac and 35 people who are employed as non-agricultural workers. For those who farm, the average holding is 13 hectares. The technology is more advanced; there are 40 tractors, artificial fertilisers are widely used and government agricultural agencies provide the seed for sowing. Consequently, yields are higher. Farmers reap 35 quintals of wheat per hectare compared with 12 quintals in Madère and 100 hecto-litres of ordinary wine versus 25 per hectare in Madère. Living conditions are also better. Of 212 houses in Cessac, 50 are less than 20 years old, 197 have gas or electric stoves, 210 refrigerators, 180 washing machines, 150 indoor toilets, 100 central heating. There are 280 automobiles – as well as 250 radios and 200 televisions. Most of the residents regularly go on holiday, and a number of them have travelled abroad. All of the children are in school.

The contrast between Madère and Cessac is apparent from the time it takes to earn money to buy specific commodities. For a kilo of butter a peasant in Madère works seven hours – which shows why they do not eat butter – while in Cessac, the wages from one and a half hours buy a kilo of butter. In Madère, it takes 8 hours to get the money for a chicken, in Cessac 45 minutes. Such details show that Cessac is a more modern, more developed village than Madère. The work is different, since tertiary employment has largely replaced agriculture as the main employer, and life is easier; automobiles, televisions and radios, as well as the economy, tie Cessac into a national society and culture. Cessac looks like a pleasant small town in a developed country, while Madère could easily be in an underdeveloped one. Yet both are in France – and, in fact, they are the same village. Madère is the village of Douelle-en-Quercy in 1946; Cessac is the same village in 1975.

The microhistory of Douelle illustrates the enormous changes which occurred in European society after the Second World War. Demographic patterns, the nature of work, the structure of society, the creature comforts of life all changed dramatically, and the contrasts between the immediate postwar period and the present are even more obvious in a lesser developed region of Europe than in industrialised France. Particularly in the countryside, more dramatic changes took place in the 30 years after 1945 than in the entire century before the Second World War. Such changes may well be considered as signs of progress, yet modernity brought attendant problems, ranging from pollution of the environment to the psychological effects of stress in consumer society. Not all benefited equally. Great disparities remained between the rich and the poor, and between cities and countryside. Old religious, ethnic and ideological disputes remained in divisive and violent form, and yet new divisions opened as well as new, or heretofore silent, groups demanded recognition.

GENERAL TRENDS

Population movements

After increasing during and immediately after the war, birth rates declined in all countries. In northwestern Europe by the early 1980s they had dropped close to or even below replacement levels. In eastern and southern Europe rates in the 1980s were close to those seen in the northwest in the 1920s. Variations in marriage rates paralleled birth rate figures. A peak following the war was followed by a steady decline. Again, the number of marriages per thousand was lowest in northwestern Europe – lowest of all in Sweden – and highest in eastern Europe, where the Soviet Union celebrated more marriages per thousand than any other European country. Cultural factors influenced marriage rates in quite straightforward ways. Overall, because they no longer had to wait until a farm or a guild mastership became vacant, Europeans were more likely to marry than they had been two centuries previously, though more open homosexuality was beginning to have a statistical impact. In countries like Sweden, the lack of social censure of non-married couples helped to keep the marriage rate low, whereas the Soviet policy of encouraging and providing various incentives for marriage helped keep the rate high. Why married or unmarried couples should have chosen to have fewer children is more problematical. Because postwar developments seem to continue trends begun in the late nineteenth century, factors specific to the postwar world (social security for the aged provided by the welfare state, for instance) are not satisfactory explanations. However, the changing role of women, increased urbanisation, higher educational requirements, the declining influence of the church and the decline of peasant society with its arranged marriages all worked to make decisions to marry and bear children more intentional in postwar Europe, which may also have had an effect on demographic patterns.

Death rates are another standard demographic indicator. The number of deaths per thousand declined almost everywhere in Europe after the Second World War. The absence of a war on the continent was one obvious factor, but improved nutrition, the control of disease and better medical care also contributed. Particularly important was the decline in infant mortality. For example, in France in 1950, 52 of every 1,000 babies born (other than stillbirths) died before the age of 1 but in 1970 only 18. Sweden, Norway, Denmark and the Netherlands enjoyed the lowest rates; Rumania, Portugal and Yugoslavia suffered the highest. The correlation between the level of economic development and the incidence of infant mortality is obvious, but not foolproof; in Bulgaria, the infant mortality rate fell from 95 per 1,000 in 1950 to 27 per 1,000 in 1970, although Bulgaria could not be considered a thoroughly modernised country.

The statistics mean that a person born anywhere in Europe in the 1970s or 1980s stood a greater chance of surviving the first year of life than at any other time in history. Europeans could also expect to live longer – life expectancy at birth in western Europe was about 75 years in 1981 and about 72 years in eastern Europe. Lower infant death rates perhaps meant that families did not feel it necessary to have so many pregnancies, since more of the children would survive to adulthood. This in turn improved life expectancy of women who were no longer exposed to the risk of repeated pregnancies. It also meant that the young constituted a larger part of the population. The new welfare state needed to address the problems associated with children and young people – housing, education, and child support – on the one hand, and those of the elderly and retired – retirement, pensions and even euthenasia – on the other. The large number of children entering adolescence in the 1960s was a demographic fact which was also connected with such phenomena as the growth of subcultures, new forms of political protest and new styles of life.

The stabilisation of national boundaries and political systems after 1950 did not end politically motivated migration. Some 2.6 million persons left East Germany to settle in West Germany between 1949 and 1961. In addition, for several western European countries decolonisation meant the repatriation of large numbers of ethnic Europeans as well as the migration of dissatisfied natives of former colonial areas. Relatively few of the white colonial elite returned to Britain, since the chronically unsatisfactory condition of the British economy made other Commonwealth countries, especially Canada and Australia, seem more attractive as new homes. On the Continent, the lack of alternatives and more buoyant economic conditions encouraged larger flows. Both the Netherlands and Belgium absorbed large numbers of persons compared to their populations. Substantial numbers of ethnic French and Southeast Asians moved to France from Indochina, and even larger numbers of persons moved to France from former North African colonies. In 1962, when de Gaulle granted independence to Algeria, 600,000 *colons* abandoned their former home to 'return' to France.

In the more stable postwar context, some old patterns of overseas migration re-emerged. From 1941 to 1950, for example, 467,000 Italians left their country, and in the next decade 858,000; relative to population, Greek emigration was equally heavy. From 1946 to 1950, 755,000 people left the United Kingdom and Ireland, followed by a further 1.5

million from 1951 to 1960. Many moved to the old areas of overseas settlement, the United States especially, but larger numbers of Italian and Greek migrants moved to Australia. Australia now has roughly a quarter of a million Greek and half a million Italian-born residents. Other flows did not resume. The eastward spread of Europe's 'migration frontier' halted, as the Soviet Union and other socialist governments discouraged emigration to western Europe and overseas and also permitted virtually no migration among themselves.

In western Europe, though not in the east, individual workers and sometimes their families began to move from overseas and from southern and southeastern Europe as the boom of the 1960s gained momentum. Indian and West Indian faces became common in British cities, and north Africans, Spaniards, Portuguese, Italians, Yugoslavs, Greeks, Turks and Lebanese flowed into the urban and industrial centres of the north and west. Of the European states, Italy sent 853,300 workers abroad annually, Turkey 686,000, Yugoslavia 606,000, Portugal 472,900, Spain 390,900, Ireland 232,000 and Greece 177,800. For North Africa, Egypt exported 519,000 workers, Algeria 363,700, Morocco 235,200 and Tunisia 77,200. These human exports accounted for more than twenty per cent of the total employment in Algeria and over fifteen per cent in Portugal and Yugoslavia. Despite the more difficult economic situation of the 1970s, the flow continued, supplemented by migration from sub-Saharan Africa and the Middle East. Compared with population, the largest numbers of migrant workers found jobs in the Low Countries and Austria, and exceptionally large numbers in Switzerland, where they made up 37 per cent of all workers in 1974. In absolute terms, however, France and West Germany absorbed the lion's share of the movement. In 1982 4.2 million foreigners resided in France, and every tenth worker was non-French, with north Africans comprising the largest group. In the same year 4.6 million non-Germans resided in West Germany, primarily Italians, Yugoslavs and Turks. Some 500,000 lived in West Berlin alone, a reflection of the West German government's policy of subsidising the isolated West Berlin economy.

Within Europe urbanisation was a major feature of the

postwar age and the culmination of a trend which had started in the nineteenth century. By 1975 most Europeans lived in cities. Athens contained almost a third of the population of Greece in the 1970s; Moscow, Paris and London had become sprawling conurbations of 7–8 million people each. Most of the population growth in cities resulted from emigration from the countryside; higher wages, better housing, more attractive employment and educational opportunities and greater varieties of recreation drew Europeans to the cities. Since the older areas of cities were incapable of accommodating new residents, suburbs mushroomed; entire new suburbs were built on the peripheries of historic cities, complete with shopping centres and towering apartment buildings. Industrial parks created on the outskirts reflected the economic boom and also provided employment. Even in the centre of cities skyscrapers – sometimes of doubtful architectural merit – arose in the midst of medieval buildings.

Occupational distribution

One of the most important demographic trends after 1945 was the changing socio-professional division of the work-force, the demographic equivalent of the change from an agricultural and industrial economy to one increasingly dominated by the tertiary sector. The decline of the farm population was the most striking of these changes. In Bulgaria, for instance, 80 per cent of the workforce was employed in agriculture in 1950 – little changed from an estimated 82 per cent in 1910 – but by 1980, only 20 per cent of Bulgarians worked on the farm; in Eire the proportion dropped from 46 per cent in 1946 to 20 per cent in 1979 and in Spain from 52 per cent in 1940 to 20 per cent in 1979. The drop in the agricultural workforce was greatest in those countries undergoing a transition to industrial society only after the Second World War, that is, primarily those of eastern and southern Europe (as well as Eire). But even in the more developed nations, the trend was the same; in Norway, the agricultural workforce dropped from 29 per cent to 8 per cent of the total from 1949 to 1980 and in Belgium from 12 per cent to 3 per cent. By the late 1970s, nowhere in Europe did agricultural workers account for a majority of the labour force, and only in Greece, Poland and Portugal did they make up a quarter of the workers. Most European countries had less than 10 per cent of their workforce in agriculture.

Generalisations about the industrial workforce are less easy to make. In countries which had already become industrialised, the labour force remained relatively stagnant or even declined. In Denmark the industrial workforce accounted for 31 per cent of the total in 1940 and 30 per cent in 1979, while in the United Kingdom the proportion dropped from 49 per cent in 1951 to 38 per cent in 1980. In industrialising nations, by contrast, the proportion of workers rose dramatically: in Yugoslavia from 16 per cent in 1951 to 52 per cent in 1980, in Hungary from 23 per cent to 50 per cent during the same period, in Eire from 15 per cent to 32 per cent. By 1980, almost everywhere, industrial workers accounted for 30 to just over 50 per cent of the workforce. Both the nations which had undergone an industrial revolution before 1900 and those which began to industrialise only later moved in the postwar years towards a 'post-industrial' social structure.

The major change occurred in the workforce of the tertiary sector. Employment here expanded rapidly; by 1980, the tertiary sector accounted for at least 60 per cent of employment in Belgium, Denmark, Norway, the Netherlands, Sweden and Switzerland, and at least 50 per cent in Austria, Finland, France, Luxembourg, and the United Kingdom. Rumania was the only nation in which the tertiary sector employed less than 30 per cent of the active population. Such demographic statements are full of social implications; white-collar work implied a certain standard of education and the actual labour was different from that in the farm and factory. Many in the service sector considered themselves middle class rather than working class, a large number lived in cities and their patterns of social mobility differed from those of farmers or factory workers.

Yet another demographic characteristic of postwar Europe was the large and increasing proportion of the workforce made up of women. The need for labour, the opening up of different types of jobs to women, higher levels of education and the rise of feminism were all important in this change. Women had always worked, but almost always in the home or on the farm, in ways which governments did not consider it worth the trouble to record. Now women worked in new social contexts, and the statistical result was a massive increase in recorded female employment. In Greece, only 18 per cent of the recorded workforce was female in 1961, but a decade later, the proportion was 32 per cent; in Hungary, the percentage of female employment grew from 29 in 1949 to 45 in 1980. Ultimately, women made up more than half of the workforce of the Soviet Union and more than 40 per cent in Austria, Czechoslovakia, Denmark, Finland, Hungary, Norway, Poland, Rumania, Sweden and the United Kingdom. Nevertheless, most women worked at the lower end of the job scale and most, 'everywhere in Europe, received lower wages than their male colleagues.

CLASS STRUCTURE

Traditional class categories became less relevant in postwar Europe. The expansion of the service sector and the development of new technologies blurred the differences between blue-collar and white-collar work, while the availability of consumer products to large proportions of the population decreased the difference between the middle and working classes. Land ownership, though prestigious, no longer conferred power, and education and rank in managerial hierarchies to a great extent replaced birth as a mark of status. With the expansion of education, social mobility, at least in theory, became much easier. The welfare state largely eliminated absolute destitution for all but a fraction of the population in both western and eastern Europe. The entry of socialist and communist parties into full political participation in most European countries transmuted the old class struggle of those having a political voice and those denied it. And the new popular culture softened the division between the literate groups holding a monopoly on culture and those whose horizons were limited to what was condescendingly called folklore. Such changes did not lead to a classless society in Europe, even in the people's democracies of the east. Birth and wealth provided privileged access to social, political and cultural power, while poverty continued to exist both in less modernised regions and for those at the bottom of the social scale in industrial society. Titles – whether aristocratic titles, university degrees, membership in ruling political parties or titles attached to particular jobs – provided both prestige and perquisites. Vast differences in income still divided Europeans into groups of haves and have-nots and created tensions which often seemed to verge on class war. Certain groups were still excluded from the mainstream of society by their marginal status as ethnic, political, religious or sexual minorities.

Elites

The new ruling class in western, northern and southern Europe was a coalition of captains of industry and commerce and those in high government positions. Interlocking directorships of businesses, the close relations between government and private enterprise and the interpenetration of finance and industry helped to bring together the controlling heights of the corporate world and the state. Such groups formed a small proportion of the population. Of a total population of approximately 50 million in the United Kingdom in the mid-1950s, only 30,000 were company directors and 3,000 higher civil servants. In France in 1954, 0.4 per cent of the population were classified as industrialists, 0.9 per cent as heads of major businesses and 3.9 per cent upper level managers and professionals. Such elites tended to be self-perpetuating, since the sons and daughters of those in the elite generally acceded to their parents' rank more easily than those from the middle and working classes. Eastern Europe, too, rapidly developed its ruling class, composed of members of the Communist Party or those with important economic functions, especially engineers. These elites were also small and tended to be self-perpetuating through promotion in the technocratic or political hierarchy. As in the west access to schooling was crucial; hence the pressure on Russian parents to secure a position in Moscow during their children's school years, for instance. Such privileges led some, such as the Yugoslav writer and Communist Party official Milovan Djilas, to speak of a 'new class', analogous to the property-owning class in capitalist societies, 'those who have special privileges and economic preference because of the administrative monopoly they hold'.

The middle class

The lines between the upper class and the middle class, whether in western or eastern Europe, were particularly blurred. Some observers denied the existence of a separate upper class except as a gradation of wealth and influence. In many ways, the middle class was the triumphant class of the postwar world, and writers during the 1950s and 1960s hypothesised that Europe and other developed regions were becoming a one-class society. Certainly, the higher standard of living for the working class and the end of legal distinctions for the upper class led to an embourgeoisement of society. Increasing job opportunities in the service sector swelled the ranks of the middle class, while greater access to education opened up the path to middle-class status. As in earlier times, this generally implied work that was mental not manual labour, a minimal level of education, payment by salary rather than by hourly wages and a number of the comforts of consumer society. The number of people who fit into this category increased, although painfully obvious divisions continued to exist between the upper and lower levels.

A case study of France will make the evolution of the middle class clearer. Lower level white-collar workers, those officially classified as *employés* and having some secondary-level education, accounted for 10.8 per cent of the workforce in 1954 and 17.7 per cent in 1975; those who had passed the examination given at the end of the secondary school (the *baccalauréat*) and were classified as holding middle level white-collar jobs (the *cadres moyens*) came to 5.9 per cent in 1954 and 12.7 per cent two decades later; those with some university-level education (the *cadres supérieurs*) and professionals, such as lawyers and doctors, accounted for 2.8 per cent of the population in 1954 and 6.7 per cent in 1975. Such statistics show both the growth of these middle-class categories and, at the same time, the small size of such groups in the population as a whole. Further examples illustrate just how small certain archetypically bourgeois groups were: in France in 1975, engineers represented 1.2 per cent of the workforce, professors and others working in scientific and intellectual activities 1.7 per cent and those working in medical and social services 1.4 per cent. The middle class, in short, remained a minority although it largely controlled politics and economics. Most of the expansion in the 'middle class' was at the lower rather than at the upper end of the scale. Only if the middle class is taken to include all those working in the service sector – a risky equation at best – did the middle class form a majority of the population anywhere in Europe.

The working class

The blue-collar working class, those employed in mining, manufacturing, transport, building and artisanal trades, lost its primacy as the largest segment of the workforce in many European societies. Certain kinds of workers were reduced in number – the number of French miners, for example, dropped by a quarter from 1962 to 1968 alone – while those associated with the newer technologies, such as automotive workers and mechanics, increased. The working class was better off than in the past, thanks to the social security provisions of the welfare state. However, though workers were eligible for subsidised housing (the 'council housing' in Britain, the HLM complexes in France), such lodging often was of poor quality and consisted of impersonal high-rise buildings located in peripheral areas of the city. Health care, family allowances, education and other social services improved the minimum standard of living for the working class, but they did not succeed in doing away with great disparities in income or certain social disadvantages. In the east the chronic shortages of housing, medical services and consumer goods made access to them one of the major defining characteristics of the elite. Social mobility indeed increased for workers but remained limited, since the child of a western bourgeois or an eastern state functionary had a much greater chance of enrolling in tertiary education and obtaining a white-collar job than the son or daughter of a proletarian in either west or east.

Of continuing importance for the working class in contemporary Europe were the trade unions. Authoritarian governments in Germany, Italy and other nations had done away with the unions in the interwar years. In the Soviet Union the Bolshevik Revolution in theory ended the need for contestatory workers' organisations, and the division of the socialist parties outside the Soviet Union into pro-Moscow groups and independent ones caused a similar split in the trade union movement. However, the years after 1945 witnessed a revival of trade unions in western Europe and an increase in their membership. In West Germany the number of unionists grew from just over three million in 1947 to just under nine million three decades later; in Britain membership increased by half; in Denmark it doubled. Not all workers were members of trade unions; in Scandinavia and Belgium fully two-thirds of the workforce was organised, but in France and Italy only between one-fifth and one-quarter. Even the unionised workers remained divided. In France three major unions, one communist, one social democratic and one Catholic, competed for members; in the Netherlands there were also three major unions, one social democratic, one Catholic and one Protestant.

Despite fragmentation and less than total adhesion from workers, trade unions were able to perform a variety of tasks. Following their nineteenth-century intentions, many provided facilities and institutions for the working class; one major West German union, for example, owned the fourth largest bank in Germany, the largest insurance company, the largest property development firm and one of the three largest travel agencies. But the most evident activity of unions remained the strike. In some parts of Europe, notably France and Italy, the right to strike was considered a constitutional right; legally, it was regarded as the suspension of a contract rather than a breaking of it. In other countries strikes were considered illegal. Strike action was a constant feature of western European politics and society after the war; certain years, like 1968, saw widespread actions, and certain unions, such as the British mineworkers, were particularly militant. In eastern Europe, although as many as 95 per cent of workers were unionised, their organisations did not generally challenge the government or engage in contestatory activities.

The peasantry

Perhaps the most striking change in European classes in the postwar period was what the sociologist Henri Mendras called the 'end of the peasantry'. Technological innovations in agriculture (particularly mechanisation), migration from rural to urban areas, and the extension of consumer society broke down the economic and cultural bases of peasant life. No longer did the peasant live in a closed universe of producing for a local market, intermarrying with and being related to those in the village and being confined to a culture of folklore. The farming population which remained had lost many of the characteristics which previously separated it from urban civilisation. Rural ways of life and rural standards of living more closely approached those of cities than at any time in the past. Radios and televisions became as common in the countryside as in the city, automobiles carried rural dwellers back and forth to the city, and levels of literacy in villages rose. What disappeared was not the rural population, although it diminished greatly, but the peasantry as a social and cultural world apart. Most of the customs associated with religious festivals or the harvest fell into disuse both because of the secularisation of society and because of the anachronism of rites and traditions associated with traditional farming. The maypole dances, the building of bonfires on hillsides at midsummer and the celebration of feast days of patron saints all seemed quaint and unnecessary when entertainment was provided by the mass media and seed and machinery by multinational corporations or government agencies.

In eastern Europe, centralised planning, the intervention of the state in the local economy and the availability of social services all put the peasant into a somewhat less precarious position than in times past but at the expense of traditional rural culture. Collectivisation and the establishment of state farms did away with the economic bases of peasant life. Even in areas such as Poland where the proportion of farmers who did not work on state farms remained high, state agencies controlled most prices and distribution. The hostility towards religion of socialist governments changed cultural loyalties, and the removal of an entrenched elite of landlords did away with the deferential society which had persisted until the middle of the twentieth century. Some aspects of traditional peasant civilisation still remained, such as the importance of the Catholic Church in Poland, but these were only vestiges of a civilisation which had disappeared.

Immigrant workers

At the bottom of the social scale in western Europe were the immigrant workers, men and women exported from less developed to more developed nations. Immigrant workers occupied low-status jobs; Italians, Yugoslavs and Turks worked in West German factories, north Africans worked as menial labourers and construction workers in France and West Indians laboured in the hotels and transport systems of Britain. These workers, therefore, formed a kind of subproletariat, taking the jobs that native workers disdained but forming a cheap reserve army of labour for the economies of the developed countries. The foreigners were often badly treated, denied political rights and housed in state-operated shelters or left to survive in shanty towns or in ghettos. Host countries attempted to exclude the families of immigrant workers. Deprived of family life, unintegrated into their host countries and lacking the financial wherewithal to make frequent visits to their own lands, they led unenviable lives. They were scorned by the natives of the countries to which they had moved, both for their inferior occupations and for their different religions and traditions. This condescension often became outright racism, and incidents of immigrants being harassed by the police, forced out of certain restaurants or beaches or physically attacked were not uncommon.

Within the European Community, immigrant workers

benefited if both their 'home' and 'host' countries belonged, for they then could appeal to the Community authorities for redress. However, despite well-intentioned advertising campaigns by various international bodies, migrant workers continued to be subject to varying degrees of prejudice and discrimination. There were serious race riots in Britain and isolated incidents of violence on the Continent. Austria and Switzerland took advantage of their status as non-members of the European Community to limit migration from other European nations, and particularly to restrict the ability of foreign workers to bring their families with them. In Switzerland serious constitutional amendments to limit migration or the proportion of migrant workers in the labour force were proposed in 1970, 1974 and 1977. West Germany welcomed foreign workers, but still placed serious obstacles in the way of those who wished to become German citizens. In West Germany, and in other host countries, foreign workers continued to be considered as 'guest' workers (*Gastarbeiter*) who would return 'home' someday. 'Home' for many of the workers, however – and certainly for their children – had become their host country. As temporary migrants became permanent residents, countries were faced with difficult problems concerning new ethnic minorities.

EASTERN EUROPE

Although eastern Europe displayed many of the same social characteristics as western Europe – urbanisation, a move towards the tertiary sector, higher levels of education, the advent of a consumer society – the underlying social ideology differed and this led to particular distinguishing marks in the social structure. In the west, governments in the welfare state period assumed responsibility for providing the population with the basics of health care and education, minimum wages and pensions; despite legal equality and a certain equality of opportunity for social mobility, however, class differences were still seen as inevitable manifestations of social and economic differences. The ideology of the eastern part of Europe, however, had a different foundation; Marxism consciously sought to evolve towards a classless society with the distribution of goods and services on the basis of individual needs not the workings of the marketplace. Therefore, the state had to level out differences and do away with the parasitical and exploitative elite. In theory, conflicting classes ought not to exist, since the socialist revolution had eliminated the need for a class struggle.

The end of classes, or at least social distinctions, did not arrive in reality in the east. Distinctions between those who lived in towns and cities and those who lived in the countryside, between white-collar and blue-collar workers, between those with basic skills of literacy and numeracy and those with secondary and tertiary education and between those with political influence and those without it were all too readily apparent. Social scientists in the east developed a theory of 'non-antagonistic classes', in which distinctions were not exploitative and were based not on the ownership of the means of production or the lack of it but rather on the relationship of the individual or group with different means of production – occupation rather than ownership. Western observers emphasised the very real differences in income and status which continued to exist, whether these were class differences or not.

A simple difference was income. In Poland in the early 1970s, for example, a technical worker in a factory earned half as much again as a manual labourer, and a mining engineer earned half as much again as an ordinary miner. In 1972 the proportion of the population earning twice the national average income was 4 per cent in Poland, 2 per cent in Czechoslovakia and 2.5 per cent in the Soviet Union (compared to 6 per cent in Britain). But differences of status and power also existed. Again in Poland in the early 1970s, 45,000 persons were statistically classified as scientific workers; only 5 per cent, however, held the powerful positions of full or associate professors in scientific establishments. An informal hierarchy of status in Poland was the following ranking, in descending order of prestige: members of the intelligentsia, skilled workers, private farmers, private businessmen, white-collar workers and unskilled workers; in Yugoslavia, the ranking was similar: qualified white-collar employees, skilled manual workers, lower white-collar employees and unskilled manual workers. (Note the differences with western nations, where almost any white-collar employee outranked a blue-collar worker.) Although eastern Europe did not have an official middle class, those who enjoyed the perquisites of their professions, including shorter hours, higher pay and greater prestige, made up a *de facto* bourgeoisie. It has also been suggested that the intelligentsia in eastern Europe performed many of the functions and held many of the ideas of a middle class, particularly in their consumption of and control over culture. Such distinctions pointed to a further difference between groups, their different patterns of consumption. The white-collar families were much more inclined to frequent the theatre and cinema than their blue-collar neighbours, who spent their leisure time at home reading newspapers, listening to radio and watching television and who went out primarily to attend sporting events. Urban residents spent their surplus income on consumer goods, particularly household appliances, while rural residents first used their money for vehicles (such as bicycles and motorbikes) and utilitarian items like sewing machines.

Without a doubt, the life of eastern Europeans became more comfortable as time passed. In 1960 the average real income of a Polish peasant was 250 per cent of the prewar level. In Czechoslovakia the average person ate 57 kilos of meat annually in 1960 and 71 in 1970; in Hungary the figures were 48 and 59 kilos respectively and in East Germany 55 and 66 kilos. Levels of education also rose dramatically; in Poland the number of people with a secondary or higher education soared from 100,000 in 1945 to 4,000,000 in 1970. Consumer goods were more widely distributed; in East Germany only 17 per cent of all households had a television set in 1960, but 75 per cent in 1972. The number of private automobiles per thousand residents almost quadrupled in the decade after 1960 in East Germany and Poland while it increased sevenfold in Hungary.

The distribution of consumer goods remained lower in the east than in the west. Nevertheless, eastern Europe may well have been more egalitarian than western Europe. Certainly, rates of social mobility were high. In Poland in 1961, 42 per cent of the blue-collar workers enjoyed a higher social position than their fathers; 20 per cent of graduates and half of all white-collar workers came from blue-collar backgrounds. Judged against the aspiration to create a classless society, the eastern countries were not total successes. Judged against the situation obtaining in eastern Europe before 1945, however, they had made great strides to increased mobility and a more egalitarian social structure despite the presence of status incongruities.

FAMILIES AND EDUCATION

With changes in law and economics, family life became less rigid in the postwar period than in the past. The family remained the basic unit of society in both western and eastern Europe. However, more women worked outside the home than ever before, while education prolonged the period of dependency of children to the teen years or later. Contraception and abortion made the limitation of families easier and the number of children per couple dropped. Liberalisation of divorce also made it easier for couples to dissolve their marriages. The social welfare system removed some of the burden of caring for aged relatives from families and also provided subventions for children and other dependents. A decreasing influence of religion and perhaps greater sexual freedom led to the increase in the number of couples living together and even having children without the legal sanction of matrimony. Therefore, the family was no longer an economic unit of complementary labour as it was in agrarian society. It was also less of a labour unit based on the division of work between the breadwinner husband and the housekeeper wife than it was in bourgeois society. This marked a major reorganisation in European society, particularly in those countries where because of economic conditions or the strength of Catholicism, the family remained the centre of life even when it had become less so in other areas.

The family shed or reduced many of the functions which it had handled in earlier periods. The change in law abolished the judicial role of the family, both the primacy of the father and the subordination of wife and children. Meanwhile, the cultural function of the family was in decline, as outside forces, including the electronic media, replaced the family as the centre of cultural life. Even the reproductive function of the family was attacked; falling birth rates, contraception and abortion undermined the functions of procreation at the same time as more liberal mores ended the ideal of sexual relations only in the context of marriage. Thus, the relationship of members of the family to each other changed, with the family moving from a hierarchical group to a more democratic partnership, and the role of families in society underwent a similar metamorphosis.

Most dramatically, the function of the family as the primary institution for the socialisation of children declined. Child care centres, nursery schools and the whole range of educational establishments appropriated much of the child-rearing responsibilities of the parents. A great expansion of education, what might be termed an education revolution, occurred in Europe after the 1940s. An emphasis on education resulted from the need for a more highly trained workforce and the desire of socially-conscious governments to develop a more articulate and more egalitarian electorate. Less developed regions also became aware of the need to become competitive on a cultural as well as economic basis. In primary education, eastern and southern Europe caught up with the north and west. Almost everywhere in Europe, primary education became compulsory and most children were enrolled in school from the ages of six or seven until fourteen or fifteen; illiteracy virtually disappeared. Furthermore, increasing numbers of students continued to secondary education. From 1945 to 1970, the number of high-school students almost quadrupled in Belgium, tripled in Czechoslovakia and doubled in Greece. In France the number of students who successfully sat the *baccalauréat* examination at the end of secondary schooling, only 1 per cent of the age group in 1900 and still only 5 per cent in 1949, rose to 23 per cent in 1974. Such a level of education gave students the skills needed for work in the service sector of the economy; basic numeracy and literacy, which would have been a distinct accomplishment in Europe at the beginning of the century, no longer sufficed for many jobs.

Even more impressive growth rates were registered in university-level education. From the late 1930s to the late 1960s, the number of university students increased from 11,000 to 69,000 in Belgium, from 26,000 to 104,000 in Czechoslovakia, from 8,000 to 53,000 in Greece and from 12,000 to 98,000 in Hungary. In Yugoslavia the number of university students grew eightfold, in Italy sixfold, in Denmark fivefold and in the United Kingdom fourfold. The baby boom increased the pool of students, of course, but more important was the larger number of people whose primary and secondary education allowed them to be admitted to universities. More flexible entrance requirements also played a part, such as the 1969 law in Italy which allowed any student who had finished secondary school to obtain a university place, instead of only those who had graduated from the 'academic' high schools. Governments established many new universities after 1950 which responded to the demand for courses; in Great Britain, there were some 28 new universities, in Portugal 5 new ones, in Spain 11. The new schools taught the traditional subjects but many specialised in technology, a subject which had previously not been taught at all in European universities or which was awarded a low status by comparison with letters. In Hungary, for example, there had been no technical training institutes before the Second World War, but between 1960 and 1967 48 were founded; a French law of 1968 established the University Institutes of Technology, of which there were 50 by 1980.

Such developments changed the composition of the student body and the sorts of subjects studied. In Hungary before the war 39.7 per cent of students studied law, 8.9 per cent engineering and technology and 5.2 per cent agriculture; in the early 1970s, the percentages were 4.3, 34.5 and 8.65 respectively, showing a massive swing towards engineering and technology. The number of women students in universities increased dramatically: in Hungary, from 14.5 per cent of the student body in the 1930s to 47.4 per cent in the 1970s, in Poland from 29.8 per cent in the late 1940s to 46.5

per cent in 1973. However, university students still came from privileged backgrounds, particularly in western Europe. In the early 1960s, a quarter of the students in Norwegian universities came from working-class backgrounds, and the same was true in Britain (although the number of working-class students was far smaller at Oxford and Cambridge); in France, 17.6 per cent and in Sweden 14.1 per cent of students were from working-class families. Elsewhere in western Europe, the proportion of students from proletarian backgrounds was less than 10 per cent. In the east, half of the students in East Germany were the children of working-class parents, and one-third in the Soviet Union; in Hungary, the proportion of proletarian students increased from 14.5 per cent of the student body in the late 1930s to 47.4 per cent in the 1970s. Such change hinted at a democratisation of higher education, but showed too that equality of opportunity still did not exist.

POPULAR CULTURE

The decades after 1945 saw major changes in the structure of European culture, some of which had direct links with the economic and social changes of the period. The new popular cultural forms of the radio and television were obviously connected to the technological possibility of the machines and to the successful marketing of receivers by major international corporations. In both eastern and western Europe, there was both an official and an unofficial (and often dissident) culture; the decade of the 1960s, in particular, witnessed an attempt to create an alternative culture.

Most striking was the culture presented through the electronic media. Radio was first used during the First World War for military purposes, but commercial broadcasts began in the early 1920s. By the time of the Second World War, most European households had access to the radio, either through ownership of a receiver or through use of a radio in a café or other communal establishment. The invention of the transistor in the 1950s allowed the miniaturisation of radio components, and the portable radio became a ubiquitous feature of everyday life. This marked an immense change in the diffusion of culture – with the flick of a switch (and the initial purchase price) every European had access to music and sport, news and documentaries; isolated rural villages now had greater access to urban culture and those who did not possess literacy could stay in touch. Partly for these reasons, governments regarded the radio as a somewhat dangerous device and therefore usually kept control of broadcasting. The radio became a tool for government propaganda; in eastern Europe, the official line of the state radios was challenged by another sort of propaganda, the American version broadcast on Radio Free Europe. In the west the establishment of illegal 'pirate' radio stations challenged state control and resulted in the establishment of independent radio stations.

Equally important was a phenomenon peculiar to the postwar world: television. Television was a great attraction of the 1939 Worlds Fair in New York, but the first set was not put on sale in Europe until the late 1940s. By the early 1970s television sets numbered 28 million in the Soviet Union, 18 million in Great Britain, 17 million in West Germany, 12 million in France and 10 million in Italy; by 1980 almost every European family possessed a television. Television performed the same functions as radio but, by adding pictures to words, had an even greater and more immediate impact. Europeans in the 1960s could thus see pictures of the war in Vietnam on the evening news, in 1968 they could watch the demonstrations in Paris and the Soviet invasion of Czechoslovakia live, and the following year they watched direct transmission of the pictures of man setting foot on the moon for the first time. Regularly they could watch sporting events, movies and news. It is not an exaggeration to say that with television, Europeans had a better familiarity with the wider world than ever before, even if that vision was filtered through the eyes of the broadcasters and the governments which controlled the television stations. The revolution of the electronic media can be compared only to the invention of the printing press, not only creating new channels of culture but also disseminating new brands of culture.

But what sort of culture were the radio and television transmitting? Certainly, the media broadcast traditional high culture; the Third Programme of the BBC set the standard for the broadcasting of 'serious' music and programmes. But the years after the war saw the birth of a new sort of popular music which often seemed to monopolise the airwaves. If the interwar years had the new music of jazz, the postwar years have had rock. Rock developed first in the United States in the 1950s, as newly-affluent white youth found in the music of American Blacks a vehicle for their self-expression. By the 1960s this brand of music and the dancing that accompanied it spread to Europe, and England gave birth to the Beatles. In the early 1960s the four singers from Liverpool (by way of Hamburg) drew audiences that in previous generations would have been reserved for popular political or military heroes. Fusing the musical traditions of the most oppressed group in American society with the cultural concerns of European working-class youth, they pioneered a new style of music with their bittersweet lyrics and compositions based on the guitar and percussion; their long hair set a new trend in male fashion. The Beatles sang about love, not the love of marriage but sexual love which previous generations would have condemned; they sang too of drugs, and of release from the constraints of convention. Musically, they were thumbing their noses at both official culture and the conservative social mores of their parents, while setting themselves up as apostles of the new youth. Rock music was part and parcel of the youth revolt of the 1960s, and by the 1970s rock music was incorporating the rhythms of folk music and Third World rhythms like reggae. Meanwhile, the Beatles had broken up, new rock groups took their place and new youth cults emerged, including the mods, skinheads and punks in England and their cousins on the Continent, groups whose dissidence sometimes extended to acts of violence. In eastern Europe, the governments disapproved of the permissive new youth culture, which also seemed dangerously 'American', but recordings of rock concerts and blue jeans penetrated eastwards despite official misgivings.

One barometer of changing customs is fashion. At the beginning of the twentieth century, respectable women were attired in shoe-length dresses and proper gentlemen sported frock coats. The liberation of women was accompanied by a shortening of skirts; shorter skirts and brassieres replaced long dresses and camisoles during the First World War partly because of the needs of women working in the munitions factories. The 'flapper' era of the 1920s saw bobbed hair and even shorter skirts; by this decade men had completely replaced their frock coats and cravats with more modern business suits and neckties. For the workers and peasants of Europe, there was less choice of wearing apparel and consequently less change in fashion.

The big change came after the Second World War. In high fashion, the French designer Coco Chanel pioneered the 'little black dress', a simplified and standard women's garment which paved the way for the fashion revolution of the 1960s. Accompanied by the music of the Beatles, the British designer Mary Quant of Carnaby Street shocked conservative publics with her mini-skirts which rose high above women's knees, and bathers on the Riviera began to wear topless swimsuits. Even men's clothing began to change with brighter colours, greater variety in styles and the disappearance of tail coats and dinner jackets except for the most formal occasions. Blue jeans became a uniform for the young; they were inexpensive, durable and informal, and women as well as men wore the trousers. Such changes in fashion also helped level social differences. The wealthy wore jeans, and those with modest means might afford off-the-rack clothing adorned with a designer label.

Also breaching the divide between popular culture and high culture were the movies. After 1945 the cinema moved in a number of directions. In Italy in the 1950s directors concentrated on realistic movies trying to convey the everyday life of ordinary people or portraying (and parodying) the life of the elite. In France in the late 1950s the 'new wave' reacted against the glitter of American movies with more thoughtful, analytical films about the human condition. Individual directors, like the Swede Ingmar Bergman, explored the inner worlds of the psyche. The cinema provided a form of entertainment for the masses of a quite new sort, even in small villages, where cinema evenings might be organised with some regularity; at the same time, the cinema provided an outlet for artistic creation, a new cultural medium complementing the printed word.

Popular music and the cinema provided a new social aristocracy of glamour in their stars and an immense economic field for individual entrepreneurs and major corporations. In the mid-1970s, for instance, Spain's 3,000 movie theatres attracted 263,000 customers annually, and Italy's 6,000 theatres served 546,000 patrons. The improved records and tapes on which the new music was available regularly sold in the millions of copies. Increasing personal income and the decreasing real price of 'stereo' equipment created another new industry with an explosive growth rate. As it expanded, the popular entertainment industry lost much of its innovational and oppositional character. Individual stars tended to become politically and socially conservative, pressured perhaps by record and film corporations whose main concern was to avoid alienating any important segment of the market.

Limitations on the maximum number of hours which employers could demand from workers gave more people the time to enjoy television, films and music; the institution of paid vacations gave them new opportunities to travel. Tourism had been the preserve of those wealthy enough and leisured enough to afford trips on the Orient Express or ocean cruisers; however, the postwar years saw a definite democratisation of tourism. Paid holidays now totalled between 20 and 30 days annually, and rising income enabled most workers to seize the opportunity. The growth of resort towns and beaches provided a magnet for vacationers. Some, such as the ski slopes of the Alps and the beaches of the Côte-d'Azur, were still largely reserved for the elite. Others, however, were more widely available. In eastern Europe governments developed resorts on the Black Sea and Adriatic for workers, and in Poland, the number of people using holiday hostels rose from 700,000 in 1960 to 2.8 million in 1972. The coach tour provided an opportunity for those of modest means to travel around their own countries or go abroad. In 1950 a British entrepreneur organised the first package tour, with air fare and accommodation included;

Horizon Holidays soon did a thriving business taking British tourists to Mediterranean beaches in Corsica, Sardinia and Spain. Also in 1950 the first Club Méditerranée was set up with its brand of all-inclusive holiday villages in exotic spots and lured tourists with hopes of sun, sand, sea and sex. Faster train links, such as the Trans-Europe Express, and the beginning of large numbers of commercial flights (and the new 'jumbo jets' of the 1970s) opened up travel to larger numbers of people. The annual holiday away from home became a standard feature of European life; workers, both blue and white-collar, accounted for 47 per cent of tourists in Spain. The proportion of those taking a holiday ranged from 53 per cent in France to 84 per cent in Sweden. Italy received the largest number of tourists of any country, 38 million in 1976, and Spain came second with 30 million; from them, the two countries earned 414 million and 1.7 billion pounds respectively. Denmark, for its part, welcomed 14.4 million visitors in 1976 – almost three times the nation's population.

Sport also provided a way of spending leisure time, although for most Europeans it now became a question of spectator sport rather than participatory recreation. Some sports still had an aristocratic cachet, such as horseracing, fox-hunting, polo and yachting. Others, such as *boules* in the Mediterranean region and cricket in Britain (and oddly, in Corfu, a relic of British imperialism) were restricted in popularity. Most sporting activities were exported from England to the Continent in the last two decades of the nineteenth century, and all sorts of sports became wildly popular after 1900. But the undoubted champion of European sport was soccer football. After the Second World War the popularity of soccer reached new heights. In Britain attendance at soccer matches in 1947–48 was already over 41 million, providing takings of 4 million pounds; pools amounted to a further 12.5 million pounds and revenues to the tax office and post office 2 million pounds more. A soccer association was formed in Germany in 1950, and by the mid-1970s counted some three million members, the highest per capita ratio in Europe. The European Cup matches began in 1955 and, along with the World Cup series, became popular television broadcasts. In 1966, the World Cup final between Britain and West

Germany attracted 400 million television viewers in the world, and the number of telespectators doubled to 800 million for the 1970 final. Meanwhile, it was estimated that the BBC's broadcast of the match of the day on Saturday drew 10 million viewers in the 1970s and that 1.5 million in Britain played soccer each weekend. Soccer was also of great importance economically; top players earned salaries higher than those of many politicians and professionals, and the construction of playing fields and stadia was often a major investment undertaken by government agencies. Major companies also invested in soccer – the Turin Juventus team was owned by the head of the Fiat Corporation.

Sports were also of great importance in eastern Europe. In 1952, East Germany set up the German College for Body Culture, and a 100,000-seat stadium was erected in Leipzig at a time when much of the city was still in rubble left from the war. The Soviet Union had always encouraged physical fitness and, also in 1952, participated in the Olympics for the first time. Soon East Germany and the Soviet Union were taking many of the medals given out, and such eastern countries as Rumania had established themselves as strong competitors in international events. If private enterprise supported sport in the west, in the east it was the state, which granted huge subsidies to gymnasia and training camps and made of athletic victors the sorts of heroes that they also became in the west. Crowds who gathered for football and gymnastics, track and field were no less numerous in the east than in the west.

Inevitably, sports became subjects for polemics and politics. In the late 1940s and 1950s sport was seen in terms of a Cold-War confrontation between the superpowers. In the year of the Berlin blockade, 1948, the Communist Party of the Soviet Union called on the nation's institutions 'to spread physical culture and sport to every corner of the land, and to raise the level of skill, so that Soviet sportsmen might win world supremacy in the major sports in the immediate future'. One party spokesman commented: 'Each new victory is a victory for the Soviet form of society and the socialist sport system; it provides irrefutable proof of the superiority of socialist culture over the decaying culture of the capitalist states'. The

Olympics became a prime focus for nationalist sentiment, not only for large nations with competing ideologies, but for national minorities seeking recognition. In 1956 the Hungarian water polo team savaged their Russian opponents, and in 1968 the victory of the Czech ice hockey team over the Russians commemorated another Soviet intervention in eastern Europe. In 1972 Palestinian terrorists murdered eleven Israeli athletes at the Olympics in Munich, and several of the gunmen died in a shoot-out with police. For better or worse, therefore, sport provided an apt illustration of many of the critical economic and political themes of the postwar period.

Yet another recreation is sex. Sexual activity, previously seen by the Church as being only for the purposes of procreation and restricted to married couples, became an obsession in the postwar world. In the 1960s, commentators talked about a 'sexual revolution' and those who were opposed to it criticised the 'permissive society'. Whether sexual activity actually increased or not, discussion of it did. Books about sex became best sellers. Cities like Amsterdam, with their liberal laws which permitted open prostitution and sale of pornographic literature, became meccas for randy tourists. Increasingly explicit films forced new definitions of obscenity. Reforms in the divorce law, the legalisation of abortion and the sale of artificial contraceptives changed the old constraints on sexual attitudes. The contraceptive pill helped to change sexual habits. Statistics showed that in western Europe in 1968 a quarter of all men and a fifth of all women had had premarital sexual experiences before the age of 21. In the Netherlands 78 per cent of men and 86 per cent of women had engaged in extramarital sex. In the United Kingdom in 1976, over 60 per cent of unmarried females had engaged in premarital sex.

Yet another, and less healthy, diversion was the use of alcohol and drugs. Alcohol was not new in Europe – moralists at the turn of the century protested about the consumption of absinthe. But addiction to alcohol remained a problem, particularly in northern Europe and the Soviet Union. The number of users of drugs, both 'recreational drugs' such as marijuana and 'hard drugs' such as heroin, increased greatly in postwar Europe. Drug-dealing became a major activity of illegal organisations, especially the Mafia, with profits accruing to the black market. Police found it difficult to stop sales of drugs and, in parts of Europe, turned a blind eye to the use of the less dangerous drugs. The use of both drugs and alcohol could be interpreted as a reaction against the pressures of modern society as well as a form of recreation which often had dire consequences for health.

RELIGION

Well into the twentieth century religion preserved much of its importance as the mainstay of popular culture through the organisation of festivals and holy days. Churches enjoyed great influence in politics and were frequently a bulwark of conservative social values. This position did not go without challenge, most obviously from Marxism but also from a general process of secularisation and de-Christianisation dating back to the Enlightenment. After the Second World War religion continued to come under attack. Figures for church attendance showed a rapidly declining proportion of practising Christians; for most Europeans church attendance was limited to baptisms, marriages, funerals and attendance at services on Christmas or Easter; regular church attendance was largely limited to the elderly, women and children. The migration from countryside to city and the availability of other cultural outlets, including cinema, television and radio, diminished the cultural role of the church to a minimal position; even such religious festivals as Christmas were commercialised by merchants and advertisers. The role of the church as a dispenser of charity was largely usurped by the welfare state. The political influence of the church also declined. Separation of church and state in the west and the active hostility of the state in the east contrasted dramatically with the situation in the generation before the First World War. Even in Italy the Vatican proved incapable of stopping legislation allowing the distribution of artificial birth control devices, abortion and divorce.

All of this did not mean, however, that the Church had

been entirely effaced. The Catholic church remained a powerful and wealthy institution. Pope John XXIII, who reigned from 1958 to 1963, was a genuinely popular leader with his message of peace and goodwill and his friendly and casual manner. His calling of an ecumenical synod, Vatican II, resulted in a substantial modernisation of the church: the rewriting of the mass and the holding of services in local languages rather than in Latin, loosening of old regulations (such as the prohibition on eating meat on Fridays) and slightly different presentation for the clergy, including the substitution of street clothes for the traditional habits of religious orders. John's pontificate and that of his more conservative successor Paul VI also saw the beginnings of rapprochement between the Catholic Church and other Christian religions, including both Protestantism and Orthodoxy. The pope remained a strong voice in society, since a substantial proportion of the European population remained nominally Catholic. Papal pronouncements on any subject, particularly condemnations of birth control, abortion and homosexuality, the refusal to ordain women priests and other social stands, provoked wide debate. The church was also able to influence opinion through schools, since a large number of Europeans attended parochial schools; the relationship between the state and these confessional institutions continued to provoke conflict.

New currents of theology and religious practice were also of importance. The phenomenon of 'worker priests', priests who took up non-clerical jobs in factories or elsewhere in order to testify to their faith among the common people, arose in the 1960s; 'liberation theology', an attempt to marry Christianity with Marxism, was influential both in Europe and the Third World and incurred the wrath of conservative Catholics (including the Vatican). Meanwhile, arch-conservative forces also challenged the church, notably the renegade Monseigneur Lefebvre who expressed opposition to Vatican II and continued to defy the pope by celebrating the mass in Latin and ordaining his own priests. In eastern Europe, the church experienced a certain revival. Nowhere was this more true than in Poland, where the Catholic church attracted millions of ardent followers; faced with official censure for most forms of dissident culture, the church provided a rallying point for those disenchanted with the regime and also a cultural outlet for them. The election of a Polish pope in 1978, the first non-Italian pontiff since 1522, testified to the popularity of religion in Poland and to the political implications of Catholic loyalty there. In other countries, the churches allied themselves with one or another political faction (generally, the conservatives) and thereby maintained some of their standing. In Protestant countries, religion was less evident, although many in the elite and middle classes paid lip service to the church.

The years since the Second World War also saw the re-establishment of Jewish communities in parts of eastern and central Europe, although the number of Jews was greatly reduced by the Holocaust. In Britain and in France, Jews still formed a major group with their cultural identity intact. They also continued to be victims of terrorism; Jewish communities were implicated in the question of the Middle East, although most Jews had no direct connections with Israel, and Palestinian terrorists were blamed for the attacks on Jews in Europe. Meanwhile, Islam was a growing religion in Europe, due largely to the arrival of Muslim workers from Africa and Turkey. Most major European cities acquired a mosque to serve these groups (as well as Muslim students, diplomats and business people). The revival of a militant Islam occasionally touched Europe; France, for example, was the home in exile of the Ayatollah Khomeini before his return to Iran after the Islamic revolution there.

THE AMERICANISATION OF EUROPE?

Many Europeans were influenced by developments in the United States. Rock music, blue jeans, the cult of the automobile and Coca-Cola were obvious signs of the phenomenon sometimes labelled the 'Americanisation' of Europe. The 'American way of life' had been presented to Europeans by the large numbers of American soldiers in Europe during the Second World War, as well as by the stories of the migrants who had gone to the New World.

Consumer durables were imported into Europe in the early postwar years, and European companies started producing motor scooters and automobiles, radios and televisions, dishwashers and other household appliances. Because of their relatively high cost, many were not immediately available to Europeans, particularly in the poorer or more devastated regions. But by the late 1950s, the consumer society had triumphed in Europe, thanks to higher wages and to successful advertising campaigns promoting the goods. Even in eastern Europe, where consumer durables were more difficult to obtain, a vogue for the new products appeared.

As well as importing American products and ideas, European societies increased exchanges among themselves. Easier transportation and the breaking-down of tariff barriers with the establishment of the Common Market made possible the flow of commodities across borders, and the mass media aided the flow of music and movies, television and radio programmes and newspapers. Such movement tended to reduce distinctions among Europeans, and the resulting 'homogenisation' of culture was often mistakenly equated with 'Americanisation'. In fact Europe and America remained culturally rather distinct, and within Europe national characteristics remained strongly marked. This sometimes took the form of an economic specialisation, as in the cases of Scandinavian furniture design or Italian clothing; sometimes it was more subtle, as in the greater distance which northern Europeans still preferred to maintain between themselves during conversations compared to Mediterranean peoples. Customs associated with a more traditional way of life persisted in contemporary society – religion remained an obvious example, but so did the long lunch break and siesta of the Mediterranean countries. Opinion polls regularly showed that most national groups were proud of their nationality, satisfied with their own traditions and had little desire to abandon their particular ways of life. Such regional and national differences contradicted the notions of both a thorough Americanisation and a complete homogenisation of Europe.

7
POLITICS AND IDEOLOGY

IDEOLOGY AND POLITICAL CONSENSUS

Along with the replacement of one party, one leader and one legislature by another, as well as the dialectic between formal and extraparliamentary politics, political activities involve theory or ideology. Ideology, according to the dissident Polish philosopher Leszek Kolakowski, 'however grotesquely remote from reality, is the main, indispensable instrument for legitimising power systems. . . . There is no other means of justifying power except adducing its ideologically established meaning; doctrine becomes a substitute for other mechanisms of legitimacy'. Thus, every actual or would-be ruler or ruling party feels obliged to adopt some statement of principle and either to align policy to that principle or rework the principle as conditions change. At some times, the ideology is not clearly defined; at other times, the ideology is largely the manifestation of the leader's will; another variation is a carefully preserved corpus of principles. The political ideologies dominant in 1900 – which traced their origins to the French Revolution – metamorphosed in the postwar period. Traditional monarchism, loyal to king, aristocracy and official religion, dissolved into a democratic parliamentarianism with a figurehead monarch. Old-style conservatism had seen itself outdistanced on the right by the ideology of fascism and its kin movements in interwar Europe; old style liberalism, meanwhile, gave way to the more interventionist Keynesian liberalism of the welfare state. Socialism, for its part, had divided into socialist and communist strands after the Bolshevik Revolution and after 1945 fragmented even further.

199

A conjunction between social group, ideology and practical politics was far from easy to make in the postwar world, and the prevalence of coalition governments, changes in theory and the exigencies of power politics made any simple scheme misleading. But the 'death of ideology' announced by some observers in the 1950s, like the equally heralded 'one class society', was premature. In both eastern and western Europe, the assertion that ideological divisions had disappeared was itself ideological, an attempt to reinforce the existing political consensus. In the east, the official argument contended that the triumph of the working class and of Marxism-Leninism had put an end to significant social and political divisions within the socialist states. In the west, a less clearly formulated but equally pervasive argument held that economic growth and the welfare state had achieved the same goal; all citizens would shortly be included in an undifferentiated affluent middle class, and political debate would be reduced to highly technical discussion of the best way to employ the tools of Keynesian economic management. In fact social classes did not disappear; the sphere of politics did not narrow but rather extended itself, and heretofore silent groups developed new ideologies to articulate their interests and demand their satisfaction.

WESTERN EUROPE

The remarkable stability of politics in western Europe in the years following reconstruction was credited to the stability of parliamentary institutions, the flexibility of the electoral process and the general economic prosperity of the time. Politically, presidents or figurehead monarchs provided continuity as heads of state, while policy was determined by parliaments elected on the basis of universal suffrage. A range of political parties contended for power; all, however, accepted the ruling consensus. Conservative parties – the Tories in Britain, the Gaullists in France, the Christian Democrats in Italy and West Germany – opposed one or more socialist parties as well as, in some states, a communist party. The socialist and communist parties had become in fact social democratic ones, reformist rather than revolutionary, and thoroughly integrated into the parliamentary process. Yet the conservative parties were as committed to the existing welfare system and to government action to ameliorate social problems as their leftist opponents. A large number of smaller parties – the lay parties in Italy, the Free Democrats in West Germany, the radicals in France – allied with one or the other of the major formations. Though they occasionally held the balance of power, none presented a serious intellectual or ideological challenge to the premises on which the system rested. Indeed no party advocated substantial change of the system, or even considered it possible. Elements of older liberal-democratic, radical and socialist creeds had been combined. The interests of private industry and commerce, farmers and unionised workers were represented in parliament and in the government bureaucracy. Through the apparatus of the welfare state the government claimed to care for disadvantaged groups as well. Those outside the consensus who posed no threat, such as aristocrats and monarchists, were considered merely quaint. Those who might prove dangerous, like radical leftists and neo-fascists, were placed under intensive surveillance and repressed.

The parties of the centre and right ostensibly favoured a free market and private ownership rather than nationalisations and a strong role for the state. However, British conservative leader Harold Macmillan argued for 'the Socialist remedy' wherever 'private enterprise had exhausted its social usefulness, or where the general welfare of the economy requires that certain basic industries and services need now to be conducted in the light of broader social considerations than the profit motive will supply'. The conservative government of Charles De Gaulle in France managed one of the most *étatiste* economies in western Europe, and through holding companies Italian Christian Democratic governments controlled fully one-third of the economy. In short, conservatives were good Keynesians, using the state as an economic entrepreneur and regulator. The idea was that the state should ensure the basic minimum through social services and that the continued expansion of the economy would create a higher standard of living for the general population. Returned to power in 1951, the British conservatives ruled for the next thirteen years, but did not attempt to dismantle the welfare provisions introduced by the labour governments of the reconstruction period. The Italian Christian Democrats, though opposing divorce and abortion, extended comprehensive social security measures to cover most Italians during a period when the country was still relatively poor and underdeveloped.

The main competitors of the conservative parties were the socialists. The socialist parties of western Europe had become thoroughly reformist ('revisionist' in Marxist terminology) rather than revolutionary. The declaration of the First Congress of the Socialist International in 1951 stated that socialism was simply 'democracy in its highest form'. The 1959 Bad-Godesberg programme of the West German SDP indicated the change in theory. The paper asserted that 'Democratic Socialism' in Europe was rooted in Christian ethics, humanism and classical philosophy – there was no mention of Marx in the document. Placing the emphasis on freedom and justice, it argued that the role of the state was to 'create the conditions in which the individual may freely develop his personality, responsible to himself but conscious of his obligations to society'. The goal of Social Democratic economic policy 'was the constant growth of prosperity and a just share for all in the national product', a life in freedom 'without undignified dependence and without exploitation'. As for ownership of the means of production: 'The Social Democratic Party therefore favours a free market wherever free competition really exists. Where a market is dominated by individuals or groups, however, all manner of steps must be taken to protect freedom in the economic sphere. As much competition as possible – as much planning as necessary'. Privileges were to be eliminated, particularly in such areas as access to education, but no reference was made to the class struggle. 'From a party of the working class the Social Democratic Party has become a party of the people.'

Socialist – or social democratic, to be more precise – practice generally conformed to theory. In the Nordic countries socialist governments had first come to power in the 1920s, and in Sweden the socialists ruled with only minor interruptions continuously from the early 1930s; however, though they introduced social welfare legislation earlier than other nations, they did not disturb property ownership. Wealth remained as concentrated in the north as elsewhere and the state sector grew no larger than in other western European countries. In Austria, Switzerland and the Low Countries, the socialists regularly participated in coalition governments. In Italy in 1963 the Christian Democrats dramatically enlarged their coalition by bringing the Independent Socialist Party into the government, and in West Germany the socialists ruled in coalition with the Christian Democrats from 1963 to 1966. In Britain in 1964 the rule of the conservatives ended and labour returned to power; in 1969 the West German socialists won an election and formed the first leftist government in the history of the Federal Republic. In 1971 Austrian socialists too won an election and formed a one-party government.

Nowhere did the inclusion of socialists or socialist rule result in dramatic changes in government policy. Nationalisations did take place, but only of certain sectors of the economy such as banking, coal, steel and a few of the largest companies. Only in Britain – ironically, the country where labour was most often accused of playing Tweedledum to the conservatives' Tweedledee – did the extension of the state sector provoke real debate, and even here the consensus regarding the welfare state and economic management remained solid. Some factions – such as Militant Tendency in the British Labour Party or CERES in the French Socialist Party – might demand a more rigorous application of socialist principles, but the moderates generally had the upper hand. Meanwhile, the socialist and social democratic parties broadened their electoral bases. No longer were they solely the parties of the factory proletariat, but found support among white-collar employees as well.

To the left of the socialist parties were the communists. In Italy the main electoral rival of the Christian Democrats was the Italian Communist Party (PCI), which benefited from its resistance to fascism and opposition to the war. It gained support from Italy's growing factory proletariat, a number of prominent intellectuals and a wide range of others dissatisfied with the pro-Catholic, pro-American and procapitalist politics of the Christian Democrats. The Italian communists had possessed in Antonio Gramsci one of the major Marxist theoreticians of the twentieth century, a thinker who also became a martyr through his imprisonment and death under Mussolini's regime. Gramsci emphasised the necessity of adapting Marxism to the exigencies of the twentieth century, and the PCI proved able to adapt theory to practice. The PCI argued that the profits of Italy's 'miracolo economico' had gone largely to the capitalist elite and that the working class had benefited less from growth. Emphasising the provision of greater social services it captured the city governments of major cities like Bologna, Rome and Venice. Communist municipal governments increased budgets for education and culture, set up child-care centres and provided free city buses. Nationally, the PCI cooperated with its rivals, although it did not join the government; internationally, the PCI criticised the Soviet Union more openly than most other communist parties.

In the Nordic countries support for the communists declined after the war – even eventually in Finland, where it was long the strongest. In 1959, however, a new party, the Socialist People's Party (SF), emerged in Denmark. It was self-consciously Marxist in domestic policy but nationalist and independent of Moscow in external policy. SF held twenty seats in the Folketing by 1966 and related movements appeared in Sweden and Norway, where in 1963 the two members in the Storting held the balance of power and within one month had overthrown and restored the labour government to office.

Urban administration in Italy and nationalist independence in the Nordic countries were two precursors of a broad reformist movement within all western European communist parties, which became grouped under the heading of 'Eurocommunism', a designation first used in 1975. The Eurocommunists were critical of the Soviet Union and also autonomous from Soviet direction. Whether stating so explicitly or not, they had all agreed to use parliamentary methods rather than class war to achieve their ends. They cooperated with non-communist groups, with the 'historic compromise' in Italy, the Common Programme in France and the Moncloa Pact in Spain. They softened the old rhetoric and their programmes did not demand the outright nationalisation of all the means of production. The fortunes of the individual parties varied, and in some states, such as Greece, the theoretical debate on communism led to a split in the communist parties; nonetheless, across western Europe communist parties had in effect joined in the ruling consensus.

Spain, Portugal and Greece seemed to stand out as glaring exceptions to the peaceful parliamentary consensus which ruled elsewhere in western Europe. Francisco Franco ruled Spain from 1939 until his death in 1975. Franco was the *generalissimo*, the *Caudillo*, head of state and prime minister. Franco relied on three major groups for support: the military, the Falange movement and the Catholic church. Military leaders participated in the government as ministers. The Falange, the right-wing movement which Franco had taken over in the 1930s, was less important as an institution than as an ideological and polemical focus exemplified by the monument to the civil-war dead in the Valley of the Fallen. In 1953 a Concordat between the government and the church made Catholicism the official state religion, and several Catholic organisations, the best known of which was the Opus Dei, marshalled support for Franco. The elected assembly, the Cortes, possessed extremely limited powers; the government was not responsible to the Cortes for its actions and election of opposition deputies was impossible because of censorship, persecution and the necessity of amassing enormous numbers of signatures to qualify for the ballot. In Portugal the authoritarian regime which came to power in 1926 weathered the depression, the Second World War and the turbulence of the immediate postwar period. Antonio Salazar, the former economics professor who had dominated the government since 1928, retained power until he was incapacitated after an accident in 1968. The 'New State', as it was called, was similar to that of Francoist Spain; a veneer of constitutionalism masked a dictatorship, though Salazar's Portugal was marginally less repressive than Franco's Spain.

In 1949 the defeat of the communists in the civil war left Greece in the western camp, but the war also left Greece with fratricidal recriminations; a large number of Greeks emigrated, and opponents of the victorious regime were kept in prison. Conservative coalition governments ruled Greece until 1963, when they were turned out of office by a party of centrists. Of most concern, however, was Cyprus. This Mediterranean island, with a population two-thirds Greek and one-third Turkish, had been a British possession until independence was granted in 1960. The constitution had tried to mollify both national groups – the president was to be Greek, the vice-president Turkish and other offices would be apportioned. A movement for *enosis*, or union with Greece, led to violence in 1964. This unsettled both the Turks in Cyprus and Turkey itself, which by the independence arrangements had the right, along with Greece and Britain, to intervene in Cypriot affairs. The Greek centrist government proved unable to provide a solution. The military was dissatisfied, both with the overall policies of the centrists and in particular with their attitude toward the *enosis* faction in Cyprus, and army leaders struck in 1967 with a coup d'état. The members of the new ruling triumverate were colonels; all were lower middle-class men whose personal frustrations were compounded by their horror at the liberalising course of Greece. They pursued an archconservative policy, dismissing teachers and professors and exiling prominent intellectuals and artists. They banned long hair and short skirts, suppressed dissent, instituted press censorship and tortured prisoners.

However, even the Mediterranean dictatorships did not escape the trend towards reform and greater representation of interests. The Greek colonels were forced to modify some of their policies in order that aid from the United States and European countries would begin to flow again. Within the Spanish government, reform-minded elements (the *aperturistas*) gained ground against the hard-liners (the *immobilistas*) who opposed any modification of the system. Certain measures began to loosen the reins of the dictatorship: 'economic' strikes, although still illegal, were no longer declared seditious, some dissent was allowed in the press, a Spanish cinema in

1962 for the first time showed a woman wearing a bikini and a new education law in 1970 toned down the ideological indoctrination of students. In the late 1950s a liberal wing also emerged within Portugal's ruling National Union. Cautious reforms followed, accelerating after Salazar's retirement; women were allowed to vote in the 1969 elections, for example.

Ruling governments and the major parties in western Europe not only became more alike in their programmes and policies; they also resembled one another in their increasing tendency to consult organised interests outside parliament regarding legislation and administration. This 'neo-corporatism' bore a strong resemblance to the ideologies of the conservative regimes of the interwar period, especially Mussolini's fascist 'corporations'. Consultation with industrial and labour organisations lay at the heart of the French style of 'indicative' planning, and was implicit in the extensive government shareholdings in private corporations in West Germany and Italy. In Switzerland the legislative process continued to incorporate the 'consultation of interests'. In the Low Countries successive coalition governments attempted to achieve consensus by cooperating with the major interest groups such as the Netherlands Federation of Labour and its Social-Economic Council and through the creation of government bodies such as the Belgian National Investment Corporation. In Austria the process of balance and compromise reached such an advanced stage that virtually all legislation was passed unanimously when it finally appeared before the parliament.

Corporatism was most completely developed in the Nordic countries under the leadership of the socialist parties. Though their partners did not always support the entire social democratic platform, basic agreement existed on the concept of the welfare state. The cooperation and compromise such governments involved were extended to major organisations outside parliament, such as the bureaucracy, farmers, labour and employer organisations. Even the communist parties participated in these corporatist activities, though rarely were they included in government. Leaders of the parties and all the major interest groups met and worked out the details of new laws and their administration. In Sweden the process frequently involved pilot projects to determine in advance the effectiveness of new proposals, and the whole process of government became known as 'Harpsund democracy' after the name of the rural retreat where the leaders met. The trend towards corporatism within each state also had its counterpart within the region itself. All professions and vocations (from tanners and foresters to doctors and bank directors) had their Nordic as well as their national organisations. The Nordic Council, which first met in 1953, brought together representatives from the parliaments of Denmark, Sweden, Norway, Finland and Iceland. Many of the Council's recommendations inspired government action as well as greater regional cooperation and rationalisation.

With so much public policy determined behind discreetly closed doors and only revealed later in the impersonal actions of the administrative bureaucracies, political change seemed to occur only in response to incompetence or scandal. In France, for instance, de Gaulle's departure from office seemed a classic case of political mismanagement. After surviving the loss of Algeria in 1962 and the year of student demonstrations and strikes in 1968, in 1969 de Gaulle sent to the electorate as a referendum a muddled proposal for changes in local administration and the powers of the Senate. He staked his regime on an approval of the measure, and when it was rejected he resigned and never returned. The point of the episode remained unclear; some said that de Gaulle was committing political suicide and others that it marked a dramatic way for him to abdicate or, conversely, an attempt to secure a new mandate.

Scandals were more straightforward, though they threw a quirky light on the concerns which preoccupied the peoples of different countries. In Britain in 1963 John Profumo, the Secretary of State for War, was forced to resign after he lied about his relationship with a female prostitute; a decade later the leader of the Liberal Party, Jeremy Steele, was made to step down after revelations of his sexual affair with another man. In West Germany Chancellor Willy Brandt resigned after one of his aides was revealed as an East German spy. French president Valéry Giscard d'Estaing was badly damaged (though not forced from office) by allegations that he had received a large diamond from one of the more flagrantly repressive African rulers. In Italy the revelation that a clandestine grouping of prominent right-wing politicians were organised into a Masonic lodge which had unsavoury connections with the underworld seemed to support the suspicions of both those who stressed behind-the-scenes deals in Italian politics and those who saw a great conspiracy of Catholics, gangsters and the political right. In Greece, the murder of a left-wing member of parliament implicated members of the government and culminated in the conservative coalition's resignation in 1963.

Another sort of scandal which could disrupt governments was the process of decolonisation. Acrimonious controversy accompanied the loss of the Dutch East Indies and the Congo in the Netherlands and Belgium; Belgium had used the revenues from the Congo to finance reconstruction and the new social security system and the Netherlands had hoped to do the same, but neither sent conscripts to fight in their colonies. In 1956 the failure of the attempt to use military force to maintain international control over the Suez Canal caused consternation in Britain and led to bitter debate in the House of Commons. Police and professional army units proved able to contain nationalist uprisings in most British possessions; however, the cost of military action and the political impossibility of using large numbers of conscript soldiers overseas rapidly convinced British leaders that the 'winds of change' were blowing in the direction of independence.

France and Portugal made greater attempts to hold their colonial possessions and paid correspondingly higher prices for failure. After the defeat at Diên Biên Phu in 1954 the French withdrew from Indochina, only to be confronted with the beginnings of the war of independence in Algeria. By 1958 France had mobilised hundreds of thousands of increasingly unhappy conscripts for service in north Africa and the expense of the war had seriously strained the economy. Still the Algerian FLN did not surrender. The United Nations provided them with a forum from which they could publicise the brutality of French troops, and Libya's complaints about French border violations foreshadowed more active United Nations involvement. Within French government circles there was absolute deadlock on Algeria. A new government patched together in April 1958 – the fourth in twelve months – seemed willing to negotiate with the Algerians. This set off an uprising among French soldiers on 13 May 1958 in Algeria; demonstrators thronged the streets of Algiers, banging pots and pans to the rhythm of 'Algérie Française'. Terrorist attacks broke out in France, and the rebels were establishing control over the island of Corsica. France seemed in danger of breaking apart. Faced with chaos, the president called on Charles De Gaulle to form a new government. De Gaulle incarnated the military leader, a war hero who had been able to hold France together during the years 1944–46. For the Algérie Française faction, he seemed to promise a maintenance of French control. De Gaulle wrote a new constitution in accord with his political philosophy; the president was to be the real power with the prime minister and cabinet instructed to execute policy. The constitution was approved by the electorate and De Gaulle became the first president of the Fifth Republic. Legislative elections gave a majority to his followers. The first four years of De Gaulle's government were concerned with settling the Algerian question. Although he made a trip to Algeria soon after his election, shouted 'Vive l'Algérie Française' and said to the white settlers 'I have understood you', he gradually moved in the direction of a more compromising stance towards the Algerian nationalists. In 1962 he agreed to grant independence to Algeria, to the fury of die-hard settlers and army officers. There were several attempts to assassinate De Gaulle and another attempt at a military uprising in Algeria, but De Gaulle clearly enjoyed the support of French public opinion and of the mass of enlisted soldiers.

Colonial war strained Portugal's limited resources past the breaking point and led to revolution. The expense of the thirteen-year war in Angola and Moçambique forced the delay of investment projects and created severe inflationary pressures in Portugal. Several hundred thousand young men left the country to escape conscription. The stalemated war, the worsening economic situation and the slowness of political reform led to opposition from within the regime itself. Disillusioned army commanders demanded a change in policy. In 1973 the Governor of Portuguese Guinea, General Antonio de Spinola, was dismissed for advocating a liberal policy towards the guerrillas; the next year, in February 1974, he published *Portugal and the Future*, an open criticism of the regime. On 25 April 1974, a revolution broke out and within a day the peaceful rebellion had brought the 46-year dictatorship to an end. General Spinola became the head of the revolutionary government. Guinea, Moçambique and Angola were granted independence, civil liberties were guaranteed, the secret police abolished, an amnesty on political prisoners declared and the armed forces purged. However, the unity of reformist forces disappeared when the more radical elements began to press for extensive nationalisations, confiscation of the property of wealthy landowners and agrarian reform, and the situation remained unstable for the remainder of the decade.

EASTERN EUROPE

The political structure of eastern Europe differed in one very important way from that of western Europe. Although the eastern nations each possessed a constitution, head of state, head of government and legislature and conducted regular elections with universal suffrage, their governments had been dominated since the late 1940s by a single party. This, of course, was the communist party, although the precise name varied from state to state, and the communists might include non-party members in the government. Furthermore, the apparatus of the party, with its congress, central committee and Politburo, complemented and even overshadowed the apparatus of the state; the head of the party, rather than the official head of state or government, when not the same person, was the dominant figure in policy-making. In the Soviet Union official power resided in the Supreme Soviet of the USSR, a large bicameral body whose membership included a carefully-balanced cross section of Soviet society. The Supreme Soviet, however, met infrequently; it elected the Council of Ministers and the small permanent Presidium which conducted its day-to-day business and whose chairman was the head of state. In theory the Communist Party was completely separate from these organs of government. Every five years a Party Congress elected a Central Committee of over 300 full and 150 candidate or non-voting members. Like the Supreme Soviet, the Central Committee met infrequently, and the Party's day-to-day affairs were in the hands of the dozen regular and half-dozen candidate members of the Party Presidium, or Politburo.

The dual structure of party and government formed the model for all of the states of eastern Europe. Officially, the relation between them was vague. The Soviet constitution referred to the Communist Party as 'the leading core of all organisations of the working people' and named it as one of the organisations possessing the right to nominate candidates for public office but did not spell out the division of functions among the Supreme Soviet, Central Committee, Presidium, Council of Ministers, Politburo and other leading organs of government and party. In fact power was highly concentrated in the Politburo. Membership was cooptive; the Central Committee and Party Congress unanimously approved the list of nominees placed before them. Politburo members had risen to the top through one or more of the centralised bureaucracies governing Soviet society, while at the same time holding increasingly important positions in the Communist Party apparatus. Politburo decisions therefore resulted from face-to-face negotiations among the senior representatives of the various ministries and interest groups. As Communist Party directives, Politburo decisions were ratified unanimously by the Central Committee and Party Congress. Legislation and the state budget passed from the Politburo and the ministries to the Presidium and Council of Ministers and then to the Supreme Soviet – where the miniscule modifications permitted before unanimous adoption gave every evidence of being carefully stage-managed.

Those who questioned the official consensus thus achieved did so at their own risk. The Leninist principle of 'democratic centralism' provided for debate before the party had made a decision but demanded absolute obedience to the party's decision once it had been made. Institutions such as the church lived in an uneasy *modus vivendi* with the party. Individual protesters such as the writer Alexander Solzhenitsyn were subject to internal exile, expulsion from the country or worse. Sporadic demonstrations occurred, and dissident intellectuals managed to criticise the regime through clandestine publications or veiled satire. But the sort of open political debate common everywhere in the west was absent in the Soviet Union and eastern Europe.

Stalin had been absolute master of the Soviet Union for nearly 30 years; his death in 1953 and the memory of the purges of the 1930s led to subtle but important changes in the Soviet system, which in turn had important consequences for east-central Europe as well. The beginning of 'de-Stalinisation' occurred in 1956. At the Twentieth Congress of the Communist Party, Nikita Khrushchev delivered an amazing speech attacking Stalin. He reported that relations between Stalin and Lenin had been very strained just before Lenin's death and read letters in which Lenin accused Stalin of being rude to him and his wife. He criticised the way in which Stalin had run the country: 'Stalin ignored the norms of party life and trampled on the Leninist principle of collective party leadership'. He spoke at length about the purges of the 1930s, including details of the elimination of Lenin's associates and the massive arrests and executions of party members, complete with falsified evidence and forced confessions:

> In those years repressions on a mass scale were applied which were based on nothing tangible and which resulted in heavy cadre losses to the party. . . . Here Stalin showed in a whole series of cases his intolerance, his brutality and his abuse of power. Instead of proving his political correctness and mobilising the masses, he often chose the path of repression and physical annihilation, not only against actual enemies, but also against individuals who had not committed any crimes against the party and the Soviet Government.

Khrushchev accused Stalin of not adequately preparing the Soviet Union for the Second World War and had said that 'had our industry been mobilised properly and in time to supply the Army with the necessary material, our wartime losses would have been decidedly smaller'. Finally, he accused Stalin of having built up a 'personality cult', extending to a new version of the official party history to upgrade his role in the 1917 revolution, the naming of cities after the leader and the rewriting of the national anthem so that the word 'communist' did not appear but Stalin was praised by name.

The speech was a shock. Although not officially published in the Soviet Union, the contents slipped out. It seemed to promise change in the Soviet Union; among communist parties outside Russia, it forced a re-examination of policies and ultimately the replacement of Stalinist leaders. It sparked the revolts in Poland and Hungary, and led to dramatic tension between the Soviet Union and two hard-line allies, China and Albania. In reality, de-Stalinisation increased the stability of the Soviet system by reducing insecurity but without major structural transformations. Khrushchev, who had been one of Stalin's most enthusiastic henchmen, used the de-Stalinisation campaign in his rise to power. However, though some of Khrushchev's followers proclaimed him to be a new leader, Khrushchev himself insisted that the Communist Party was supreme, and that the Politburo was a collective body in which he wielded only a single vote and whose decisions he would have to obey. Khrushchev's rivals were demoted and transferred, but they were not arrested or shot and in several cases continued to occupy responsible official posts. In turn, when Khrushchev lost power in 1964, the coup was quick and peaceful; he was sent into retirement but not charged with any crime or brought to trial.

Such structural differences meant that the political process differed in west and east as well. In the east opposition to the governments in power came either from within the party or from dissident groups not organised into rival parties. Elections were confirmations of the party and its orientation rather than debates on programmes; they proved to potential enemies − both internal and external − that the movement remained united, and they provided an important means of overcoming apathy and indifference. Similarly, debate over policy was confined to meetings of the party (or the executive of the party) and the legislature confirmed decisions already taken. Eastern politics did not fit the western model; such, however, was not the intention of the communist revolutionaries of the 1940s or of those who framed the constitutions of the 'people's democracies'. If in practice they silenced opponents and restricted human rights, they argued that they had achieved a greater measure of equality and economic rights than the politicians of the west. Furthermore, they argued that the multi-party system of the west was merely a façade which kept the ruling bourgeois elite in power.

An important characteristic of the ruling parties in eastern Europe was the regular renewal of membership. At the grass-roots level, this took the form of a 'verification' of membership cards; those whom the leadership wanted to be rid of were not given new cards. This resulted occasionally in a reduction in party membership by as much as a third. At the upper levels renewal took the form of reshuffling of the Central Committees and Politburos or, more drastically, of purges. In the late 1940s and early 1950s purges took place in each of the socialist countries, and those eliminated were generally imprisoned or executed. A second round of purges took place after the death of Stalin in 1953 and during the de-Stalinisation programmes beginning in 1956, but the losers this time were generally not treated so severely. Being purged no longer necessarily ended a member's political career and several of eastern Europe's leaders returned to power after being discredited or even imprisoned by their colleagues. In postwar Poland, for instance, the victorious communist party was led by Wladyslaw Gomulka, son of a worker, party militant during the interwar years and head of the clandestine communist party in Poland during the war. Gomulka consolidated his authority by eliminating the influence of non-communist groups in the coalition and then by unifying the communist and socialist parties and purging potential rivals. Yet Gomulka himself fell a victim to a purge in 1948. He was dismissed from office on the grounds of 'nationalist deviationism' and in 1951 was arrested. Nevertheless, following the suppression of the riots in 1956 the head of the party resigned in favour of none other than Gomulka. He ruled for the next fourteen years, but in December 1970 mass demonstrations by workers in the Baltic cities of Gdansk, Gdynia, Sopot and Szczecin turned into riots that, according to the government, left 45 killed and over 1,000 wounded.

Gomulka was a political casualty of the riot; he resigned, his roller-coaster career finally at an end.

Renewal and purges provided a means of changing personnel and policies in a collegial fashion; since elections were symbolic demonstrations of unity, this internal rearrangement in part served the function of elections in non-communist nations. Purged individuals were always accused of ideological impurity, but more often their fall resulted simply from their inability to solve economic problems or deal with dissent; in fact it was widespread discontent which most often led to a change in leadership. Khrushchev's fall followed the disappointing results of his economic policies. The Polish riots of 1956 had been touched off by hopes for reform; Gomulka in turn alienated students and intellectuals with a new 'offensive on the cultural front' which began in 1963, and the 1970 demonstrations began as protests over increases of up to 30 per cent in the price of basic food items announced shortly before Christmas.

In addition, the ties of clientelism and patronage were not absent in eastern Europe. Stalin provided the model which all aspiring Soviet leaders attempted to emulate, carefully fostering the careers of his supporters as he moved towards absolute power. Politburo members thus represented not only the interests of the institutions they led, but also those of the personal cliques they had welded together on their road to the top. In most eastern European nations, a division emerged in the 1940s between those who had spent the war years in the Soviet Union (the 'Muscovites') and those who had been in prison in their own countries. Ethnic divisions also continued to play a role, for instance between Czechs and Slovaks in Czechoslovakia and between Jews and non-Jews in Poland and Hungary. Even family ties could play a part. In East Germany the wife of the party head became Minister of Education; in Rumania the leader's spouse was made a member of the communist party's executive committee. In Bulgaria the daughter of the leader in 1971 assumed the role of the 'first lady' on her mother's death; four years later she was made chairman of the Committee on Culture with ministerial rank and responsibility for cultural affairs, education and propaganda. In 1979, two years before her death at the age of 39, she was made a full member of the Politburo and delivered a major address at the United Nations. The party leader's female companion subsequently became a candidate member of the Politburo, minister of education and deputy prime minister. In Albania in the early 1960s, according to Soviet reports, at least half of the 53 members of the Communist Party's central committee were related by family ties, and members included four pairs of husbands and wives.

Certain individuals displayed remarkable longevity in power; in East Germany Walter Ulbricht ruled until 1971, in Yugoslavia Tito until 1980, in Albania Enver Hoxha until 1984. Nonetheless, gradually the old cadres of the interwar period gave way to a new generation; this had to do with the replacement of ageing leaders but also with a new emphasis on technocracy instead of simple party militancy. A toning down of ideological stridency and a rapprochement with the capitalist west accompanied this evolution. Khrushchev spoke of 'peaceful coexistence' and signed a treaty limiting the testing of nuclear weapons. Though east and west did not simply 'converge', there was a parallelism of certain sorts of development: an interest in problem-solving rather than ideological purity, departure from insularity with greater international contacts, economic experimentation (with nationalisations in the west and the reinstallation of profit incentives in the east), the growth of the service sector and its white-collar functionaries, and the maintenance and spread of extraparliamentary political activity. Thus, although theories and structures remained different, the practice of statecraft showed decided similarities.

MARGINALS AND THE WIDENING SPHERE OF POLITICS

The sphere of politics expanded dramatically during the postwar years. In both east and west governments assumed responsibility for wide areas of economic and social life. At the same time new groups entered into active politics. Where they did not exercise it already, almost everywhere in Europe women were given the vote during or immediately after the war (Portugal and Switzerland finally followed in 1969), and beginning in the 1960s many governments lowered the voting age for both men and women from 21 to 18. These measures greatly enlarged the electorate, though in the one-party states of eastern and southern Europe the immediate effects were minimal. In western Europe many women voted for conservative candidates; thus, the reign of the Christian Democratic parties depended in part on this enlargement of the electorate. This was counterbalanced in turn by the increased presence of youth, who overall tended to vote more 'leftist' than their elders and whose votes contributed to the increasing strength of socialist and communist parties. The decades after 1945 also saw a greater parliamentary presence for the working classes. Theoretically, the regimes of eastern Europe were workers' governments; the successes of the socialist parties in western Europe also gave an increased importance to the concerns of the working class. Leftist parties gave prominence to social questions and were characterised by a high level of participation on the part of the traditional blue-collar working class and the new white-collar working class. The proletariat and lower middle class were thereby incorporated into parliamentary politics in a substantially new fashion.

The widening of parliamentary politics by no means meant the end of extraparliamentary activity. Trade unions continued to exert strong political influence and to mount their independent actions, such as strikes. Britain and Italy saw continual rounds of strikes by various unions protesting against government policy; in eastern Europe, where unions were firmly under the control of the ruling parties, strikes could disrupt and even topple governments. Violence, both collective and individual, was a recurring feature of extraparliamentary politics which called into question the official ideologies of political consensus and social stability. Demonstrations and riots were frequently put down by police. When the police failed, the army moved in; street battles took place in Budapest in 1956, in Prague and Paris in 1968 and in Athens in 1973; Northern Ireland was a continual battleground. Kidnapping, bombing and assassination played counterpoint to incidents of mass violence. From 1968 to 1975, there were annually in Britain 81 bombings and 34 letter bombs; in Italy, 24 bombings, 5 skyjackings and 4 political murders. In France, several attempts were made to assassinate President De Gaulle; in Spain, the prime minister was assassinated by Basques; in Italy, a former prime minister and head of the Christian Democratic Party was taken hostage and later killed by a far-leftist group; in Britain, the queen's uncle was murdered by Irish terrorists.

Groups using terrorism systematically included the Basque ETA separatists, the Italian Red Brigades, the Irish Republican Army (IRA) and the German Baader-Meinhof group. Such groups argued that they were employing direct action against their political and class enemies and that violence was a legitimate means of overthrowing the establishment. Such war could be waged against the system as a whole or against representatives of the system – thus, the kidnapping and 'kneecapping' (the practice of shooting the victim in the knees) of Italian businessmen and political figures. Acts of terrorism posed questions about the response of the state and society. The British government's refusal to treat with the IRA led to the deaths of hunger strikers and the West German government was accused of mistreating imprisoned dissidents; the Italian government's refusal to negotiate with kidnappers led to the death of some of the hostages. In eastern and southern Europe, political dissidents were imprisoned or exiled. Here the state itself could be an agent of terror to its opponents and individual rights counted for little. In western Europe too, however, police demanded and received broad powers of search and detention in cases of suspected terrorism, and all citizens found their privacy and freedom correspondingly reduced.

One of the most important developments of the postwar period was the emergence of special groups as social and political forces and their use of both parliamentary and extraparliamentary means to make their grievances felt. The student protests of the 1960s and 1970s provided a prototype for the formation of these groups among dissatisfied elements in society; the women's movement was a prime example. Other groups, whose diversity ranged from ethnic groups to immigrants, from homosexuals to followers of religious creeds, demanded recognition and improvements in their status. Some groups contended that they were 'marginal' – different from the majority of the population because of their customs, beliefs or behaviour and therefore relegated to a peripheral and inferior status in a society which sought either to reject them or 'normalise' them into the mainstream of conduct and ideology. Others saw themselves as a product of 'internal colonisation', exploited politically and economically by the dominant groups. Yet all saw in their status a positive focus for self-identification and the basis for a cultural resurgence and political protest.

Youth and the crisis of 1968

The education system, particularly the university sector, trained future members of the elite, whether the middle class of the west or the intelligentsia of the east. It is not surprising therefore that as university enrolments exploded unrest among university students should reflect broad movements in the surrounding society. In Berlin in 1948 students demanded a more democratic university administration after the expulsion of a student journalist critical of administration policy and the level of teaching at the school. The University of Berlin was located in the Soviet sector of the divided city, and support for the demonstration by the western powers led to the establishment of a 'Free University' in their sector. The 1946 charter of the French students' union, UNEF, asserted flatly that 'the student is a young intellectual worker', and in 1949 UNEF successfully demonstrated for the extension of various social security benefits to the student population.

The 1950s and 1960s saw an increase in protest. Some student discontent arose out of the conditions of the universities themselves. In Milan in 1963, students in the Faculty of Architecture demonstrated to demand a review of the curriculum, and four years later the students occupied the faculty and (with the support of a number of professors) ran the faculty for an entire academic year. Such protests were responses to overcrowded classes and inadequate facilities – the older universities were generally located in old, cramped buildings in city centres and the newer ones in monolithic, impersonal developments on the outskirts. But they also were protests against rigid curricula, which emphasised rote learning instead of independent work and formal lectures rather than discussion. Subjects were also traditional; only one Italian university, Trento, had a department of sociology in the 1960s, and that university was one of the sites of demonstrations in 1965. University staff were sometimes sympathetic; they were badly paid and an enormous gulf existed between the lowly-paid lecturer and the professor, who had almost authoritarian powers, including control over finances, subjects and teaching assignments.

But student protests were not restricted to academic matters. Since the state controlled the universities in all European countries, protest against the university administration was, indirectly, a blow at the government. Furthermore, national political questions could also spill over into university politics. When the German student union, the SDS, disagreed with the Socialist Party's 1959 Bad-Godesberg manifesto which adopted a revisionist line (and, in the students' eyes, betrayed Marxism), the party expelled the organisation, which then became the spearhead of university protest. At the University of Rome in 1965 a student was killed by neo-fascists and the resulting demonstration toppled the rector. The Algerian War politicised French students against the conservative government, while the unsuccessful revolutions in eastern Europe in 1956 were vital to the formation of the so-called New Left in Britain in the years afterwards. The American war in Vietnam was a catchpan of protest with widespread demonstrations against colonialism in general and American imperialism in particular.

Student movements also expressed a range of ideas on social issues. At the University of Uppsala, Sweden, for example, the Verdandi Student Society (which dated from 1882) organised a 1961 meeting of atheists from which Christian apologists were excluded; four years later the group held a four-day symposium on sex roles and in 1966 a teach-in on Swedish class society; in Stockholm a student symposium in 1964 on sex and society included the showing of a six-minute pornographic film. In the Netherlands a student group known as the Provos disrupted the wedding of the crown princess in 1966 and later organised a series of street 'happenings' combining carnival with political protest. In eastern Europe students were among the most prominent protesters against the communist regimes. In Hungary the Petofi Circle, founded in 1956, organised meetings for students on political and cultural topics and became the centre of protest which culminated in the anti-Russian uprising. In Czechoslovakia students battled Soviet troops sent in to crush the reforms of 1968, and in 1969 a student immolated himself to protest the abandonment of liberalisation. In Poland students and intellectuals played a part in the change in government in 1970.

The mixture of carnival, social protest, demands for university reform and confrontation with the government came together in 1968. Almost every university in western Europe was affected. Demonstrations at the Universities of Milan and Trento spread and the Italian university system was virtually paralysed by February; a riot and mass arrests followed in Rome. In West Germany the attempted assassination of a student radical, 'Red' Rudi Dutschke, provoked massive protests by students. In Copenhagen 20,000 students protested.

The longest and most important demonstrations were in Paris. The French tertiary system was particularly rigid, and a plan to reform the universities had increased government control over students' education. A particular point of friction was the University of Paris campus in the suburb of Nanterre, a poor neighbourhood with a large number of immigrant workers and a half-finished university. In 1966 and 1967, there had been numerous protests against the rigidity of the system; rumours held that the government was keeping files on student activists. An attempt was made to transfer one of them, Daniel Cohn-Bendit, from Nanterre to the central Sorbonne campus. By March 1968 tension was high, and a committee in sympathy with the Viet Minh had organised protests against American establishments throughout Paris at the same time. On 22 March about 600 to 700 students led by Cohn-Bendit organised a meeting and occupied the Nanterre administration building; the head of the university closed the school 'temporarily'. Easter recess interrupted the demonstrations, but they began again when students returned from the vacation late in April. Cohn-Bendit was arrested, allegedly for assaulting a right-wing student, but soon released.

In May the demonstrations spread to the Sorbonne, the oldest part of the University of Paris, located in the central Left Bank. Students congregated in the University's main hall; the rector ordered it evacuated; police arrested between 500 and 600 students. The Latin Quarter exploded. Barricades went up in the neighbourhood on 6 May, demonstrators occupied other buildings (including the Odéon Theatre and the École des Beaux-Arts), 20,000 students massed in the Latin Quarter and between 30,000 and 50,000 marched down the Champs-Elysées singing the *Internationale* on 7 May. On 10 May, the protest turned nasty, as students and riot police confronted each other across the 60 barricades on the Boulevard Saint-Michel and the Boulevard Saint-Germain. The students hurled paving stones, and the police used tear gas, rifle butts and clubs against the students; at the end of the night 400 had been injured and 460 arrested, and 188 automobiles had been damaged or destroyed.

Now one of the trade unions came to the defence of the students, and a general strike on 13 May brought between 500,000 and 1,000,000 protesters into the streets of Paris – by now, every university in France was the site of demonstrations and most businesses in the country were closed. Four days later, while strikes continued, the Renault car factories were occupied. On 24 May the communist-affiliated trade union organised its own demonstration, which drew 150,000 participants, and another demonstration grouping students and those in non-communist unions drew 100,000. Again there was violence in which one person was killed and hundreds wounded. The same day General De Gaulle, who had recently returned from a foreign trip, announced that an electoral consultation would be held. On the following day, however, some ten million workers were still on strike. The Minister of Education resigned, and the leftist leader and later president François Mitterand called for the establishment of a provisional government.

Meanwhile, De Gaulle vanished from Paris – some assumed he had gone to his country estate to write his own resignation. In reality, he made a quick trip to Germany to speak to the commander of the French troops there; the purpose of his visit was uncertain, but critics were unanimous that it was not unconnected with the disturbances back in Paris. De Gaulle returned to Paris on 30 May and went on television to declare that the assembly would be dissolved and elections held. Disturbances continued in Paris for the next fortnight, marked by demonstrations and the death of a young striker killed by the riot police. The government outlawed the far-left political groups, and on 16 June the police occupied the Sorbonne. A week later, the Gaullists won an overwhelming victory in the general elections, and by the end of the month the would-be revolution had come to an end.

The posters of May 1968 graphically portrayed the feelings of the students. One was a silhouette of General De Gaulle with his hand over a boy's mouth and the slogan: 'Be Young and Shut Up' – a commentary on the fact that the legal age of majority was still 21. Another well-known poster showed a brick with the caption, 'For those less than twenty-one years old: here is your voting ballot'. Another was a conjugation exercise: 'I work, you work, he works, they profit'. Some were humorous banners showing the intellectual currents of the times: 'Free contraception, free aphrodisiacs and free psychoanalysis'. The meetings in the Odéon Theatre and the Sorbonne amphitheatres mixed political grievances against the heavy-handed Gaullist regime and the ossified university system with a profusion of social and cultural demands by the student masses influenced by the philosophies of the New Left, Trotskyism, Maoism and the inheritance of Sartre's brand of existentialism. 1968 is best seen not as a *révolution manqué*, but as a crystallisation of the social and political trends of the 1960s – from the expansion of universities to the politics of neocolonialism.

The level of student activity of the 1960s, tied both to the political context and the education revolution of which it was a part, was not repeated. Governments quickly learned to combine concession with repression. Specific reforms robbed radicals of part of their constituency. Protest could also be cut off at the source; Sweden reduced annual university admissions by a third, the cuts coming in the arts faculties and leaving science, engineering and medicine unaffected. The harsher economic climate of the late 1970s had the same effect. Most importantly, however, in any violent confrontation between unarmed protesters and armed police or military units, the latter always won. However, the student demonstrations provided the tactics for future protests, including petitions, posters and organised marches, and they provided the début of many later activists. The majority chose the techniques of highly-publicised but non-violent confrontations; a minority chose selective acts of terror to publicise their causes.

Women and feminism

One of the most important changes in postwar society was the emergence of women as a distinct social group demanding political and economic rights. Women's place in European history had generally been marked by legal inferiority. The simple granting of the vote was a long process, completed only in 1969. And even this political emancipation was slightly misleading, for few women attained positions of political power. The paradox in the 1940s was that women were gaining a political voice and were becoming more important in the workforce and at the same time suffering legal discrimination and social inferiority. Simone de Beauvoir's *The Second Sex*, published in 1949, highlighted the plight of women who for centuries had been reduced to the role of free household servants, childminders and sexual objects; the submission had nothing to do with their physical or mental capacities but to the domination of women (and of society) by men. De Beauvoir – herself one of France's leading intellectuals – thus sounded a clarion call for an autonomous movement of women's liberation to redefine women's social role and to work for an equalisation of their status. Several decades passed before the call was translated into action; only in the 1960s, in the wake of the student rebellions of 1968, did the women's liberation movement begin to produce ideological works, pamphlets, petitions and demonstrations as women took their campaign into the streets. Significant numbers of women became feminists after being patronised and exploited by the male leaders of radical student movements.

Gradually, law courts did rule that constitutions gave equal legal rights to women and men, and new laws replaced the old ones which had made women inferior to their husbands. Other statutes dealt with matters affecting women such as divorce, abortion and illegitimate births. Divorce had always been a serious source of contention in European society because European religions saw matrimony as a life-long union, uniting husband and wife 'until death do you part'. Grounds for divorce or annulment of the marriage were traditionally restricted to such conditions as non-consummation or adultery. Gradually the grounds were broadened in the nineteenth and early twentieth centuries to include such problems as life imprisonment, mistreatment of the spouse or insanity, but the guiding principle was still that divorce was a judicial procedure in which some degree of fault or guilt must be proved. After the Second World War, however, substantial legal changes made divorce easier to obtain and also non-judgmental. In Britain and the Netherlands, for instance, 1969 laws permitted divorce on the basis of the irretrievable breakdown of marriage and allowed divorce by mutual consent. Divorce was instituted for the first time in Italy in 1970 over the opposition of the Catholic Church; Belgium revised its divorce law in a more liberal direction in 1974 and France followed suit the next year. In Sweden, marriage became a simple private contract, dissolvable at will. In eastern Europe, there was also some liberalising of divorce. In the Soviet Union, for example, the law was changed in 1968 to make divorce an administrative act rather than a judicial one. The result of the changes, predictably, was an increase in the incidence of divorce. In the Soviet Union, where divorce was least common, there were 1.3 divorces per thousand residents in 1960, and 6.6 twenty years later. In western Europe one-third to one-half of all marriages ended in divorce by the 1970s.

Even more contentious than divorce was abortion, which various groups considered outright murder, but which many women demanded as a civil right. The Soviet Union had become the first country to permit abortion on the request of pregnant women in 1920, but fifteen years later abortion was prohibited. Both Denmark and Sweden passed laws permitting abortion in 1937. Other countries loosened regulations – partly because of the number of illegal abortions taking place and the frequent danger to the life of the woman. Hungarian and Polish laws were liberalised in 1956, Czech in 1958 and Yugoslav in 1969; the east was far less restrictive than the west. Laws generally set certain limits on abortion, allowing it to take place, for example, only during the first twelve weeks of pregnancy and requiring a doctor's certification that the woman's physical or mental health was endangered by the unwanted pregnancy. Even in countries with stricter regulations, abortion was often allowed in the case of foetal abnormality, rape or incest.

Another legal problem affecting women was the issue of children born out of wedlock and their rights to support and inheritance. Sweden was the most liberal in this as in many other social areas, and the lack of opprobrium attached to single-parent households or unwedded parents was apparent in statistics of illegitimacy. In 1956 10.2 per cent of Swedish children were born outside wedlock, but the figure was 21.7 per cent in 1971 and 37.5 per cent in 1979. The proportion of illegitimate births was almost as high in other Nordic countries and showed the same tendency to rise; in the late 1970s the rates began to increase in western and southern Europe as well.

These social and legal changes did not assure equality for women; most women were still underpaid and underrepresented in the higher social echelons. In the late 1970s, only 38 of 518 deputies in the West German Bundestag and only 19 of the 635 Members of Parliament in Britain were women. But the laws did begin to correspond both with women's demands and with the new social trends in Europe. If they did not guarantee women's accession to levels of political and economic importance commensurate with their skills, they did at least abolish traditional legal restrictions to their advancement.

The position of women in eastern Europe differed from

that in the west. The Bolshevik Revolution of 1917 promised to liberate women, and Lenin's government set up a women's section in the Communist Party, headed by his colleague Alexandra Kollontai. Immediately following the revolution, divorce and abortion were legalised, civil marriages replaced religious ceremonies and illegitimate children were given the same rights as those born in wedlock. Under Stalin, however, most of these measures were reversed, and the women's section disbanded. The aim of the Communist Party under Stalin was to ensure the entry of all women into the workforce; the demands of the Soviet industrialisation campaign mandated such an approach. That effort was largely successful; in the postwar years 86 per cent of Soviet women worked outside the home. Soviet officials prided themselves on the integration of women and the equal opportunities offered; 44 per cent of all engineers were women, 75 per cent of all medical personnel, 39 per cent of all scientists. Yet a distinct occupational segregation continued to exist; of the medical personnel, 90 per cent of pediatricians were women and almost all nurses, but only 7 per cent of surgeons; of the women engineers, only 1.4 per cent worked at managerial levels. Women typically earned between two-thirds and three-quarters of the average man's wages at the same level of expertise, about the same ratio as in the west. Furthermore, women were still expected to do all the household chores in a resolutely patriarchal society, imposing a 'double day burden' of labour inside and outside the home, again as in the west. An embryonic women's liberation movement protested the situation in 1979; its leaders were exiled or otherwise silenced.

Homosexuals

A similar creation of a cultural presence and political contestation issued from an entirely different quarter. Homosexuals came into public attention immediately after the war with the publication of the report *Sexual Behaviour in the Human Male* in 1948. The author, Alfred Kinsey, contended that fully 37 per cent of the male population had some homosexual experience and 4 per cent were exclusively homosexual. Nine years later a British parliamentary commission published the Wolfenden Report, which recommended that the laws which made homosexual behaviour an offence should be abolished. Meanwhile, a number of law reform organisations had been born, including the revival of the Sex Education Society in Britain in 1947 and the Homosexual Law Reform Society founded in 1958; in France a new homophile organisation, Arcadie, was established in 1954; similar organisations were set up in the Netherlands and Denmark. These groups demanded changes in legislation which would remove homosexual behaviour between consenting adults from the list of crimes. Changes in laws took years to achieve; in Britain, the law was not changed until 1967 and in France not until 1982. Such law reform resulted from the work of the groups established in the 1940s and 1950s, but also from a new militancy born in the 1960s and early 1970s. In 1968 homosexual tracts and petitions were distributed by some of the student rebels. In 1969 a well-known New York homosexual bar, the Stonewall Inn, was raided by police, and the clients fought back, an incident which marked the beginnings of the contemporary 'gay rights' movement. This movement advocated not assimilation into heterosexual society, as did the old reformist organisations, but the creation and maintenance of a gay identity – evidenced by the word 'gay' preferred to the old terms of homosexual and homophile. The gay movement also demanded more than just the abolition of outdated laws; it insisted on guarantees of equal opportunity and protection of rights as well. Very often, the gay rights groups were allied with the new left or with renegade political parties.

Along with political militancy went cultural manifestations of gay life. A number of philosophical and historical works began to analyse homosexuality and social attitudes to it from the homosexual's point of view; Guy Hocquenhem's *Le Désir homosexuel*, published in 1972, began with the challenging statement: 'What creates a problem is not homosexual desire, but the fear of homosexuality' on the part of the majority. In the 1970s a wave of publishing saw the appearance of gay newspapers in most west European nations and a number of novels with gay themes. In major cities gays congregated in certain neighbourhoods, complete with bars, discotheques, restaurants, bookshops and areas for casual encounters; such 'gay ghettos' marked the maturation of a gay subculture, and cities like Amsterdam, Paris and Munich gained reputations as gay centres in Europe.

These changes did not end discrimination; in Eire, Gibraltar, Rumania, the Soviet Union and parts of Yugoslavia homosexual acts were still illegal; elsewhere in Europe, the age of consent ranged from 15 to 21 and was often different for homosexuals and heterosexuals. Gays were still frequently forbidden to hold certain jobs, particularly posts in the military or certain branches of the public service. Harassment of gays continued by police and by right-wing Christian groups – most churches still condemned homosexuality. But the emergence of homosexuality and the establishment of a gay subculture created, for the first time in modern European history, a militant and open group campaigning for an alternative sexuality. The emergence of gay liberation, as well as the visibility of other contestatory factions, showed the close link between social and political developments and pointed to some of the specific characteristics of postwar Europe.

National minorities

A widespread and dramatic example of the resurgence of marginals was that of ethnic groups. Despite decades and sometimes centuries of work by centralising states, particularly through educational institutions attempting to create or impose a 'national' language and culture, most European states remained mosaics of cultural groups, divided by language especially, but also by religion, social customs, levels of economic development and political attitudes. The policies of central governments varied, but ethnic resurgence continued and spread, new groups awakened and protests continued against government programmes regarded as half-hearted or incomplete. In few cases were the national questions resolved, and nationalism, a centrepiece of European culture and politics since the French Revolution, remained a divisive issue.

Such contestatory actions affected almost all of Europe. In the United Kingdom the old civil war in Ulster continued between the radical Provisional IRA representing the Catholics and the paramilitary bands of Protestants. Assassinations, bombings and street violence became regular features of life in Belfast despite the drastic repressive measures taken by British forces, and the violence was exported to Britain. Attempts to 'solve' the Northern Ireland question failed; the issue dominated Irish politics and kept relations between Eire and the United Kingdom delicate. The Irish government supported unification of Ulster with Eire but maintained a strong line against the Provisional IRA and its terror tactics; a poll in 1979 found that one in five Irish citizens supported the aims of the Provisional IRA. Meanwhile, new autonomist groups in Scotland and Wales demanded regional political powers and greater support for their language and cultures, demands related to claims for better treatment for the depressed mining areas of Wales and the economically undeveloped highlands of Scotland. Politically, militancy crystallised in the election of Members of Parliament from the Scottish Independentist Party and in calls for 'devolution', the creation of regional assemblies. One major attempt was made to reorganise the administration of Britain by creating regional parliaments for Scotland and Wales. Parliament was not keen on the initiative, constitutional questions were unresolved and the electorate lacked enthusiasm; voters in Wales rejected the proposal, while those in Scotland failed to give it the necessary majority.

In Belgium the expansion of the central government bureaucracy, far from fostering national unity, only stressed the growing polarity between the southern French-speaking Walloons and the Flemings in the north, and the growing resentment of both against Brussels. This divisive issue dominated the postwar era and coloured the debate over all other questions – even the granting of independence to the Congo. It also led to the fragmentation or polarisation on linguistic lines of the old political parties such as the Christian Social Party and Socialist Party. The divisiveness of the issue emerged immediately in the postwar period over treatment of suspected collaborators and in the so-called 'royal question' when Leopold III was forced to abdicate in 1951, as Flemings supported him while Walloons did not. Later administrative, educational and economic policies proved equally contentious. In the background lay the continued economic decline of Wallonia, especially its steel industry. In 1960 the government's austerity programme, largely a response to the loss of revenue from the Congo, led to strikes in Wallonia on the grounds of economic discrimination and to the recall of some NATO troops from Germany. In 1966 there was similar trouble and in 1968 the country divided dangerously again over an attempt to impose linguistic rules on the Catholic University of Louvain. In 1971 a new constitution reduced the power of the central government and in 1980 further constitutional changes created separate regional governments for Flanders and Wallonia.

Similar protests took place in France, a nation with distinct ethnic groups on all its borders, including Basques, Bretons, Flemings, Alsatians, Catalans and Corsicans. A cultural resurgence included the establishment of schools to teach the 'national' languages, which in many cases are entirely different from standard French – Breton, for instance, is a Celtic language – and the publication of literature and documentation in these languages. In the case of the Corsicans and Bretons, the most militant of the national groups in France, cultural revival was accompanied by violent political protest, including bombings (the château of Versailles was damaged by Breton nationalists). Although violent acts were punished by the state, the government made some gestures to regional groups, such as the Breton cultural charter issued by the French president during his visit to the region in 1977 and the establishment of a university in Corsica.

Spain also had a history of regional protest and violence. Regional autonomy was an important issue in the civil war. Franco revoked the statutes of autonomy granted by the republican government to Catalonia and the Basque region but failed to extinguish separatist sentiment. Protest in the Basque lands was particularly violent. A wealthy, heavily industrialised area which spilled over the Pyrenees into France, the region maintained some particular characteristics, such as the large number of agricultural and industrial cooperatives which had succeeded in reorganising much of the Basque economy. But the distinguishing characteristic of the Basques, or Euskadi as the Basques call themselves, was their language, a difficult language unrelated to any other European tongue and of uncertain origin. The Franco regime attempted to suppress the language and local culture and milked the region of profits to support less developed areas. In 1959, Basques organised a clandestine society, the Euskadi Ta Azkatasum (ETA) – Basqueland and Liberty – to fight for their rights. ETA adopted a hard line, claiming Basque independence and employing terrorist tactics. In the ten years after 1965 the organisation assassinated close to 40 high-ranking Spanish officials, including Spain's prime minister in 1973, as well as perpetrating numerous kidnappings, bombings and acts of sabotage. Industrial unrest added to separatist sentiment. In 1962 some 45,000 Andalusian miners went on strike for two months, and they were followed by 70,000 Catalan and 50,000 Basque strikers, the beginning of the wave of protests by workers against the regime. Only after the death of Franco did Madrid relent; in 1977 the Basques were allowed to fly their national flag and in 1979 regional statutes of autonomy were voted by the Cortes. But ETA argued that such measures did not satisfy its national aspirations, and violence continued.

Eastern European nations such as Czechoslovakia, Yugoslavia and Bulgaria also suffered from conflicts among ethnic groups. In the Soviet Union Stalin had pursued a ruthless policy of outright Russification of the Soviet Union's numerous national groups. Khrushchev's de-Stalinisation speech of 1956 included a repudiation of his predecessor's national policies, which opened the door to a number of local ethnic movements and repressed nationalisms, including the Baltic peoples, Byelorussians, Georgians and Jews. The Ukrainians experienced a cultural revival after 1956 which began in the intelligentsia and spread to the masses. Ukrainians felt that they were being demographically submerged in the Russian population, and that they were suffering economic discrimination as well. Of over 4,400 instructors at the 8 universities in the Ukraine, only about half were Ukrainians and fewer than 1,500 lectured in the Ukrainian language. Soviet authorities were unhappy with the Ukrainian revival, which questioned some of the tenets of Marxism-Leninism, attacked the authority of the state and might have inspired other nationality groups. In 1961, seven dissident Ukrainian lawyers were put on trial and in 1963, Moscow suppressed celebrations of an important Ukrainian holiday. Dissent continued, and Khrushchev's failure to deal forcefully enough with Ukrainian nationalism played a role in his overthrow in 1964. The Brezhnev government stepped up the anti-Ukrainian campaign. The library of the Ukrainian Academy of Science and the historic Vydebetski monastery burned under suspicious circumstances, and many Ukrainian dissidents were exiled to Siberian labour camps.

8
THE CONTINUING CRISIS

THE PATTERN OF DEVELOPMENT

The experience of the 1970s and 1980s contrasted sharply with that of the 1950s and 1960s, though again the suspicion that conditions might have changed spread only gradually. A recession in 1970–71 was quite widespread and long-lasting, and Swedish output actually declined, but the boom seemed to return in 1973. Then in 1974–75 total output declined in nearly all western European countries for the first time since the 1930s. Another boom year followed in 1976, but recession returned in 1977 and again from 1979 to 1982, when most countries experienced declines in output. 'Recession' began to sound less like an analytical concept and more like an official euphemism intended to divert attention from some unpleasant facts. In all western European countries average rates of growth of total output were lower and fluctuations in the rates greater during the 1970s and 1980s than during the late 1950s and 1960s. Some of the contrasts were striking; for instance, during the 1970s Swiss industrial output grew at less than one-tenth the rate maintained during the 1960s. Moreover, though the eastern European economies had continued to expand relatively rapidly until the mid-1970s, beginning in the late 1970s they too slowed. In both western and eastern Europe the new lower rates of economic growth were accompanied by substantial increases in prices – 'stagflation', a new phenomenon which tested the ingenuity of both neoclassical and Marxist economists.

As the great boom resulted in part from a number of relatively fortuitous factors, so the slower growth of the 1970s and 1980s resulted in part from the disappearance of those same factors. Population grew more slowly, and the initial explosive increases in consumer durables passed; consequently, aggregate demand increased at lower rates. The share of agriculture in total employment declined to the point that large increases in productivity could no longer be expected from the simple shift of workers into industry; the rise in the share of the service sector in turn tended to reduce productivity, since workers in the very heterogeneous 'tertiary' areas were on average less productive than workers in industry. Slower growth of world demand reduced potential export markets; the rise of new competitors and a resurgence of protectionism worked in the same direction.

One of the roots of Europe's problems during the 1970s was the high and rising prices of primary products. Western European dependence on petroleum from the Middle East and north Africa suddenly catapulted into the headlines in 1973, and the Organisation of Petroleum Exporting Countries (OPEC) became a convenient scapegoat for the sins of both inflation and depression. However, the OPEC cartel was only effective because widespread development had proceeded to the point where oil was no longer plentiful. Metals, paper, cotton and food were also in short supply, and each contributed to the generally increasing level of prices. In the ensuing years Europeans discovered that supplies of any given resource could be made available if there was a will to find them and if prices rose high enough to warrant their exploitation. The huge deposits of natural gas in the Netherlands, the North Sea oil deposits and Soviet pipelines to deliver oil and natural gas to eastern and western Europe were cases in point.

The financial and political costs of exploiting new resources could be extremely high. After 1973 the Soviet Union began to press other eastern European countries to help finance new oil exploration, new processing plants and new pipelines as the price for continued supplies of Soviet petroleum. Even successful discovery and exploitation of resources sometimes brought problems. The Netherlands, Norway and Britain all suffered from the 'Dutch disease', a depression resulting from exports of primary products. Natural gas and petroleum development created relatively few jobs but produced substantial domestic inflationary pressures. High world demand for gas and petroleum increased the value of the producing countries' currencies, which raised the price of other exports. Higher prices meant poor market prospects, while inflation led to high interest rates; together these factors reduced investment, slowed growth and created stubborn pockets of unemployment.

Prices of raw materials and some agricultural products declined in the mid-1980s. Increased production and the depression of the late 1970s and early 1980s reduced the price of petroleum; countries which had become dependent on petroleum revenues increased output as the prices fell, which only tended to depress the price further. Nearly 9 per cent of the British government's tax revenue was derived from oil, for instance, and British North Sea output rose from 1.8 million barrels a day in 1981 to 2.6 million in 1986. Britain did not belong to OPEC, but even within the cartel members openly exceeded their production quotas in the hope of maintaining their incomes. Other attempts to control international commodity prices also failed; on average primary producers received twenty per cent less for their products in 1986 than in 1980. In the case of sugar, the very high subsidies paid to producers by the United States and the European Community robbed other exporters of their major markets, and the world price of sugar plummeted from 45 US cents a pound in 1980 to less than 5 cents in 1985.

Nevertheless, prices in western Europe continued to increase at an average of some five per cent annually. Food prices rose dramatically, continuously in western Europe and in sudden jumps in eastern Europe. In western Europe this partly reflected world conditions, but in the European Community it also resulted from a complex system of subsidies and intergovernmental payments, the compromise Common Agricultural Policy (CAP) which had replaced the previous national systems of subsidies, tariffs and import quotas. The intent of the CAP was to maintain the incomes of farmers in all member countries. The direct cost absorbed nearly the entire Community budget, and the result raised food prices to consumers far above world levels. The decline in world sugar prices, for instance, did not benefit consumers in the European Community at all. Overall, western European farmers remained more efficient than their eastern European counterparts, but the protective system maintained production of a number of products, especially sugar, wheat and meat, which overseas sources could supply far more cheaply and occasionally led to the production of goods which could not be sold at all, notably the 'butter mountain' and the 'wine lake'.

In eastern Europe, agricultural planners continued to confront the dilemma that agricultural inefficiency resulted in periodic food shortages and unrest in urban centres, but that increases in the food supply required increases in incentives for the farmers, which resulted eventually in rising prices and again in unrest in urban centres. The Russian agricultural plan for 1976–80 was particularly disappointing, as extremely heavy investments and increased incentives resulted in only a nine per cent increase in output. Large grain imports from the United States, Canada, Australia and Argentina covered the deficit but also absorbed foreign exchange which could have been better spent as well as proving subject to political pressure. Nature was unhelpful; eastern Europe suffered fourteen years of bad weather from 1960 to 1980, including some of the worst years on record. Nonetheless, despite the large reductions in the agricultural labour force in both east and west and the ostensibly large scale of eastern European collectives, the problems were similar. There remained too many small farmers, with too little capital, often producing the wrong products. In both east and west the necessary investment and reorganisation were hampered by the opposition of the farmers and by the often delicate political balance on which they exercised disproportionate influence.

Previous long upswings in the European economy had been connected with the introduction of new technologies permitting more efficient use of existing resources. During the 1950s and 1960s Europe benefited from the opportunity to exploit a backlog of new techniques developed during the 1930s, but in addition the stream of new developments continued to widen and deepen. Technological change no longer depended on isolated individual inventions but had become a virtually automatic process dependent only on a perceived need and sufficient funding for the necessary research. It was not an exhaustion of technological options which ended the great boom; however, the changing direction of technological change may have contributed indirectly to the slower rates of growth. Beginning in the 1970s the world economy began to be transformed by the application of electronic technologies in the handling of information through electronic data processing and in the automation of industrial processes through the use of industrial robots. Whether this 'third industrial revolution' would result in an upswing comparable to the second industrial revolution before the First World War or to the boom of the 1950s and 1960s remained in doubt, and Europe's position in the changed economic system also remained unclear. Most of the growth of employment following the Second World War had occurred in the tertiary or service sector of the economy, particularly those areas concerned with collecting and maintaining stores of information and records. A large fraction of those jobs disappeared as information and record keeping was 'computerised', as did other traditional service jobs such as sales clerks and bank tellers. Manufacturing industry, to remain competitive, was forced to adopt new, computer controlled, automated techniques, reinforcing the tendency for manufacturing employment to decline. Belgium's steel industry, for instance, lost some 25,000 jobs between 1978 and 1985, with no firm guarantee that even this planned rationalisation would make the industry truly competitive.

Overall, Europe was not in the forefront of the new technological advance. Though seemingly limitless in extent, the river of technical innovations sprang from only a few restricted origins. A study commissioned by the Organisation for Economic Cooperation and Development in 1970 identified the 100 most significant innovations introduced since 1945; of these 'major innovations', 60 had been introduced in the United States, 14 in Britain and 11 in West Germany, with the remainder scattered across the rest of western Europe and Japan. In the 1980s the United States continued to lead in the development of new techniques, particularly the creation and use of more powerful computers, and Japan had forged ahead in the production of industrial robots and inexpensive production of electronic products. Western Europe enjoyed a few notable successes, such as the application of electronic technology in automobiles, but also suffered some embarrassing failures, such as the expensive attempt to produce a 'French' computer, finally dropped by the French government as an economy move during the recession of 1975. Eastern Europe, especially the Soviet Union, lagged far behind except in certain areas of military importance.

However, electronic technologies declined in price extremely rapidly; in many areas their introduction was therefore not especially costly, and the results could be surprising. For instance, the Italian Benetton firm, founded in 1964, used computers to calculate size variations for its ready-made clothing, to determine the arrangement of pieces for cutting which minimised waste fabric and to control the automatic cutters. The franchised shops were located after computerised market surveys, including analysis of pedestrian flows; stock was ordered at the beginning of each season by computers which also monitored inventories and sales. In 1984 there were some 3,000 Benetton shops throughout the world, and a new one was opening somewhere every day. Benetton employed very few workers in its automated factories. A new firm, it could introduce the new computerised techniques directly and therefore avoided both the expense of modernising outmoded plants and the labour conflicts resulting from changed work patterns and firing of redundant workers which plagued its competitors. For the Italian clothing industry, and for Europe as a whole, the third industrial revolution created opportunities for some but also created conditions for substantial conflict between workers and employers and reduced employment opportunities in older sectors. For relatively small outlays of new capital, certain sectors of the European economy could become vastly more productive; whether the resulting decline in the prices of goods and services would create the conditions for expansion sufficient to absorb all workers remained an open question.

As the boom of the 1960s called forth theories of economic growth, so the 'crisis of the seventies' stimulated discussion of stagnation and decline and revived interest in 'long' cycles of economic development. One of the more interesting and comprehensive analyses of the boom and the subsequent crisis was advanced by Walt W. Rostow. Known in the 1960s for his theory of the 'take-off' into sustained growth, he concentrated his efforts during the 1970s on the elaboration of a model of long economic cycles. Underlying short-term economic fluctuations, argued Rostow, were cycles of 50 years in the prices of primary products – food, energy and industrial raw materials. These price movements in turn reflected investment in the primary sector, which generally could only be undertaken in extremely large units and which had an exceptionally long lead time. The size of the required investments, their long period of gestation and the resulting delays in availability of new primary output all affected the rate of aggregate growth. Thus, the 1950s and 1960s enjoyed low costs of food, energy and raw materials, low rates of interest, generally stable prices and rising real wages. Conversely, the 1970s and 1980s suffered from increasing costs of primary products, rising prices, declining real wages and increasing interest rates reflecting the redirection of capital into large-scale and long-term investment in crucial primary products. Rostow's vision was implicitly optimistic, for the development of new sources of primary products and the introduction of more efficient technologies would eventually result in a new upswing, but his was an optimism of the long run, with little comfort for planners, employers or workers in the immediate future.

Those Marxists such as Ernest Mandel who concerned themselves with the long run took a less optimistic view than Rostow. For Mandel, the successive crises of the 1970s were inherent in the logic of capitalist development, because the 'principal motor forces of the expansion were beginning to wear down'. The high rates of investment maintained through the 1950s and 1960s and the thrust of technical change had a double effect. First, though output increased dramatically, so too did the organic composition of capital, the ratio of fixed capital and raw materials to wages. Second, the boom raised employment and workers' incomes, but in doing so it reduced the rate of exploitation, the ratio of surplus value to wages.

Because capitalist profits were a positive function of the rate of exploitation and a negative function of the organic composition of capital, these developments increased the 'contradictions' in the system. Capitalists had to introduce new technologies to survive, but in doing so as a group they produced more goods than could be sold profitably and lowered the average rate of profit.

Mandel argued that the capitalist economies suffered from excess capacity even during the 'boom' phases of the late 1960s, despite very heavy military expenditures, and that rates of profit were declining continuously after about 1965. The 1970–71 recession was longer and more serious than any seen during the great boom, and the 1974–75 depression was a 'classic over-production crisis' in which production could not be sold at prices which would realise the anticipated rates of return. Normally, prices would have declined; Mandel blamed inflation on the influence of capitalists on governments, which increased the money supply even as they claimed to be combatting inflation in order to maintain capitalist profits.

Mandel foresaw a long period of slow growth, indeed a crisis of the capitalist system itself. In contrast to Rostow he did not expect substantial declines in the price of energy and raw materials, partly because capitalists wanted to protect their investment in high-cost alternative sources. Mandel believed that technical change was continuing to increase capital intensities of production and therefore the organic composition of capital. He also noted that the depressions of the 1970s and 1980s did not reduce the money value of the existing capital stock, because of inflation and because governments did not allow large firms to fail. Finally, strong and increasingly militant labour organisations would resist the attempt of capitalists to raise the rate of exploitation. These factors all lowered the rate of profit; Mandel hoped for revolutionary change, 'rejecting the capitalist system and initiating the construction of a qualitatively different economic system'.

Finally, and even more pessimistically, there were those who suspected that the increased prices of raw materials and high unemployment of the 1970s and 1980s could not be overcome either by the introduction of new technologies or by political change. Projecting increases in demand into the future, they wondered whether the depletion of natural resources had accelerated to a rate which would outrun attempts to overcome rising costs with either new technologies or any conceivable reorganisation of production. They wondered as well whether economic development had already done irreparable harm to the ecological system. Even though estimates of the extent of mineral resources varied according to the assumptions made, 'non-renewable' sources of energy and raw materials were by their very nature finite. Among 'renewable' resources, to take only two examples, the forests along the borders of West Germany, France and Switzerland were in steady decline as a result of atmospheric pollution, and in the Mediterranean several species of fish were threatened by a combination of excessive fishing and pollution.

ECONOMIES IN THE CRISIS

Western Europe

By the late 1960s discussion of Britain's economic problems had produced a substantial pile of books and articles. Nonetheless, even the most pessimistic observers were not prepared for the difficulties Britain experienced in the 1970s and 1980s. The devaluation of the pound in 1967 should have increased the competitiveness of British exports, joining the European Community in 1973 should have opened new markets, and the beginning of production of oil in the North Sea fields should have provided a new export and alleviated the effects of higher energy prices. Instead, devaluation failed to have any appreciable effect until 1969, and then British exports declined during the general recession of 1970–71; membership in the European Community was followed by a further decline in exports due to the world depression of 1974–75; the flow of oil increased export earnings, but other exports sank again in the depression of 1979 and the early 1980s. British exports depended relatively heavily on imported raw materials, and therefore the 1967 devaluation and subsequent downward 'float' of the pound actually increased the costs of producing British exports during the early 1970s. On the other hand, the increased value of the pound caused by oil exports increased the price of other British exports during the late 1970s. Membership in the European Community resulted in large net payments by Britain which went largely to support Irish and Continental farmers, increased British food costs (which led to upward pressure on wages) and increased competition from Continental manufactured goods in the British home market. In consequence, Britain suffered from slower growth (about two-thirds the relatively low level of the 1960s), high rates of inflation (over 24 per cent in 1975) and heavy unemployment (one million or more in most years during the 1970s, rising to four million in the early 1980s).

Britain's problems might be explained as the unique product of historical circumstances and bad luck; however, the difficulties besetting the French economy clearly reflected broad trends. In agriculture, the dramatic increases in efficiency of the 1950s and 1960s had been purchased at the cost of a heavy burden of debt. Tractors were expensive and required further investment in ancillary tools and chemical fertilisers; the rising expectations of farmers and their families had led to further borrowing for improved housing and consumer durables. In the 1970s and 1980s higher interest rates and stagnant demand undermined the farmers' position and led to unrest. French farmers' demands for protection against foreign competition, such as Italian wine and British lamb, led to recurrent crises in the European Community. Outside of agriculture, rates of profit declined throughout the 1970s, and private investment declined absolutely in every year from 1975 to 1982 and stagnated thereafter. France's state sector began to suffer from the same problems which had plagued Britain's nationalised industries a decade earlier, and the demands for increased prices and subsidies contributed to inflation directly as well as crowding private firms out of capital markets. Prices rose at over twice the rate of the 1960s, industrial output increased at only a little over half the rate maintained during the boom and unemployment had risen to over 10 per cent of the labour force by the mid-1980s.

In the 1970s and early 1980s the West German economy remained relatively strong, though only growing at a rate approximately two-thirds that of the 1950s and 1960s. Because of its size, West Germany was often identified as an 'engine of growth' for the world economy; however, West Germany depended heavily on exports, which equalled nearly one-third of its gross national product in the mid-1970s, and therefore its strong 'recoveries' from recessions remained suspect as long as there was no sustained expansion elsewhere. In the early 1980s West Germany suffered especially from Japanese competition in export markets. West German technology appeared stagnant, and in some areas such as electrical machinery and electronics the West Germans had slipped badly. The 'easy' gains in productivity realised by shifting workers from agriculture to industry had ceased, and the heavy subsidies paid to the remaining farmers imposed a burden on the rest of the economy. The institutions which had appeared 'stable' now began to appear 'rigid' and 'inflexible'. Waves of strikes tended to be led by migrant workers who felt the unions did not represent their interests; at the same time, very high unemployment benefits could lead to a combination of unemployment and a labour shortage, as in 1977–78. The large industry and banking groups tended to protect existing investment rather than introduce new techniques. The government removed the controls on interest rates in 1968, and competition among banks for deposits tended to drive all rates up. The government also attempted to control inflation, and prices in West Germany in fact rose at only five per cent a year through the 1970s and around two per cent in the 1980s, compared to an average for western Europe of nine per cent in the 1970s and five per cent in the 1980s. However, the restrictive monetary policy which helped to contain inflation also raised interest rates, reducing the attractiveness of investment. Fixed capital in manufacturing rose by only a third from the early 1970s to the early 1980s. Slower growth of capital stock meant slower introduction of new techniques, and lower investment meant unemployment, which fluctuated around one million through the 1970s, rose to two million in 1982 and remained at nine per cent of the labour force in the mid-1980s.

The 1970s and 1980s brought slower growth and inflation to the small countries of western Europe, though Switzerland and Austria fared better than the Low Countries, largely because they were able to dismiss thousands of migrant workers and send them home. Swiss and Austrian industry lost export markets, partly because low rates of inflation raised the value of their currencies but also because of changing technology; for instance, watches and sewing machines changed from complex assemblies of mechanical gears and linkages to relatively simply-constructed electronic devices, and the Swiss lost their previous advantage. Nevertheless, Switzerland still enjoyed the highest per capita income in Europe, and Austria also appeared relatively fortunate. Though Swiss industrial output declined by ten per cent from 1974 to 1975, the number of registered unemployed persons rose from a mere 64 to 6,527; most of Swiss unemployment was in fact 'exported' to Italy. In Belgium and the Netherlands, the necessity to support relatively larger numbers of unemployed workers and subsidies to ailing industries led to government deficits, which contributed to the general increase in prices. The Belgian steel and textile industries suffered particularly heavy losses, and Dutch industrial exports were hampered by the effects of the new natural gas industry. In both countries government borrowing restricted the capital available to industry.

By the early 1970s the Nordic countries had all developed affluent economies, but all also were precariously balanced on the edge of uncontrolled inflation combined with slumping exports and unemployment, and all were finding the balance increasingly difficult to maintain. All attempted to halt inflation indirectly through intermittent 'austerity' programmes and directly through price freezes (imposed by Denmark and Sweden in 1970, Finland in 1974, Sweden again in 1977 and Norway in 1978), and all failed. The commitment of all four to full employment and expanding social welfare measures, high levels of taxation (Sweden's value added tax and Denmark's income tax were the highest in Europe) and rising prices charged by the large and expanding government sectors all pressed the price level upwards. In addition, affluence led to higher per capita levels of energy consumption, and Finland, Sweden and Denmark all required large energy imports. Norway possessed large petroleum reserves but oil exports 'overheated' the small domestic economy and led to inflation; Norwegian exports other than oil did poorly, and the government used oil revenues to subsidise export industries, purchased distressed shipyards and coal mines outright and finally resorted to devaluation in 1978. Denmark's membership in the European Community did not improve the Danish balance of payments; inflation and unemployment both remained high. Finland stagnated through the mid-1970s, recovered in 1979 following a large devaluation and then slumped again as world demand declined. Swedish export industries collapsed in 1977; Swedish industry had fallen behind in the introduction of new techniques, and wages were high. A devaluation brought some recovery, but unemployment and attempted cuts in government spending led to labour unrest. In 1980 one-fourth of the Swedish labour force was either on strike or locked out, the worst disputes since the agreement between unions and employers signed in 1938. Through the mid-1980s Sweden was locked into a pattern of slow growth accompanied by moderately high inflation. Official unemployment was low, but the figures omitted those enrolled in government 'retraining' programmes.

The decline in the western European economies hurt the south; export markets and tourism declined and a large number of migrant workers returned. Imports continued, however, and increased in price; the southern countries imported some four-fifths of their energy requirements, and Italy's food imports had risen from one-tenth to two-fifths of consumption since the mid-1960s. In the context of slower growth, the large state sectors in the south proved themselves relatively inefficient. Prices therefore rose even more rapidly than elsewhere, roughly trebling from the early 1970s to the early 1980s. Unemployment – partly the result of repatriation of migrant workers – was high and labour unrest chronic. In Italy, militant labour union activity led large unionised firms to subcontract large amounts of work to small non-unionised firms; this tendency, added to the extensive government subsidies paid to 'artisan' firms (actually, any firm with ten or fewer employees), led to a substantial expansion of small firms in northern and central Italy where the demand for their services was greatest. The expansion of small firms in Italy was also connected to another feature of economic life prevalent throughout the south, the evasion of taxes. Unreported small businesses and second jobs – the so-called 'black economy' – remained by their nature unquantified, but estimates ranged as high as 15 per cent of the Italian labour force and 30 per cent of the Italian gross national product. Attempts at tax reform and elimination of tax evasion, as in Italy in 1971 and Greece in 1978, had little noticeable impact. Membership in the European Community, though bringing net payments to the agricultural sectors of Greece, Spain and Portugal, could have little positive impact so long as the economies of western Europe remained depressed.

Eastern Europe

Soviet growth through the 1970s and 1980s, though more rapid than that of western Europe, was substantially slower than before. The goals of the 1971–75 plan were modest: annual industrial growth of 7.9 per cent, safely under the 8.5 per cent rate maintained since 1961, and a slight increase in the output of consumer goods. Even these limited aims proved impossible to achieve, however, and the targets were revised downward to avoid the embarrassment of a failure to fulfil the plan. Subsequent plans announced even lower targets, and these had to be revised downward as well. The Soviet system continued to do well at those things at which it traditionally excelled. The planning agencies could make and effectively enforce the large-scale decisions affecting allocation of resources among sectors and industries. They also continued to enjoy success in expanding the output of basic industries and fuels – sectors which were often owned by governments in western Europe as well. Finally, where cost was no object, even the most advanced techniques and most delicate sorts of production were well within Soviet capabilities; this was most obviously the case in space research and military technologies. However, the system also continued to do badly at those things at which it had never excelled. Agriculture, starved of capital and with large numbers of workers still labouring under premodern conditions, stagnated. Consumer goods, especially consumer durables, remained in short supply and of poor quality. With the exception of limited types of military hardware, Soviet manufactured goods remained uncompetitive in world markets, and the Soviet Union therefore continued to depend on exports of raw materials to pay for imports of advanced machinery and of food.

In 1979 another round of changes in the management of manufacturing enterprises gave managers greater authority to redeploy labour within their firms (though not to fire workers), instituted new bonuses for precise fulfilment of contracts and increased the importance of quality and increased productivity relative to the quantity of output. However these changes, as had the 'Liberman' reforms of fifteen years before, failed to overcome the essential dilemma confronting Soviet managers. Plan targets remained rigid and often unrealistic, supplies of raw materials and intermediate products remained unreliable and workers remained chronically unresponsive and inefficient. In order to achieve the goals imposed on them by the planning agencies, managers bribed suppliers to ensure delivery and purchased extra supplies on the black market. To pay for bribes and black market purchases managers sold their own products on the black market, and to maintain morale and efficiency among their workers they either ignored or actively connived at black market operations with which the workers supplemented their incomes. Trading for private profit, stealing state property and falsifying state accounts of course were highly illegal, but such 'economic illegalities' were a pervasive and even necessary part of the system, so long as more realistic and flexible means for allocating scarce commodities did not exist.

Soviet authorities knew that hierarchical planning led to rigidity and that the increasingly diverse range of products required not only greater flexibility but also more rapid responses by planning agencies. The data problems were formidable; over six million individual prices were administered by all-union or republic agencies. The solution, obviously, was computers to speed response and improve the interaction of parallel systems. In 1971 the Party Congress authorised the creation of an 'All-State System for the Collection and Processing of Information for Reporting, Planning and Management of the National Economy', and in 1973 a reorganisation of the central ministries was proposed to facilitate the task of central data processing. However, computerisation of economic planning encountered the same problems which bedevilled the economy itself. The main computers had to be modelled on American patterns, and the necessary 'peripherals' remained in short supply because the norms and calculations of bonuses in the plan did not give enough weight to them. Each agency defended its autonomy; this could take a petty form, as for instance in the insistence of the Ministry for Wood and Wood-Processing on producing an 1800-page list of codes for its own products, but took more a serious form in conflicts over the control of the system itself. The structure of the system could not be separated from its effects on the balance of power, for instance in the balance between regional and industrial groupings, central and local power, and civilian and military requirements implicit in the way in which information was collected and utilised. Managers of enterprises at all levels remained unenthusiastic; computerisation did not promise them any tangible rewards but did promise more effective surveillance of their performance – which might hamper their efforts to achieve results with unauthorised or illegal methods.

The economies of east-central Europe continued to grow rapidly through the mid-1970s. However, in the late 1970s all slowed dramatically. Total product actually declined in Poland in 1979 and in both Poland and Hungary in 1980, and throughout the east rates of growth stagnated in the 1980s. The high rates of growth maintained until the mid-

1970s and the low rates thereafter can be explained with reference to rates of investment. Beginning in the 1950s all the eastern economies invested very large fractions of their annual product. The actual amounts are difficult to measure because of official pricing policies – turnover taxes inflated the value of consumer goods, while the prices of capital goods were held artificially low by subsidies. Thus, although the official rates of investment in Czechoslovakia and Poland in 1953 were around 20 per cent of net material product, one western authority calculated that they actually were investing an astonishing 44 and 48 per cent of gross national product respectively. Over time, however (and regardless of whether eastern or western definitions are used), capital-output ratios declined in all the eastern economies. Not only did investment result in continuously smaller increases in output, but labour productivity also rose slowly and remained low compared to western Europe. The east, it appears, overinvested in the favoured heavy industrial sectors while not introducing technological advances rapidly enough. Then in the 1970s rates of investment declined (Poland's capital stock actually declined after 1977 and only recovered slightly in the early 1980s), partly because of the continued drag of backward agricultural sectors and partly because of the need to increase the availability of consumer goods. The declining rate of investment in turn led directly to sharp reductions in the rate of growth of total output.

East-central European governments were as aware of their difficulties as their Soviet counterparts, and during the 1970s all embarked on conscious attempts to increase the efficiency of their economies by importing advanced technology from the west. However, because of their high prices and the generally low quality of their manufactured goods, it was very difficult for them to earn sufficient income to pay for new machinery directly, and they therefore began to borrow from western banks, governments and international agencies. The west was happy to lend, because increased trade with the east was viewed as an opportunity to encourage the growth of 'free market' impulses in the eastern European economies and to loosen the ties binding eastern European governments to the Soviet Union. Both sides proved to have been overly optimistic. The eastern Europeans had no intention of changing their systems and remained dependent on the Soviet Union not only politically but also for supplies of raw materials and energy resources. Some in the east also misunderstood the west; Rumanian authorities, for instance, expected the 'monopoly capitalists' who had lent them money to force a lowering of western tariffs on Rumanian goods so as to ensure repayment of the loans. The slower growth and decline of the world economy which marked the late 1970s and 1980s made it very difficult for the eastern countries to repay their loans, and the burden of debt contributed to the severe economic crises in Poland, Rumania and Yugoslavia and to increasingly difficult conditions throughout the east.

SOCIETY AND POLITICS IN THE CRISIS

Social and political responses to the economic crisis were Janus-faced, looking back to the happy days of the great boom while peering forward from the difficult 1970s and 1980s into an uncertain future. Some important trends continued, giving evidence of the essential stability and resilience of structures which emerged from the Second World War and reconstruction period. However, new tendencies emerged from the crisis as well. Social problems which had seemed vague and distant disturbances suddenly appeared much more tangible and threatening. They challenged the comfortable consensus, and the challenge was made more severe by the scarcity of both economic and political resources. Dissatisfied groups could no longer be absorbed into the system painlessly; as economic growth slowed new payments obviously threatened existing interests. The faith in economic planning, both the western Keynesian and the eastern Soviet models, weakened, and so too did the faith that society and politics could be 'managed' in ways analogous to the economy. But alternative approaches, though they might win elections in the west or force changes of government in the east, only further undermined the consensus without solving the underlying economic problems.

Social trends

Trends in population and social structure continued. The postwar 'baby boom' was now a memory from the previous generation; the decline in birth rates below replacement levels spread from the northwest to the south and east. In the Soviet Union, for instance, low birth rates among the 'Great Russians' tipped the balance in favour of the Islamic peoples in the south and east for the first time. Europeans continued to marry, though often their unions were not formal. Swedish studies suggested that unmarried couples behaved in ways remarkably similar to married couples. Homosexual households became more common and received tacit recognition in some western European countries. The tendency for couples to dissolve their unions also increased. Statistics were unreliable, both because they generally did not include unmarried couples and because where divorce remained unobtainable (for instance in Eire) they did not include separations or the formation of new unions. In northern and western Europe, however, over half of all unions were being ended either by divorce or separation, and the tendency was spreading to the south and east. By placing pressures on less affluent households the economic crisis reinforced these trends; children had become an expensive luxury, and financial problems often lay behind separation.

Fewer births meant a declining share of young people in the population, reversing the movement of the 1950s and 1960s and therefore reversing the economic, social, political and cultural impact of youth. Continued medical advances worked in the same direction; significantly, the area of prime concern for medical researchers shifted to the problems of the old. Fewer new households meant a slower growth of total demand, while the different needs of the elderly assumed a greater importance in the economy. Voting populations aged, despite the general reduction of the voting age to eighteen, and as they did members of the ruling elite adjusted their policies and their styles accordingly. Funds for child care and education declined relative to payments for medical treatment and pensions.

Trends in occupational structure continued, though their

rate and perhaps their significance altered. The number of farmers declined, but slowly; although a small fraction of the labour force, they still made up a large and important interest group. The farm population aged rapidly, for young people left the countryside and showed no inclination to return. Two-fifths of all farmers in the European Community were over 55 years old in 1986, and half of these farmers had no potential successor. Inefficient by world standards, the middle-aged and elderly farm population was also immobile; changes in technique and organisation were difficult and expensive, and the transfer of these older workers to other sectors was difficult. In the west these problems were compounded by the extremely heavy subsidy payments to farmers, particularly the least efficient ones working the worst land. Unable to reduce the subsidies because of the farmers' political importance, the European Community resorted to dumping agricultural produce on the world market, which contributed to the world depression by lowering prices.

The share of manufacturing employment continued to decline, and the numbers of factory workers declined absolutely in several western European countries. Again, the economic crisis accelerated this trend. Industrial workers were one of the main groups affected by the mass unemployment of the 1970s and 1980s. Many of those thrown out of work were older and with limited education and training, precisely the ones who found it most difficult to compete for white-collar technocratic jobs. The service sector continued to increase its share of total employment, but with slower growth the total number of jobs rose less rapidly, and the computerisation of record keeping and sales actually eliminated thousands of the sort of positions which those without extensive training or experience might have filled.

Along with factory workers, it was women and young people who paid the price for the depression. Despite changes in legislation and attitudes, women still found themselves pressed into certain categories of jobs, especially detailed assembly-line work, secretarial and clerical positions and sales, and these were the categories of employment which contracted under the double influence of depression and computerisation. In addition, because women almost always retained custody of children, the rising incidence of divorce and separation forced increasing numbers of women to cope with children alone even as they struggled to earn a living in an increasingly hostile economic environment.

For the young, slower growth most obviously meant fewer jobs, but in addition the thrust of economic change meant proportionately fewer of the available jobs were suitable for those with little experience. A book published in 1984, *No Future: Youth and Society*, summarised the research and conclusions of many sociologists, who argued that long spells without work and the absence of meaningful activity to occupy their time had led to a 'paralysis of ambition' among the young. Compulsory schooling to train them for jobs which would never exist seemed massively irrelevant to many of the young, and discipline in the schools accordingly became more difficult to maintain. Although social welfare payments might cover bare necessities, decent housing and the comforts of consumer society remained outside the reach of the chronically unemployed. As in the 1930s, many therefore turned to petty and not-so-petty crime or came into conflict with the authorities in other ways. Groups of young 'squatters' occupied disused apartment houses in the decaying central city districts, notably in Britain, the Netherlands and West Germany. Violence between the young squatters and the police sent to evict them escalated into serious rioting in Amsterdam in 1980. For others, the weekly soccer matches provided a periodic release from boredom. Pitched battles between supporters of rival clubs seemed to appear on television screens almost as frequently as the matches themselves. For still others, drugs provided a periodic but very expensive escape.

Sociologists also reported an increase in racism among the young, but the young were not alone in seeking scapegoats for economic and social problems. Ethnic minorities, and migrant workers especially, were objects of discrimination and sometimes violence even during the great boom. Despite unemployment and slower growth, western Europe continued to expand the area from which migrant workers were drawn in the 1970s and 1980s. A new tier of countries in the former

French colonies of sub-Saharan Africa and a new group of countries in the Middle East began to send 'guest' workers to take the jobs which western Europeans did not want. In that sense at least the European economy was still expanding. However, in response to the arguments that migrants were taking jobs from local workers and that migrants were becoming a burden on the underfunded and overloaded welfare systems, governments began to attempt to reduce the flow. Britain's 1982 Nationality Act was intended to prevent persons with black, brown or yellow skins from migrating to Britain from former colonies. France pursued a much less restrictive policy until the mid-1980s, but unemployment then led to moves to expel 'illegal' migrants.

Political structures

The economic crisis and the resulting social problems had no impact on the structure of European politics. Indeed, the only three cases where government institutions changed actually represented a further extension of the sort of political consensus which was such a marked feature of the great boom. The three cases were in the south: Spain, Portugal and Greece. Politics in the south after the Second World War differed significantly from the model of northern and western Europe. In Spain and Portugal, dictatorships established in the interwar years endured until 1975 and 1974, respectively; in Greece, the fragile parliamentary system of the early 1950s and 1960s was subverted by the installation in 1967 of a dictatorship which lasted until 1974. Some political scientists, historians and sociologists linked this pattern with particular features of Mediterranean society. These nations were less wealthy than their neighbours to the north; they had small industrial and service sectors, high rates of emigration and high rates of illiteracy. The army maintained a major role in public life, as did the church. The middle classes were small groups in a population still dominated by the peasantry. Clientelism and patronage remained more important connections than more institutionalised relations. These features led some to speak of politics in these three countries in terms of incomplete modernisation; others, particularly

Marxist critics, placed the evolution of southern Europe in the context of imperialism and the division of labour in the capitalist economy.

However, if the presence of authoritarian governments in Spain, Portugal and Greece was striking so was the rapid transition to a parliamentary form of government after the fall of the dictators – a transformation which Italy had made immediately after the war and which now continued. Civil rights were guaranteed and free elections held, and by the mid-1980s all four countries had elected socialist governments. In Spain, Portugal and Greece the previously banned communist parties had deputies in the assemblies; in Italy the communists were allied with the Christian Democrats from 1977 to 1979. All four parties were 'Eurocommunist' and thoroughly reformist. Practically overnight, southern politics had been remodelled on western European lines; membership in the European Community promised greater economic coordination with western Europe as well. Further, easy equations linking parliamentary government to rapid economic growth did not explain southern development, for the transition came in the teeth of the crisis.

In retrospect, the dictatorships in Portugal and Spain were being destabilised by colonial war and violent labour unrest respectively well before the deaths of Salazar and Franco. With the old authority figures gone, none of their would-be successors could maintain the old systems. The coalition of moderate leftists and radicals which seized power in Portugal in 1974 was divided, especially on the question of land reform. However, in contrast to the likely outcome during the interwar years, there was no unbridgeable polarisation of opinions, and there was no rightist counterrevolution. Coalition governments succeeded one another in Italian fashion, the dominant group by the end of the 1970s being the Democratic Alliance (AD). Policy gradually moved away from the more radical measures of the first years of the revolution; the government encouraged foreign investment, an economic austerity programme was adopted in 1977 and Portugal maintained its membership in NATO and applied for membership in the European Community. In 1982 Portugal saw its first general strike in 50 years, and at the end of the year the AD broke up. Nonetheless, elections in 1983 gave the largest number of seats to the socialists, who returned to power.

In Spain certain changes had been made even before Franco's death. The prime minister was assassinated in 1973, but his successor pushed on with a hesitant reformism. In 1974 the government permitted the formation of political associations; however, the new associations were legal only if they had a minimum of 25,000 members in at least fifteen provinces (thus banning Basque parties). Meanwhile, industrial action and political violence increased; 1974 saw the greatest number of strikes in Spanish history, and in the first eight months of 1975 eleven policemen were killed. Then, on 20 November 1975, Franco died. The question was whether the liberal *aperturistas* or the conservative *immobilistas* would have the upper hand in the new Spain. The young king Juan Carlos, Franco's protégé, tested the waters for the first six months under Franco's old prime minister and then, with the appointment of Adolfo Suarez in July 1976, began a programme of reform. Political parties were permitted, and in 1977 even the Communist Party was legalised. Elections in 1977, the first democratic elections in Spain since 1936, brought fully four-fifths of the eligible voters to the polls. The voting gave only eight per cent of the vote to the neo-Francoist Popular Alliance (AP) – proof positive of the readiness of the electorate for change – and only nine per cent to the Communist Party. The big winners were Suarez' Union of the Democratic Centre (UCD) with 34.2 per cent and the Socialist Party (PSOE) with 28.5 per cent.

In October 1977 the parties, including both the victorious UCD and the right and left-wing opposition, met together and signed the Moncloa Pact. This agreement pledged loyalty to the king and resolved to preserve democratic government in Spain; the government promised structural reform of the economy in exchange for increased taxes and wage ceilings; socially, there was accord on the decriminalisation of adultery and the legalising of contraceptives; freedom of assembly and press were guaranteed. Suarez was also working towards an attempted solution of the regional question. In September 1977 the old Generalitat or self-government of Catalonia was re-established, and the government granted a measure of autonomy to the Basque region. Culminating the reform came a new constitution in 1978 which defined Spain as 'a social and democratic state ruled by law', guaranteed the right of nationalities to their autonomy, abolished the death sentence, lowered the voting age to eighteen, no longer recognised Catholicism as the official religion of the state and gave full legal recognition to political parties and trade unions. The whole Francoist system, in short, had been dismantled.

In February 1981 conservative supporters of Franco attempted a coup d'état by marching into the Cortes and firing shots, but quick action by Juan Carlos in stating his commitment to the government and demanding loyalty from the army stopped further action. Violence in the Basque region also continued, and the government proved unable to master Spain's economic difficulties. Meanwhile the UCD was weakened by defections; in 1982, several centrists (including Suarez) withdrew. The elections in that year gave 25 per cent of the vote to the conservative AP, only 7.3 per cent to the UCD and about 4 per cent to the communists; the winner in the election was the PSOE with 46 per cent of the vote and the majority of seats in the Cortes and their leader formed the first socialist government in Spain for 50 years. The new prime minister had to deal with problems new and old, but his mandate was renewed in 1986; in historical terms, the metamorphosis from the Spain of the Franco years was remarkable.

The colonels who seized power in Greece in 1967 moved from coercion to outright terrorism, imprisoning, torturing and murdering their opponents, and opposition to the regime grew steadily and became more desperate as the colonels' tactics became more severe. The funeral of George Papandreou in 1973 was an occasion for a large demonstration against the junta. In the same year, massive protests began at the Athens Polytechnic and other universities; the government sent troops to the Polytechnic, and they killed 34 persons, most of whom were students. Inflation foiled attempts at price controls, and strikes also marked 1973. But it was Cyprus which, having played a role in the colonels' rise to power, proved their undoing. Archbishop Makarios accused the colonels of trying to foment a coup against him to effect union between Cyprus and Greece. In July 1974 a coup did take place. Makarios fled and Turkish troops invaded Cyprus. In Greece the failure of their policy led to loss of support for the colonels within the army, and the junta fell.

With the overthrow of the colonels, former prime minister Constantine Karamanlis returned to Greece from exile. Following a decisive victory in national elections, Karamanlis ended censorship, restored civil liberties and issued a new constitution; he kept up the alliance with the west and campaigned for Greek admission to the European Community. A referendum was held which ended the monarchy; the Communist Party was again legalised. In 1980, Karamanlis was elected president and succeeded as prime minister by another member of his conservative New Democracy Party. The following year, Karamanlis' New Democracy lost the legislative elections to the Panhellenic Socialist Movement (PASOK), whose leader, Andreas Papandreou – son of the former prime minister and himself an American-trained economist of international reputation – became the new head of government. Papandreou had campaigned on a promise to bring democratic socialism to Greece and to adopt a more neutralist line in international affairs. He also promised to stimulate the economy and to introduce wide-ranging social reforms. The new government's policies were somewhat less strident than Papandreou's rhetoric; for instance, American military bases remained in Greece. Meanwhile, economic problems continued to loom and the Cypriot situation remained a stalemate. But Greece, the only country in western Europe to experience a coup since the Second World War, had made the transition again to a parliamentary style of government with conservative and social democratic parties vying electorally for power.

In western, northern and eastern Europe, governments changed but their structure did not. In the west and north the left and right parties alternated in power, but in view of the uniformly dismal economic news neither left nor right succeeded in generating genuine enthusiasm among the voters. This was unfortunate, but those opposed to the ruling consensus threatened to undermine the existing basis of stability without presenting a viable alternative. As the crisis continued the demagoguery of ambitious leaders on the extreme right became increasingly seductive for certain threatened groups, including small shopkeepers, clerks, farmers and unemployed youths. In Britain the National Front's racist opinions appealed to those who blamed coloured immigrants for Britain's woes, and anti-Semitism reappeared in West Germany and Austria. In France the grouping of rightists around Jean-Marie Le Pen achieved substantial success in the conservative electoral victory in 1986. On the left, the British Labour Party deteriorated into open disarray after losing office in 1979 and split into a moderate Social Democratic Federation and a more militant majority which retained the official support of the labour unions. In other countries parties emerged whose prime concern was the environment, of which the West German Greens were the most successful, but without any clear social base in the electorate they seemed doomed to permanent minority status, gaining at most ten to fifteen per cent of the vote. Extraparliamentary protest also continued, some in favour of national minorities within Europe and some directed to issues outside of Europe, for instance the question of Palestine or the revolt in East Timor against Indonesian overlordship. These divisions led some to conclude that western European society had become 'ungovernable' through parliamentary institutions and to hope for a further extension of 'neo-corporatist' representation of interest groups as an alternative.

In the east, another changing of the guard in the Kremlin occurred in the early 1980s. In 1982 Brezhnev died while still in office, as did his two successors in 1984 and 1985. Death and resignation reduced the numbers of the generation that had come to power following the purges of the 1930s. The new leader, Mikhail Gorbachev, typified a younger group whose entire adult lives had been lived in the postwar period. Nevertheless, the Communist Party retained absolute dominance over politics. Where eastern European leaders felt secure they might embark on some cautious reforms.

Bulgarian economic planning was liberalised in 1979, and in Hungary beginning in 1985 the Communist Party put forward more than one candidate for most elected posts. However, in Czechoslovakia many of those who signed the reformist 'Charter of 77' were arrested.

The main challenge to the ruling consensus in eastern Europe came in Poland. The disturbances of 1970 had brought to power Eduard Gierek. For a few years Poland seemed to be back on course. Yet problems multiplied in the 1970s. The 1973 oil crisis had untoward effects on the Polish economy. From 1975 shortages of essential items, especially meat, again appeared. In 1978 the introduction of a production-linked pension plan sparked resentment. In 1980 Polish workers in Gdansk began large-scale protests; in particular they demanded the right to form independent labour unions. A free trade union, Solidarnosc (Solidarity) emerged, headed by a worker named Lech Walesa; Walesa had strong ties with the Catholic Church, and his efforts were blessed by Cardinal Wojtyla, the Catholic primate of Poland. Gierek retired and the new leader who emerged in January 1981 was an army general, Wojciech Jaruzelski. The following year saw a continuation of troubles. Solidarity held a congress which demanded wide-ranging reforms. A farmers' union emerged as well, demanding higher incomes and greater freedom for the small farmers who still predominated in the rural sector. Food shortages continued, which gave rise to 'hunger marches' and further strikes. In December, Jaruzelski imposed martial law and suspended union activities; Walesa was put under detention. The state of martial law lasted for almost a year, during which 10,000 people were detained. Walesa was awarded the Nobel Peace Prize, and Cardinal Wojtyla, now Pope John Paul II, paid a triumphant visit to Poland, but the elite and the system had maintained themselves once again.

POLICY IN THE CRISIS

The Keynesian arguments which seemed to work so well during the great boom were brought into question during the 1970s and 1980s. There arose a new brand of conservatism, variously called monetarism or neoliberalism. Basing their analysis on such thinkers as Frederick Hayek and Milton Friedman rather than Keynes, advocates of the new conservatism argued for a lessening of the role of the state in the economy and expansion of private enterprise. They favoured tax concessions for investors and 'privatisation' of nationalised industries. Private investment would end unemployment, they said, and controlling the growth of the money supply would end inflation. Keynesian deficit spending was out, the balanced budget in; although defence spending was appropriate, welfare schemes were suspect. The neoliberal, conservative and antisocialist groups drew large support from the middle classes and, in Catholic countries, from devout believers. Their ties were with management rather than labour, and they lacked the trade union connections of the socialists and communists. They placed more emphasis on nationalism than the leftist parties, and they adhered to the Atlantic alliance with greater conviction. However, monetarist and neoliberal policies did not solve the economic crisis, and the new ideology remained unsubstantiated in practice.

If economic planners were roughly treated by monetarists and neoliberals and eastern and western political elites by their constituencies, they had largely their own pretensions to blame. In the 1950s and 1960s, although growth in both east and west occurred for reasons often outside the range of government policy, governments willingly took credit and consistently promised even better things for the future. During the 1960s increasingly well-organised groups of farmers, businessmen, workers of all types, consumers, pensioners and would-be pensioners all accepted for debating purposes the principle that governments could create economic growth sufficient to satisfy their demands. In addition, the greatly increased numbers of public employees, not only more traditional forms of bureaucrats but also workers in government and semi-public enterprises, formed another powerful interest group with rising expectations. Military establishments also pressed for larger allocations of resources. To reduce the subsidies, incomes and pensions on which these groups depended became progressively more difficult. To pay for the increasing range of transfer payments, governments in both east and west opted for politically expedient taxes on each enterprise's turnover (in the east) or on value added by a firm in the course of manufacture (in the west – the value added tax or VAT) and increased charges for publicly produced goods and services. Turnover and value added taxes were less obvious in their incidence than taxes on income and property, and hence easier to levy and increase, but they were regressive and directly inflationary. Increased charges for government goods and services affected only limited groups directly and thus aroused little general opposition, but they too were inflationary.

Rising prices were therefore built into the very structure of government policy. In the west, prices began to increase rapidly in most countries in the late 1960s, well before the increases in energy costs which later took most of the blame. In 1968 the governments of Denmark, Finland, France and Spain all froze both wages and prices, Britain and the Netherlands imposed controls on wages in 1968 and in 1969 Greece and Norway both froze prices. In addition, all western governments introduced harshly restrictive monetary and fiscal policies; this resulted in substantial unemployment but did not lower wages or prices, which rose again as soon as controls were lifted.

During the 1970s most western governments pursued 'stop-go' policies similar in form and impact to British policies of the 1960s. Hoping to reduce the rate of inflation and stimulate exports, governments restricted credit, reduced spending and attempted to limit wage increases. The resulting recessions brought unemployment, but prices continued to rise. 'Stagflation' appeared mysterious after the boom of the 1950s and 1960s, but can be seen to have resulted from structural changes which had occurred during the boom years. Governments found themselves confronted by well-organised interest groups which insisted on maintaining the personal incomes of their members. Unemployment and social security payments increased during recessions, as did subsidies to ailing industries, and governments therefore found themselves unable to reduce large segments of their budgets. Temporary freezes aside, governments also found themselves unable to control wages and prices. Interest groups in fact learned to anticipate not only inflation but also increased taxes and government charges, and wage and price settlements therefore acquired a substantial upward bias. Prices set by public and private monopolies or oligopolies of course increased during recessions, and workers employed by government or semi-public enterprises struck for wage increases without compunction since they did not fear unemployment. As a result, prices, wages and government spending tended to increase during recessions. Having failed to halt inflation, governments nonetheless found themselves confronted by heavy political pressure to reduce unemployment and typically responded by easing credit and increasing spending, which increased employment but also raised the rate of inflation.

Thus the response to inflation in 1973 was generally restrictive, the response to the recession and unemployment of the mid-1970s generally expansionary and the response to increased rates of inflation in the late 1970s generally restrictive. The effects on economic growth were apparent; domestic product in western Europe (in constant prices) grew six per cent in 1973, grew two per cent in 1974 and actually declined in 1975 as unemployment swelled. Real growth averaged over three per cent in the three succeeding years then slackened in 1979. In the early 1980s western European economies were in decline, and unemployment had grown to levels not seen since the 1930s. In contrast to the 1930s, however, depression did not bring declining prices. Prices rose at an average of over ten per cent during the recession of 1975 and continued to rise during the depression of the early 1980s. Governments now considered themselves successful if they held annual inflation under ten per cent, yet as recently as the late 1960s increases of five per cent were described as a 'cancer' which would destroy the world's economic fibre. The 'recovery' which began in 1983 finally saw the rate of inflation in western Europe decline to five per cent, but output increased by only three per cent each year and over ten per cent of the labour force was unemployed.

In the east, with prices set by central institutions, inflationary pressures could be concealed but not forever. In the Soviet Union and other eastern European countries prices fixed at artificially low levels resulted in periodic shortages, especially of high-quality foods, medical supplies and consumer durables. Rather than continuously rising prices, eastern European consumers had to contend with sudden violent readjustments in the entire price structure. All eastern Europeans suffered from the doubling of Russian oil prices in 1975 (though the prices remained below western levels). The Hungarian government increased gas and construction material prices from 20 to 50 per cent in 1975, and the Czech government imposed similar increases in the prices of foods and consumer durables in 1977 and energy and clothing in 1979. Sometimes the response was violent as well. The Polish government tastelessly announced large increases in prices of basic food items and consumer durables two weeks before Christmas in 1970, and the ensuing riots toppled the government; similarly in 1980 increased meat prices and warnings of further rises contributed to disorders which again forced a change in government. In the Soviet Union prices increased substantially after 1977, though less dramatically than in Poland and elsewhere. The Russian government blandly insisted that rising prices were 'not inflation' but merely reflections of increasing production costs. Comparison with the west was difficult, and often hampered by discrimination between regions in the distribution of available products. Rural areas in the Soviet Union sometimes suffered real privation in order that supplies in Moscow and other urban centres could be maintained, though official prices remained uniformly low. Overall, however, it was clear that inflationary pressures in the east resembled those in the west, both in their origins and in their severity.

The problems of the period of slow growth were immediate and serious, but across the entire political spectrum those in positions of authority failed to deal with them adequately. In Britain, Margaret Thatcher's conservative government blamed the rising money supply – incorrectly – for inflation and promised to reduce prices, taxes and government spending. Under her administration the money supply, taxes and government spending all increased dramatically, and nearly four million British workers were unemployed in early

1983. Prices continued to rise as well. In France, François Mitterand's socialist government, having retreated from its originally announced goal of egalitarianism and nationalisation, instituted a series of 'austerity' measures to reduce prices – yet government expenditure rose 27 per cent in 1982 and prices continued to rise. In the Soviet Union, Brezhnev's successors did not succeed in improving the low productivity of Russian workers. As Yuri Andropov remarked in an early speech, 'miracles, as they say, don't happen'. Official figures showed Russian growth in 1982 to be the lowest of any year since the Second World War. The new pipeline to export natural gas depended on western European capital and American technology, pointing to the east's triple dilemma of low export income, capital shortage and backward technology, interrelated problems which exhortations to greater effort had done little to alleviate.

NEW RESOURCES AND THE PROBLEM OF NUCLEAR ENERGY

Given that the exogenous factors which promoted growth in the 1950s and 1960s had weakened or disappeared, Europe required increased investment to seek out new resources. To some extent this was happening. Conforming to the prediction of Rostow's theory of long swings, very large investments had been undertaken to discover and deliver raw materials and energy from new sources. The North Sea petroleum discoveries and Dutch and French natural gas were examples. In the mid-1970s a 2,000-kilometre pipeline began to move oil from western Siberia to consumers in eastern Europe and the new natural gas pipeline from Russia to western Europe was an even greater undertaking. Soviet investment, often in cooperation with other eastern European governments, went to exploit Russian raw materials more completely. In the west, meanwhile, much of the flow of funds through the Eurocurrency market was directed overseas into projects designed to fill western Europe's need for raw materials. The resulting expansion of production was one of the factors responsible for the decline in the prices of primary products in the mid-1980s. There were therefore some grounds for optimism; if western Europe's unemployed could be put back to work, the resulting increase in demand might end the depression in eastern and southern Europe and overseas as well.

However, in the case of nuclear energy, the problems inherent in the introduction of a promising new technology appeared likely to short-circuit the flow of benefits. Indeed the debate on nuclear power exemplified the malaise affecting Europe's economy, society and political structures. During the great boom the 'nuclear alternative' seemed to provide an answer to the question of how growth would continue when the limits of available energy resources were reached. The problems – the high cost of nuclear reactors and the direct connection of nuclear technology with atomic weapons – could be solved by investment undertaken by government agencies, in short by planning. In the east the Soviet Union cooperated with other governments to plan a large expansion of nuclear power while keeping supplies of the critical raw material firmly under its own control. In the west the Euratom agency was absorbed into the European Community structure, but American attempts to retain control over nuclear energy were hotly disputed by the French, whose ambitious nuclear power programme was closely connected to De Gaulle's insistence that France must possess its own nuclear weapons. In the west and east the results were similar; the creation of large, largely secret and highly secretive organisations which committed very large amounts of money to the erection of nuclear power stations with little or no public discussion.

In the west extraparliamentary opposition to nuclear power mounted during the 1970s. In part it spilled over from campaigns against nuclear weapons such as that organised by the British Campaign for Nuclear Disarmament, but it focused on questions of safety – not only the possibility of accidental release of radiation, but also the difficult questions of waste disposal, the relatively short life of reactors and the very expensive and difficult process of decommissioning worn or outmoded plants. In West Germany the Greens and an environmentalist faction within the socialist party campaigned against nuclear power, and in 1977 public protests and riots forced the government to cut its plans by a third and in effect halted new construction. In Austria in 1978 a referendum banned nuclear power altogether. In Sweden antinuclear demonstrations in 1977 led to a cabinet crisis the next year and to a referendum in 1980 which greatly restricted the nuclear programme. Only France pressed ahead; in 1986 France possessed 44 reactors and planned 17 more, while the other countries of western Europe together had 100 reactors in operation but plans for only 6 new plants. Fully committed to nuclear energy, the French government's electrical power agency refused to consider alternatives; committed to preserving France's position as a 'nuclear power', leaders of both the Gaullist and socialist parties relied on the agency's arguments and stifled discussion. Unhampered by the public protests which slowed reactor construction in the west, eastern European governments relied increasingly on nuclear power. In 1986 the Soviet Union had 51 reactors and planned an additional 34, and the 16 reactors operating in east-central Europe were to be joined by 26 more.

In 30 years the nemeses of a serious accident struck twice, both times in the Soviet Union. In the 1950s the region around Kyshtym, in the central Ural mountains, was contaminated by radioactive wastes, either because of a chemical explosion in a waste storage tank or because of leakage of wastes from a production plant. The Soviet government refused to discuss the incident, but the names of thirty villages disappeared from Soviet maps. In 1986 a nuclear power plant at Chernobyl, north of Kiev, exploded. The resulting cloud of radioactive dust drifted across east-central, northern and western Europe, contaminating food crops and animals as it went. West German authorities reported radioactivity readings up to 60 times higher than normal and restricted sales of farm products, but the French government denied the radioactive cloud had passed over France and assured its citizens that a similar explosion was impossible in a French reactor. In the aftermath of the Chernobyl explosion a large number of 'incidents' and close escapes came to light. Virtually all countries with nuclear power stations had either experienced a serious radiation leak or come dangerously close, and in virtually every case the responsible authorities had attempted to conceal or minimise the seriousness of the event. One of the worst cases was a near-explosion in a nuclear power station at Bugey, near Lyon, in 1984, when three of the four systems powering the reactor's cooling system failed, and the single remaining diesel generator prevented the contamination of a wide area of central and southern France.

Epilogue

THE THIRD WORLD WAR

A number of problems confronted Europe in the 1980s; foremost among them was the possibility of nuclear war. No one could say whether or when a nuclear war might erupt. Nevertheless, the possibility of nuclear war led to the creation of projections or 'scenarios' analysing the different types of nuclear war and their efforts. The most optimistic, popular in both east and west, foresaw a limited nuclear 'exchange' which then would lead to internal instability and the collapse of one side. One western version emphasised national divisions within the Soviet Union; in reply to a Soviet nuclear attack the west could destroy the capital of one of the federal republics, and the fear this would engender would result in uprisings against the Great Russians and the dissolution of the Soviet Union into its component nationalities. Eastern versions foresaw either a limited nuclear exchange leading to the collapse of anarchic capitalist societies as fear led to uncontrollable rioting, or the fear of using nuclear weapons at all leaving the west helpless against the Soviet Union's vastly superior conventional forces. In turn western military leaders relied on 'tactical' nuclear weapons to redress the imbalance in numbers of soldiers, and most scenarios therefore predicted some form of nuclear exchange on the battlefield. The initial battlefield, all agreed, would be West Germany; what would happen thereafter was more speculative.

War between superpowers was almost certain to be nuclear; worse, there was a very high probability that the use of nuclear weapons would 'escalate' into a general exchange. In

1983 the Soviet defence minister said bluntly: 'If they think in Washington that we will retaliate only against targets in western Europe, they badly delude themselves. Retaliation against the United States will be ineluctable'. In addition, restricting the use of nuclear weapons to tactical exchanges on the battlefield or to carefully selected and measured strategic targets required extremely rapid and reliable communication among political and military leaders and between them and the technicians handling the weapons. However, at least in the case of the United States, the communications networks were actually extremely vulnerable and likely to break down completely even during a limited nuclear exchange. It seemed highly unlikely that the Soviet forces were better equipped in this regard. Many observers therefore concluded that both sides would be tempted to move directly to a general exchange, using all their nuclear weapons while they still could and before the other side decided to use theirs.

Estimates of the effects of a nuclear war varied with the assumptions made, the most basic being the extent of the exchange. Britain, for instance, might be able to cope with the destruction of several medium-sized cities, as the British and Germans had coped during the Second World War, but anything beyond that would be highly problematical. In addition to the direct destruction of the blasts, survivors of a general exchange would confront the virtually complete dislocation of communications, power, water and sewerage systems, disruption of food supplies and breakdown of medical services. Fallout – radioactive particles thrown up by the explosions – would expose survivors to radiation sickness. More conventional epidemic diseases could be expected as well, partly because of the millions of bodies which the survivors would be unable to bury. Attempting to rebuild, they could find their food supplies cut even more drastically by a 'nuclear winter', as the dust thrown into the atmosphere blanketed the earth, reduced the amount of sunlight reaching the surface and lowered temperatures far below normal, possibly to the point where crops would simply not grow. Whether machinery and chemicals would continue to be available depended on the assumptions made, as did predictions of the long-term effects of radiation on the survivors and on future generations. It was these medium and long-term effects which seemed to make a hypothetical Third World War qualitatively different from the air war of the Second World War.

AN AGENDA

Obviously the tension between the superpowers had to be reduced to a level where war was unlikely, and hopefully to the point where they would feel secure in reducing their nuclear arsenals. Looming on the near horizons as well was the multi-faceted question of environmental degradation. Here technical research, international cooperation and sufficient funds to repair past damage and redirect labour and capital into non-destructive employment – for instance in the industries around the Mediterranean – were an equally obvious requirement. In western Europe, continued mass unemployment led to chronic domestic social problems, but in addition dragged down the economies of eastern Europe and the Third World by reducing demand for their products. Unemployment raised the spectre of social unrest in Europe, and continued depression seemed very likely to lead to continued confrontation with the Third World. To raise employment would require new investment, though exactly how much would depend on the rate at which Europe could absorb and develop new technologies. The technological gap opening between western Europe and the United States and Japan was another of the ominous problems which Europe had to confront. Agriculture was another; clearly the sector needed to decline further in size and become more efficient at producing high-quality speciality products.

In eastern Europe, unemployment did not pose a problem, but overstaffing, underemployment and inefficiency did. The east lagged badly in industrial technology and was having increasing difficulty paying for the necessary imports of new, more efficient machinery. The situation in agriculture was worse, and the need to import basic foodstuffs imposed a heavy drain on several eastern economies. As in the west, the sector needed to decline in size, but in addition eastern agriculture required a quantum increase in capital intensity to raise its efficiency. Planners in the east needed to avoid the temptation to rely excessively on a technological 'quick fix' such as nuclear power, and they needed to discover some way to build more flexibility and responsiveness into their systems.

Without denying the difficulties of both western and eastern Europe, it should be noted that the 1970s and 1980s had not brought the sort of depression and suffering which marked the 1930s or the periodic crises of the nineteenth century. Even the poorest countries of southern and southeastern Europe enjoyed standards of living far higher than the most affluent countries of western Europe at the beginning of the century. Further, Europe's institutional, social and ideological resources were more adequate to deal with economic problems than was the case in the preceding generation. Not the least of those resources was the fundamental recognition that governments had an important role to play in economic and social life. Equally important was the commitment to international cooperation to meet economic problems, despite the tendency for cooperation to be hampered by the pressures of existing interests within all countries. All governments continued to feel the pressure of demands to improve employment opportunities and raise living standards, and this pressure was likely to force national governments and international bodies to take the lead in the necessary redirection of resources.

MAPS

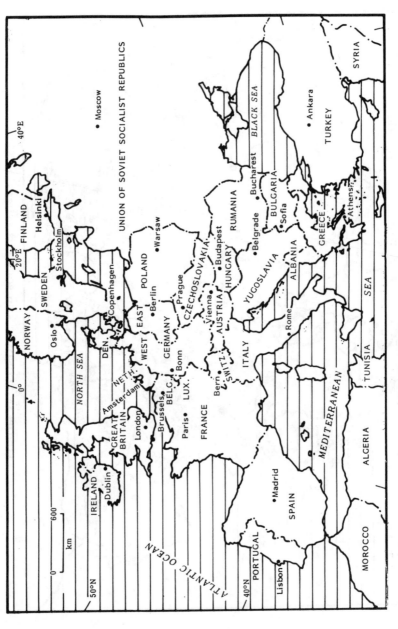

CONTEMPORARY EUROPE

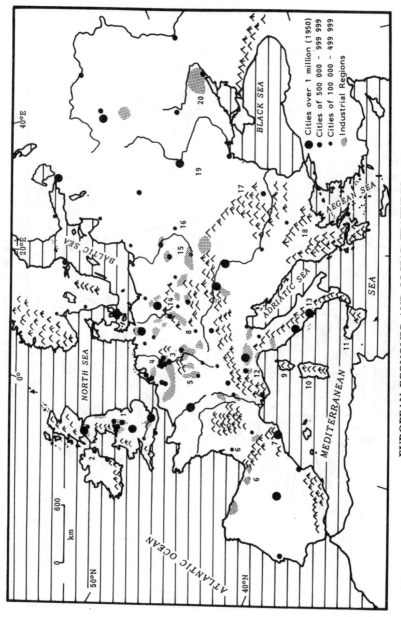

EUROPEAN ECONOMIC AND SOCIAL FEATURES

EUROPEAN SOCIAL AND ECONOMIC FEATURES:
KEY TO REGIONS

1. Midlands
2. Ulster
3. Rhineland
4. Ruhr
5. Alsace-Lorraine
6. Basque country
7. Catalonia
8. Bavaria
9. Corsica
10. Sardinia
11. Sicily
12. Milan-Turin-Genoa triangle
13. Mezzogiorno
14. Bohemia
15. Silesia
16. Galicia
17. Transylvania
18. Macedonia
19. Ukraine
20. Donetz Basin

FURTHER READING

This bibliography has two purposes: to list the books referred to or quoted from in the text and to suggest books for further reading and research. By no means is the list exhaustive. However, it includes books on almost all topics and gives preference to those that should be relatively easily available in English and, except for works of historiographical interest, published in the last twenty years. The bibliographies of these works will give references to older and more monographic sources. Journal articles may be found by consulting *Historical Abstracts*, which provides summaries of most articles in most journals. Recent events are conveniently summarised in *Europa Year Book* and *Statesman's Year Book*. The most convenient source of quantitative information is B. R. Mitchell, *European Historical Statistics, 1750–1975*, 2nd ed. (London, 1981) which gives extensive references to the publications of individual governments. Publications of international agencies are usually catalogued under the agencies' names. The League of Nations produced much material relevant to the Second World War and reconstruction period. The statistical series and specialised studies of the United Nations have become standard; the publications of the UN Commission for Europe are particularly relevant. A wealth of information is available for western Europe from the Organisation for Economic Cooperation and Development (OECD) and the European Communities (EC). Publications of the EC continue those of the European Coal and Steel Community (ECSC), Euratom and the European Economic Community (EEC). Eastern Europe poses more of a problem; the Council for Mutual Economic Assistance (CMEA, also known in the west as Comecon) publishes a statistical yearbook, but this should be supplemented by a western guide such as P. S. Shoup, *East European and Soviet Data Handbook* (New York, 1981) or R. A. Clarke and D. J. I. Matko, *Soviet Economic Facts, 1917–1981*, 2nd ed. (London 1983).

Aldcroft, D. H., *Britain's Economic Growth Failure, 1950–1980* (Brighton, 1984).

——, *The European Economy, 1914–1980* (London, 1980).

Andrews, W. G., and Hoffman, S. (eds), *The Impact of the Fifth Republic on France* (Albany, N.Y., 1981).

Anel, L., *Recession, the Western Economies and the Changing World Order* (London, 1981).

Archer, M. S. and Giner, S. (eds), *Contemporary Europe: Class, Status and Power* (London, 1971).

Ardagh, J., *France in the 1980s* (London, 1982).

Armstrong, P. *et al.*, *Capitalism Since World War II: The Making and Breakup of the Great Boom* (London, 1984).

Ausch, S., *Theory and Practice of CMEA Co-operation* (Budapest, 1972).

Bain, G. S., *Profiles of Union Growth: A Comparative Statistical Portrait of Eight Countries* (Oxford, 1980).

Bairoch, P., *The Economic Development of the Third World since 1900* (London, 1975).

Baker, W. J., *Sports in the Western World* (Totowa, N.J., 1982).

Berend, I. T. and Ránki, G., *Economic Development in East-Central Europe in the 19th and 20th Centuries* (New York, 1974).

Berger, S. (ed.), *Organising Interests in Western Europe: Pluralism, Corporatism and the Transformation of Politics* (Cambridge, 1982).

Berger, S. and Piore, M. J., *Dualism and Discontinuity in Industrial Societies* (Cambridge, 1980).

Bianco, L., *Origins of the Chinese Revolution, 1915–1949* (Stanyard, 1971).

Biddiss, M. D., *The Age of the Masses: Ideas and Society in Europe Since 1870* (Harmondsworth, 1977).

Black, C. E., *The Dynamics of Modernization: A Study in Comparative History* (New York, 1966).

Bond, B., *War and Society in Europe, 1870–1970* (Leicester, 1983).

Bracher, K. D., *The German Dictatorship* (Harmondsworth, 1970).

Brandt, J. A., *Toward the New Spain* (Philadelphia, 1983).

Braverman, H., *Labour and Monopoly Capital: The Degradation of Work in the Twentieth Century* (New York, 1974).

Bugliarello, G. and Doner, D. B. (eds), *The History and Philosophy of Technology* (Urbana, Ill., 1979).

Bullough, V., *Homosexuality: A History from Ancient Greece to Gay Liberation* (New York, 1979).

Callahan, D., *Abortion: Law, Choice and Morality* (New York, 1970).

Calvez, J. Y., *Politics and Society in the Third World* (Maryknoll, N.Y., 1973).

Carew, A., *Democracy and Government in European Trade Unions* (London, 1976).

Caron, F., *An Economic History of Modern France* (New York, 1979).

Cashmore, E. E., *No Future: Youth and Society* (London, 1984).

Castles, S., *Here for Good: Western Europe's New Ethnic Minorities* (London, 1984).

Chester, R. (ed.), *Divorce in Europe* (Leiden, 1977).

Childs, D., *The GDR: Moscow's German Ally* (London, 1983).

Chirot, D., *Social Change in the Twentieth Century* (New York, 1977).

Cipolla, C. (ed.), *The Fontana Economic History of Europe*, vols 5–6 (Glasgow, 1976).

Clough, S., *The Economic History of Modern Italy* (New York, 1964).

Crouzet, M., *The European Renaissance since 1945* (London, 1970).

Davidson, B., *Let Freedom Come: Africa in Modern History* (Boston, 1978).

Davis, L. E. *et. al.*, *Institutional Change and American Economic Growth* (Cambridge, 1971).

Delzell, C. F., *Mediterranean Fascism, 1919–1945* (New York, 1970).

Derfler, L., *Socialism Since Marx* (London, 1973).

Derry, T. K., *A History of Scandinavia* (London, 1979).

Deutscher, I., *Stalin: A Political Biography* (New York, 1979).

Djilas, M., *The New Class: An Analysis of the Communist System* (New York, 1957).

Drewnowski, J., (ed.), *The Crisis in East European Economies: The Spread of the Polish Disease* (London, 1983).

Duus, P., *The Rise of Modern Japan* (Boston, 1976).

Franko, Lawrence, *The European Multinationals* (London, 1976).

Geertz, C. (ed.), *Old Societies and New States* (New York, 1963).

Griffiths, R. T., *The Economy and Politics of the Netherlands since 1945* (The Hague, 1980).

Hardach, K., *The Political Economy of Germany in the Twentieth Century* (Berkeley, 1976).

Harman. C., *Class Struggles in Eastern Europe, 1945–83* (London, 1983).

Hilberg, R., *The Destruction of the European Jews* (Chicago, 1961).

Hodne, F., *The Norwegian Economy, 1920–1980* (London, 1983).

Holland, R. F., *European Decolonization, 1918–1981* (New York, 1985).

Hsü, I. C. Y., *The Rise of Modern China* (New York, 1970).

Hughes, H. S., *The Sea Change: The Migration of Social Thought, 1930–1965* (New York, 1977).

Ienaga, S., *The Pacific War: World War II and the Japanese, 1931–1945* (New York, 1978).

Jackman, R., *et al.*, *The Economics of Inflation* (Oxford, 1981).

Jelavich, B., *History of the Balkans: Twentieth Century*, vol. 2, (Cambridge, 1983).

Jones, H. G., *Planning and Productivity in Sweden* (London, 1976).

Kane, D., *The Eurodollar Market and the Years of Crisis* (London, 1982).

Kaser, M. and Zielinsky, J., *Planning in East Europe* (London, 1970).

Kaser, M. C. and Rodice, E. D. (eds), *The Economic History of Eastern Europe, 1919–1975* (Oxford, 1984).

Kenwood, A. G. and Lougheed, A. L., *The Growth of the International Economy, 1820–1980* (London, 1983).

Kiernan, V. G., *European Empires from Conquest to Collapse, 1815–1960* (Leicester, 1982).

Klein, G. and Reban, M. J., *The Politics of Ethnicity in Eastern Europe* (New York, 1981).

Knapp, W., *North West Africa: A Political and Economic Survey* (Oxford, 1977).

Korpi, W., *The Working Class in Welfare Capitalism* (London, 1978).

Kranzberg, M. and Purcell, C. W. (eds), *Technology in Western Civilization* (New York, 1967).

Lacqueur, W. (ed.), *Fascism: A Reader's Guide* (London, 1976).

Lapidus, G. W. (ed.), *Women, Work and Family in the Soviet Union* (Armond, N.Y., 1982).

Lawrence, P., *Managers and Management in West Germany* (London, 1980).

Leptin, G. and Melzer, M., *Economic Reform in East German Industry* (Oxford, 1978).

Lieberman, S., *The Growth of the European Mixed Economies, 1945–1970* (Cambridge, Mass., 1977).

Mack, Smith, D., *Mussolini's Roman Empire* (New York, 1976).

Maddison, A., *Economic Growth in the West* (New York, 1964).

——, *Phases of Capitalist Development* (Oxford, 1982).

Maier, C. S., 'The Two Postwar Eras and the Conditions for Stability in Twentieth Century Europe', *American Historical Review*, vol. 86 (1981).

Mandel, E., *Marxist Economic Theory* (London, 1968).

——, *The Second Slump* (London, 1980).

Marwick, A., *Class: Image and Reality in Britain, France and the USA Since 1930* (London, 1980).

McCauley, M., *The Soviet Union Since 1917* (London, 1981).

McNeill, W. H., *The Metamorphosis of Greece since World War II* (Chicago, 1978).

Mendras, H., *The Vanishing Peasant* (Cambridge, Mass., 1970).

Milward, A. S., *The Reconstruction of Western Europe, 1945–51* (Berkeley, 1984).

——, *War, Economy and Society, 1939–1945* (Berkeley, 1977).

Mitterauer, M. and Sieder, R., *The European Family* (Oxford, 1982).

Mouzelis, N., *Modern Greece: Facets of Underdevelopment* (London, 1978).

Nove, A., *An Economic History of the U.S.S.R.* (Harmondsworth, 1982).

Nove, A. (ed.), *The East European Economies in the 1970s* (London, 1981).

Oliver, R. and Fage, J. D., *A Short History of Africa* (Baltimore, 1966).

Pendle, G., *A History of Latin America* (Harmondsworth, 1976).

Peterson, E. N., *The American Occupation of Germany: Retreat to Victory* (Detroit, 1978).

Pluvier, J., *South-East Asia from Colonialism to Independence* (Kuala Lumpur, 1974).

Podbielski, G., *Italy: Development and Crisis in the Post-War Economy* (London, 1974).

Pollard, S., *The Development of the British Economy, 1914–1980* (London, 1983).

Rakowska-Harmstone, T. and Gyorgy, A. (eds), *Communism in Eastern Europe* (Bloomington, Indiana, 1979).

Raychaudhuri, T. and Habib, I. (eds), *The Cambridge Economic History of India* (Cambridge, 1981).

Rostow, W. W., *The Stages of Economic Growth: A Non-Communist Manifesto* (Cambridge, 1960).

——, *The World Economy: History and Prospect* (London, 1978).

——, *Why the Poor Get Richer and the Rich Slow Down: Essays in the Marshallian Long Period* (Austin, Texas, 1980).

Rumble, G., *The Politics of Nuclear Defence* (Cambridge, 1985).

Rusinow, D., *The Yugoslav Experiment, 1948–1974* (London, 1977).

Salt, J. and Clout, H. (eds), *Migration in Post-War Europe: Geographical Essays* (London, 1976).

Scammel, W. M., *The International Economy since 1945* (London, 1983).

Scott, H., *Sweden's Right to be Human* (London, 1982).

Singleton, F. and Carter, B., *The Economy of Yugoslavia* (London, 1982).

Smith, A. D. S., *Nationalism in the Twentieth Century* (Oxford, 1979).

Speer, A., *Inside the Third Reich* (London, 1970).

Spiro, H. J., *The Politics of German Codetermination* (Cambridge, Mass., 1958).

Stearns, P., *European Society in Upheaval: Social History since 1750* (New York, 1975).

Stotera, G., *Death of a Utopia: The Development and Decline of Student Movements in Europe* (New York, 1975).

Sturmthal, A., *Left of Center: European Labor Since World War II* (Urbana, Ill., 1983).

Svennilson, I., *Growth and Stagnation in the European Economy* (Geneva, 1954).

Taylor, A. J. P., *The Origins of the Second World War* (London, 1969).

Triffen, R., *The Evolution of the International Monetary System* (Princeton, 1964).

Vincens Vives, J., *Approaches to the History of Spain* (Berkeley, 1972).

Wallich, H. C., *Mainsprings of the German Revival* (Greenwood, 1976).

Weeks, J., *Coming Out: Homosexual Politics in Britain, from the Nineteenth Century to the Present* (London, 1977).

INDEX